July

To Maddie:

A special friend on a special
birthday.

Love

To Maddie

A special friend on a special

Chocolate Lovers Cookbook

Chocolate Lovers Cookbook

Audrey Ellis

DEANS
INTERNATIONAL
PUBLISHING

Acknowledgments

The publishers would like to thank the following companies for their help in supplying some of the photographs for this book:

Baxters of Speyside (page 114)
British Sugar PLC (pages 25, 70)
Cadbury Typhoo Food Advisory Service (pages 42, 45, 52, 72, 76, 82, 101, 121, 131, 135, 137, 140, 160, 168, 169, 177 and back cover)
Du Pont, manufacturers of 'SilverStone' non-stick coating (pages 33, 38, 39, 186, 187)
Flour Advisory Service (page 154)
Gale's Honey and Curds (page 132–133)
General Foods (pages 37, 60, 86–87, 116, 117, 122–123, 127, 142–143, 147)
The Kellogg Company of Great Britain Limited (page 63)
Libby McNeil and Libby (page 109)
Lyons Tetley Limited (pages 64–65, 95, 106, 110–111)
McCormick Foods (UK) Limited (pages 82, 160)
McDougalls Flour (pages 73, 78, 79, 81, 99)
McVitie's (page 125)
National Dairy Council (pages 9, 105)
The Nestlé Company Limited (pages 184–185)
Ocean Spray Cranberries (pages 22–23, 85)
Pyrex by Corning (page 112)
Stork Cookery Service (pages 162–163)
United Rum Merchants (page 53)
Wall's Carte d'Or Double Dairy Ice Cream (page 145)
Whitworths Holdings Limited (pages 96–97, 102–103)

Useful addresses

Sugarflair Colour Limited,
Brunel Road, Manor Trading Estate,
BENFLEET, Essex, SS7 4PS
— Suppliers of gold leaf sheets and flake

Lakeland Plastics,
Alexandra Buildings,
WINDERMERE, Cumbria, LA23 1BQ
— Suppliers of Easter egg and festive novelty moulds

Front cover: (Top) Double chocolate gâteau; (right) Chocolate walnut boxes; (bottom) Moist chocolate pudding (Paul Williams)
Back cover: Clockwise from top right; Jigsaw roll; Flake treats; Swirled mallow fudge; Miniature Florentines
Titlespread: (Left) Chocolate butterflies; (centre) Profiteroles with liqueur filling; (right) Lemon cream crunch pie (Paul Williams)

The author's special thanks to her invaluable assistant, Christine Curphey

Line illustrations by Kate Simunek

Published by Deans International Publishing
52–54 Southwark Street, London SE1 1UA
A division of The Hamlyn Publishing Group Limited
London·New York·Sydney·Toronto

Copyright © The Hamlyn Publishing Group Limited 1985
ISBN 0 603 03667 8

Printed in Italy

Contents

Useful Facts and Figures

Notes on metrication

In this book quantities are given in metric and Imperial measures. Exact conversion from Imperial to metric measures does not usually give very convenient working quantities and so the metric measures have been rounded off into units of 25 grams. The table below shows the recommended equivalents.

Ounces	*Approx g to nearest whole figure*	*Recommended conversion to nearest unit of 25*
1	28	25
2	57	50
3	85	75
4	113	100
5	142	150
6	170	175
7	198	200
8	227	225
9	255	250
10	283	275
11	312	300
12	340	350
13	368	375
14	396	400
15	425	425
16 (1 lb)	454	450
17	482	475
18	510	500
19	539	550
20 (1¼ lb)	567	575

Note: When converting quantities over 20 oz first add the appropriate figures in the centre column, then adjust to the nearest unit of 25. As a general guide, 1 kg (1000 g) equals 2.2 lb or about 2 lb 3 oz. This method of conversion gives good results in nearly all cases, although in certain pastry and cake recipes a more accurate conversion is necessary to produce a balanced recipe.

Liquid measures The millilitre has been used in this book and the following table gives a few examples.

Imperial	*Approx ml to nearest whole figure*	*Recommended ml*
¼ pint	142	150 ml
½ pint	283	300 ml
¾ pint	425	450 ml
1 pint	567	600 ml
1½ pints	851	900 ml
1¾ pints	992	1000 ml (1 litre)

Spoon measures All spoon measures given in this book are level unless otherwise stated.

Can sizes At present, cans are marked with the exact (usually to the nearest whole number) metric equivalent of the Imperial weight of the contents, so we have followed this practice when giving can sizes.

Notes for American and Australian users

In America the 8-oz measuring cup is used. In Australia metric measures are now used in conjunction with the standard 250-ml measuring cup. The Imperial pint, used in Britain and Australia, is 20 fl oz, while the American pint is 16 fl oz. It is important to remember that the Australian tablespoon differs from both the British and American tablespoons; the table below gives a comparison. The British standard tablespoon, which has been used throughout this book, holds 17.7 ml, the American 14.2 ml, and the Australian 20 ml. A teaspoon holds approximately 5 ml in all three countries.

British	*American*	*Australian*
1 teaspoon	1 teaspoon	1 teaspoon
1 tablespoon	1 tablespoon	1 tablespoon
2 tablespoons	3 tablespoons	2 tablespoons
3½ tablespoons	4 tablespoons	3 tablespoons
4 tablespoons	6 tablespoons	3½ tablespoons

An Imperial/American guide to solid and liquid measures

Imperial	*American*	*Imperial*	*American*
Solid measures		**Liquid measures**	
1 lb butter or margarine	2 cups	¼ pint liquid	⅔ cup liquid
		½ pint	1¼ cups
1 lb flour	4 cups	¾ pint	2 cups
1 lb granulated or caster sugar	2 cups	1 pint	2½ cups
		1½ pints	3¾ cups
1 lb icing sugar	3½ cups	2 pints	5 cups (2½ pints)

American terms

The list below gives some American equivalents or substitutes for terms and ingredients used in this book.

British/American
Equipment and terms
cake tin/cake pan
cling film/plastic wrap
deep cake tin/spring form pan
double saucepan/double boiler
flan tin/pie tin
frying pan/skillet
greaseproof paper/waxed paper
grill/boil
liquidize/blend
loaf tin/loaf pan
palette knife/metal spatula
piping bag/pastry bag
stoned/pitted
Swiss roll tin/jelly roll pan

British/American
Ingredients
bicarbonate of soda/baking soda
biscuits/crackers, cookies
cocoa powder/unsweetened cocoa
cornflour/cornstarch
cream, single/cream, light
cream, double/cream, heavy
essence/extract
flour, plain/flour, all-purpose
glacé cherries/candied cherries
icing/frosting
lard/shortening
milk chocolate/sweet chocolate
plain chocolate/semi-sweet chocolate
shortcrust pastry/basic pie dough
sultanas/seedless white raisins
yeast, fresh/yeast, compressed

NOTE: **When making any of the recipes in this book, only follow one set of measures as they are not interchangeable.**

A cocoa plantation in Brazil

The Chocolate Story

The fascinating facts about chocolate sound almost like a fairytale. In the early 16th Century Cortez, the great Spanish merchant adventurer, invaded Mexico and conquered the Aztec indians. He observed the defeated emperor Montezuma consuming a hot, pungent drink from a golden cup which was handed to him with much ceremony, and decided to taste it for himself. It was something of a curiosity; certainly not the delicious beverage we know today, for it was unsweetened and mixed with peppery spices. But when Cortez enquired how the drink was made, he found that pods from the cocoa or cacao tree, as large as melons, were harvested twice a year and split open to extract the precious beans. These were fermented, dried in the sun, roasted and then finely ground. The cocoa powder was mixed with boiling water, strained, and the resultant brew highly spiced.

On his return to Spain, Cortez took with him a supply of the beans and introduced them to the court. The Spaniards experimented with the drink, substituted milk or cream for the water, and sweetened it with sugar. The import of cocoa beans was jealously restricted to Spain, and the secret of how to make the drink closely guarded for nearly a hundred years, until 1655. When the Infanta of Spain arrived in France to wed King Louis, she brought with her many fine jewels and dresses, and a supply of cocoa beans for her favourite breakfast drink.

Soon the secret was out, merchants of other nationalities were buying the beans, then growing them in many countries where the climate was suitable. Chocolate houses appeared in Paris, and the fashion soon crossed the Channel. Samuel Pepys in the reign of Good King Charles sampled the drink, and dubbed it 'delicious, but rather expensive'. In those days, there was no solid chocolate to eat and another century was to pass before any attempt was made to introduce it in this form. The Swiss claim that finally they developed a method that worked. The cocoa bean naturally contains too much cocoa butter to be converted directly into a powder which would suit modern tastes for drinking, and not enough to make a chocolate block for breaking off pieces to eat. When separating out cocoa butter was discovered, both processes became possible.

The method used is not very different from that employed by the Aztec indians. The beans are roasted, broken down and the shells removed, leaving only the centres or 'nibs'. These nibs are ground until they are transformed into a liquid paste with the consistency of thick cream. The heat of grinding melts the cocoa butter and as the mixture cools it solidifies. If the mass is intended to make cocoa powder, about half the butter is then pressed out, leaving a solid block which is ground very finely and sifted. If it is going to be made into plain chocolate (U.S. semi-sweet chocolate), extra cocoa butter and sugar are added. The mixture is heated until it becomes liquid again. The mixing and grinding process continues for days until the texture suits the manufacturer's standards, and possibly additional flavourings are added. Finally, it is poured or extruded into moulds, allowed to set and is then ready for packing. Milk chocolate (U.S. sweet chocolate) is made in special factories where the cocoa mass is combined with full cream milk and sugar. White chocolate is really a misnomer. Certainly it contains cocoa butter, sugar, milk solids and vanilla but none of the mass. However, it behaves like true chocolate when heated and melted for decorating purposes. Cake coverings, which are usually less expensive than 'eating' chocolate, do not always contain any cocoa butter, relying on the inclusion of vegetable oils. This gives them the advantage of melting and resetting more than once without losing their gloss.

Clockwise from top: Dark secret (recipe page 139). After dinner cups (recipe page 55). Macaroon ice cream dessert (recipe 141). Ginger and almond florentines (recipe page 47). Chocolate crunchy cake (recipe page 132)

Various Methods of Melting Chocolate and Making Decorations

The secret of success is to begin by melting the chocolate slowly without exposing it to a high heat.

In a bowl over hot water Choose a bowl which fits a heavy-based pan conveniently so that it does not touch the bottom of the pan. Pour in enough water to come at least 2.5 cm/1 inch up the side of the bowl. Break up the chocolate, place in the bowl. Heat the water to simmering point, put the bowl over it and adjust the heat carefully so that the water does not actually boil. When the chocolate is almost melted, remove the bowl from the pan and stir until it is smooth.

In a double boiler Follow the same method as above, with water in the lower part of the double pan and chocolate in the upper part. Again, keep the water below boiling point.

In a microwave cooker Break up the chocolate and place in a non-metallic container. Cover and cook on medium power for 1–2 minutes, according to the quantity. Uncover, shake the container gently and if the chocolate is not completely melted, reprocess for a further 30 seconds and shake again.

In liquid over direct heat This method is not recommended unless you have a good non-stick pan and the recipe calls for the chocolate to be melted in liquids such as milk or coffee. It also works with unsalted butter.

Not recommended Melting in a pan over direct heat because the chocolate tends to become overheated, goes grainy and loses its gloss. Do not be tempted to add water to melted chocolate that is too thick. Instead, thin it with a teaspoon or so of cream.

Adding decorative touches

Not all these require the chocolate to be melted first. But where chocolate needs melting, there is sure to be a certain amount left over. Gather together any trimmings and remelt so that nothing is wasted.

Avoid finger contact with any completed chocolate decorations as even this amount of warmth tends to melt them.

Making chocolate curls
Ensure that the chocolate is at room temperature as the curls will break if the chocolate is chilled. Draw a vegetable peeler firmly along the edge of a block of chocolate or, for extra large curls, along the flat side of the block.

Grating chocolate
Use the coarsest side of your grater and scrape the edge of the chocolate bar against it. Place the grater on a sheet of greaseproof paper (U.S. waxed paper) so that you can easily collect the grated chocolate together. It is difficult to transfer from a board.

Making chocolate caraque
Spread melted chocolate directly on to a laminated or marble surface and allow to set but do not chill. Using a sharp knife with a long straight blade, place it at an angle of 45 degrees to the surface and scrape it along, removing the chocolate in long scrolls as you go. Put in place using tweezers or the side of a small palette knife (U.S. metal spatula).

Making fancy chocolate cut-outs
Cover a board with a sheet of non-stick baking parchment (U.S. waxed paper) and spread melted chocolate into a rectangle or square as directed above. Leave to set. Stamp out shapes with cocktail cutters. If the chocolate shape lifts up inside the cutter, release very gently with finger pressure or it will bend. If the cutter lifts out cleanly, slip a palette knife (U.S. metal spatula) between the chocolate and parchment to help you remove the shape.

Making chocolate leaves
Collect a number of small perfect rose leaves, all about the same size, or use ivy leaves. The houseplant variety produces small enough leaves to be used for this purpose. Wash the leaves thoroughly and pat dry carefully with absorbent paper towel. Coat the underside of each leaf thoroughly with melted chocolate and place chocolate-side up on a board to set. Then carefully peel the leaf away from the chocolate shape.

Making chocolate squares and triangles
Cover a board with a sheet of non-stick baking parchment (U.S.

waxed paper), ensuring that the surface is absolutely flat. Spread melted chocolate over it evenly. Allow to set. Using a ruler and sharp knife, trim the chocolate to a perfect square or rectangle. Mark into large squares such as those required for chocolate boxes, or small squares for decorating gâteaux. Cut through the shapes and lift off carefully with a palette knife. If desired, cut the squares diagonally to make triangles.

Piping melted chocolate

This can be done direct on to the surface of an iced cake, or over fruit. Use a small greaseproof paper (U.S. waxed paper) piping bag. Pour in the melted chocolate and fold down the top taking care not to over-fill the bag, otherwise it may burst when you exert pressure on it. Snip off a very small piece from the point and use in the same way as a writing tube when icing. If the chocolate hardens in the bag, place in a bowl suspended over hot water until the chocolate softens again. Don't attempt to remove the chocolate from the bag, or put the bag directly into water.

Making piped chocolate decorations

Trace suitable outlines such as swan, flower, leaf or geometric shapes on non-stick parchment (U.S. waxed paper), ensuring that you have enough tracings to carry out your design. Turn the parchment over and lay it flat on a board. Pipe the outlines. These can be filled in with petals, leaf veins or latticework. Always make extras, as these shapes break easily when moved. The best method of removing the shapes from the parchment is to draw the sheet over the edge of the board and support the shape with a palette knife (U.S. metal spatula) while you peel the paper away from underneath.

Making piped and flooded chocolate shapes

Carry out the instructions for making piped chocolate decorations to the point of completing the outlines. Flood the centre of each outline with chocolate, easing it into the shape with the tip of a wooden cocktail stick (U.S. toothpick). Remove from the parchment as above.

Making chocolate cones

Take a 25-cm/10-inch square of greaseproof paper (U.S. waxed paper), fold in half diagonally then in half diagonally again and cut into 4 triangular shapes along the fold lines. Make into piping bags (see line drawings) and secure each one with a staple or adhesive tape. Brush the inside of the paper bag generously with melted chocolate, to make an even cone shape, leaving the point of the join free of chocolate so that you can hold it conveniently. Trim off the top of the bag and invert the cone on a wire rack. Leave until set. Carefully peel off the paper.

Making chocolate cups

These can be made in paper bun cases, or in sweet cases for petits four. Use the paper cases double to keep them firm during coating. Brush inside the inner paper case generously with melted chocolate. Prepare several of these. You can then use the outer paper cases from this first set to support further cases for coating. If liked, when the cases are completely cold, brush over again with more melted chocolate. When dry and set, peel off the paper cases, taking care not to crack the edges of the cups. Fill the centres with ice cream or a creamy filling, but not for example with fruit in syrup, as this will dissolve the chocolate. If possible, only fill the larger cases just before serving.

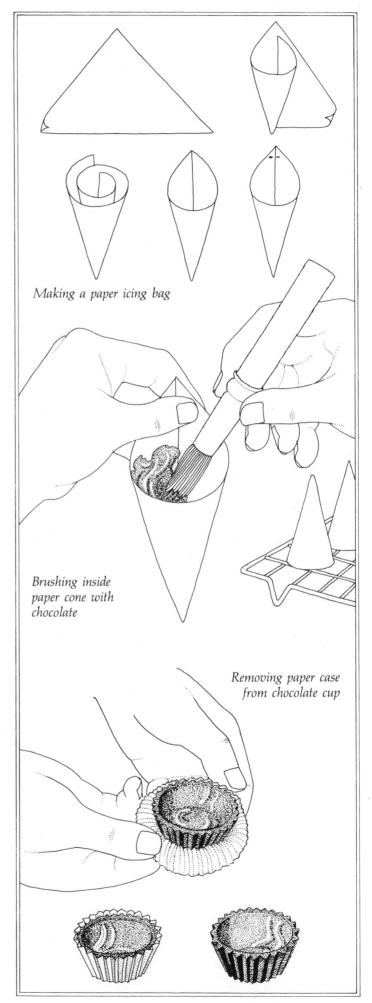

Making a paper icing bag

Brushing inside paper cone with chocolate

Removing paper case from chocolate cup

Using Chocolate in Cooking

Few people can resist the enchantment of chocolate. It is almost certainly the number one favourite in flavour throughout the world. Melted chocolate is invaluable to make all sorts of decorations and as an ingredient in the richest cakes and desserts. However, it can be temperamental, and requires some expertize on the part of the cook to achieve the best results.

Cocoa powder (U.S. unsweetened cocoa) can also be used to impart that attractive dark colour and rich aroma to all sorts of confections. In some cases, the flavour is more intense than when melted chocolate is added to other ingredients, and it is certainly cheaper.

If dry ingredients such as flour form part of the recipe and it is to be thoroughly cooked, as in baking, or steaming, the simplest method is to sift cocoa in with the flour. Combining it with fat or oil is also satisfactory. If the recipe is uncooked, it is better to add sufficient boiling water to the cocoa powder (U.S. unsweetened cocoa) to form a thick cream. It will then blend with other ingredients more easily.

Using chocolate chips and dots
These are useful, just as they come from the pack, as decorations, particularly when topping swirls or rosettes of piped cream. They can also be melted down using any of my recommended methods, and used as you would block chocolate, but this would be rather expensive. These versatile small chocolate pieces can be folded into cake mixtures or desserts and remain virtually whole during cooking.

Using couverture
This is ideal for coating centres to make your own chocolates. The surface dries with a really glossy appearance because of its high cocoa butter content. It is less sweet than dessert chocolate and is really only palatable when used to coat a sweet centre.

Using cake coverings
Check carefully when buying block chocolate and block cake coverings, to make sure what you are getting. Milk, plain and orange chocolate flavoured coverings are available, made mainly, or at least partly, from sugar, vegetable fat and flavourings. They are not intended to be cheap substitutes for chocolate itself, but are excellent for the intended purpose; that is, covering cakes and making decorative shapes.

Using chocolate spreads
These are very suitable to use as fillings, especially to sandwich together rather plain cakes which need a richly flavoured filling. They can be combined with buttercream or could be thinned with milk to make a drink, or warmed and used in the concentrated form as a pouring sauce.

Using chocolate syrups and dessert toppings
These are similarly constituted to cake coverings and spreads and are really only suitable to be used exactly as indicated on the pack.

Using powdered cocoa (U.S. unsweetened cocoa)
For a change, fill a vanilla or orange-flavoured layer cake with chocolate butter icing, and sprinkle cocoa powder (U.S. unsweetened cocoa) through a lacy doiley on to the top to decorate. Fix the doiley at one point with a wooden cocktail stick (U.S. toothpick) so that it will not move and blur the design. Lift straight up and away to keep the pattern clear. As a variation, mix equal quantities of cocoa powder (U.S. unsweetened cocoa) and instant coffee powder, and use in the same way on a chocolate layer cake with a coffee filling.

Using white chocolate
Cover cup cakes or a round layer cake with chocolate glacé icing (see page 73). Fill a paper icing bag with melted white chocolate, and when the surface of the dark chocolate icing is quite set, drizzle a zig-zag pattern from one side to the other, taking the line out to the edge each time, so that the size of the 'zig-zag' is widest across the centre of the cake and then diminishes again to form a matching pattern. A chequer-board pattern of squares, made by piping one set of parallel lines, and then another set crossing them at right angles, is also most effective, as you can then position pieces of nut or glacé cherries (U.S. candied cherries) in the squares, or in alternate squares.

Making chocolate decorations

12

Family Cakes

While you might expend a lot of time and artistry on decorating gâteaux for special occasions, the first requirement for a family cake is that it should be easy and quick to make. Also, of course, that the ingredients do not make too many demands on the household budget. This section brings you a wide choice of large and small cakes that fall into the right category, and yet are tempting in appearance and taste. Some require sugar and fat to be creamed first, others are prepared by the one-stage method which makes mixing almost no chore at all. Butter sometimes needs beating to give it a creamy consistency and is not essential although it may be suggested. Soft margarines are helpful alternatives, easy to blend even straight from the refrigerator. Most of my recipes adapt to the use of a food processor, which is particularly speedy if you prepare a larger-than-usual quantity of cake mixture or batter.

For family consumption, it is more economical of time and often of oven heat to batch-bake, rather than make just one item. Double up the ingredients, but not necessarily to make two similar cakes. Two tray cakes, for instance, can be decorated differently. Cut one up into fingers for same-day serving, and foil-wrap the other to produce later in the week. Here's another good example. When you make up the Marble rose ring recipe (see page 16), double the basic ingredients, colour and flavour as directed, and bake the extra mixture in little paper cases standing securely in bun tins. Top the pink and green buns with chocolate icing, and top the chocolate buns with white glacé icing flavoured peppermint. The result—a plateful of assorted fancies, with the minimum extra time taken to prepare them. Keep small quantities of chopped nuts or glacé cherries (u.s. candied cherries) for an expensive-looking decorative touch.

Another good tip to remember is that the flavour of a cake with a high fat content will mature and develop for several days after it is baked, especially if wrapped to enclose moistness. Don't be in a hurry to put it on the table. A fatless sponge, however, dries out rapidly and does not improve with keeping. But it is the ideal texture, whether baked in a shallow pan to make a Swiss roll (U.S. jelly roll) or in round layers, to be filled or sandwiched together with jam, seedless jellies, whipped cream or buttercream.

Above: Lemon topknots (recipe page 19). Below: Ginger iced buns (recipe page 32)

Chocolate butterflies

(Illustrated on pages 2–3)

*75 g/3 oz self-raising flour (U.S. ¾ cup all-purpose flour sifted
with ¾ teaspoon baking powder)
pinch of salt
2 tablespoons cocoa powder (U.S. 3 tablespoons unsweetened
cocoa)
100 g/4 oz (U.S. ½ cup) butter or margarine
100 g/4 oz caster sugar (U.S. ½ cup granulated sugar)
2 eggs, beaten
little icing sugar (U.S. confectioners' sugar)*
FILLING
*75 g/3 oz (U.S. ⅓ cup) butter or margarine
175 g/6 oz icing sugar, sifted (U.S. 1⅓ cups sifted confectioners'
sugar)
1 teaspoon vanilla essence (U.S. vanilla extract)*

Heat the oven to 200°C/400°F, Gas Mark 6 and stand 12 paper cake cases in bun tins (U.S. muffin pans) if possible, or on a baking sheet (U.S. cookie sheet).

Sift the flour with the salt and cocoa. Cream the butter and sugar in a bowl until light and fluffy. Gradually add the egg, beating well after each addition. Fold in the dry ingredients. Divide the mixture among the paper cases.

Bake for about 10 minutes, or until just firm to the touch. Place the cakes, still in the paper cases, on a wire rack to cool.

To make the filling, cream the butter until soft, add the sugar and vanilla essence and beat until smooth. Transfer to a piping bag fitted with a large star tube.

With a small pointed knife, cut off the top of each cake, slanting the knife into the centre so that when the lid is removed, the cake has a slight hollow in the middle. Pipe a large rosette of buttercream into each hollow. Cut the cake tops in half, and press one half into each side of a rosette, to make the butterfly wings. Sift the wings lightly with icing sugar.

Marble rose ring

(Illustrated opposite)

*15 g/½ oz cocoa powder (U.S. 2 tablespoons unsweetened cocoa),
sifted
2 tablespoons boiling water
225 g/8 oz plain flour (U.S. 2 cups all-purpose flour)
4 teaspoons (U.S. 2 tablespoons) baking powder
225 g/8 oz caster sugar (U.S. 1 cup granulated sugar)
225 g/8 oz (U.S. 1 cup) soft margarine
4 eggs
1 tablespoon triple distilled rose water
few drops red food colouring
25 g/1 oz (U.S. ¼ cup) ground almonds
few drops almond essence (U.S. almond extract)*

Heat the oven to 180°C/350°F, Gas Mark 4 and generously grease a 20-cm/8-inch plain ring tin.

Mix the cocoa powder with the water until smooth. Leave to cool. Sift the flour with the baking powder into a bowl and add the sugar, margarine and eggs. Beat vigorously until well blended.

Transfer about one third of the mixture to a second bowl and mix in the blended cocoa. Place a further one third of the cake mixture in another bowl, stir in the rose water and tint pink with food colouring. Add the almonds and almond flavouring to the remaining cake mixture. Spoon the 3 mixtures alternately into the prepared tin and run a knife blade through them once in each direction. Do not be tempted to over mix or the three-colour effect will be spoiled. Tap the tin sharply on a working surface to settle the mixture.

Bake for about 45 minutes, or until firm to the touch. Leave in the tin for 5 minutes then turn out on a wire rack to cool.

NOTE Colours and flavours can be varied in many interesting ways such as, for instance, colouring and flavouring one third of the mixture orange instead of rose pink, or green with pistachio instead of almond.

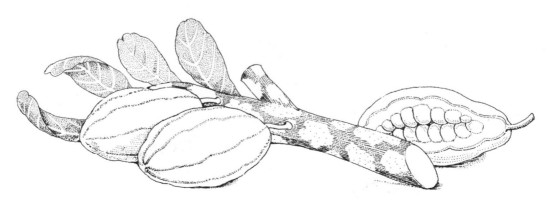

Marble rose ring

Hazelnut madeleines

(Illustrated below)

40 g / 1½ oz (U.S. 3 tablespoons) butter or margarine
2 tablespoons hazelnut chocolate spread (U.S. 3 tablespoons filbert chocolate spread or melted chocolate)
40 g / 1½ oz caster sugar (U.S. 3 tablespoons granulated sugar)
2 eggs, beaten
50 g / 2 oz self-raising flour (U.S. ½ cup all-purpose flour sifted with ½ teaspoon baking powder)

Heat the oven to 190°C/375°F, Gas Mark 5 and generously grease 12–14 fluted madeleine tins or shallow bun tins (U.S. shallow muffin pans).

Put the butter, hazelnut chocolate spread and sugar in a bowl and beat until soft and fluffy. Gradually add the egg, beating all the time. Sift the flour over the creamed mixture and fold in lightly but thoroughly. Divide among the prepared tins, filling them just over half full. Tap the filled trays sharply on a working surface to settle the mixture.

Bake for about 10 minutes, or until just firm to the touch. Invert the tin and ease the madeleines out carefully, allowing them to drop on to a wire rack. Leave to cool but serve freshly baked.

Fruity nut bars

75 g / 3 oz plain flour (U.S. ¾ cup all-purpose flour)
½ teaspoon baking powder
¼ teaspoon bicarbonate of soda (U.S. baking soda)
½ teaspoon salt
25 g / 1 oz (U.S. 1 cup) cornflakes, lightly crushed
50 g / 2 oz (U.S. ½ cup) chopped walnuts or pecans
100 g / 4 oz (U.S. ½ cup) butter or margarine
225 g / 8 oz soft brown sugar (U.S. 1 cup light brown sugar)
1 egg, beaten
1 teaspoon vanilla essence (U.S. vanilla extract)
100 g / 4 oz plain chocolate dots (U.S. ⅔ cup semi-sweet chocolate chips)

Heat the oven to 180°C/350°F, Gas Mark 4 and grease a 22.5-cm/9-inch loose-based square cake tin.

Sift the flour with the baking powder, bicarbonate of soda and salt and mix with the cornflakes and nuts. Put the butter in a large pan and heat gently until melted. Remove from the heat. Stir in the sugar then the egg and vanilla essence. Gradually add the dry ingredients, beating well with a wooden spoon until evenly combined. Fold in the chocolate dots. Transfer to the prepared tin and level the surface.

Bake for about 15 minutes, or until the cake shrinks slightly from the sides of the tin. Cool in the tin then cut into 18 bars measuring 7.5 cm/3 inches by 4 cm/1½ inches.

Lemon topknots

(Illustrated on page 14 and below)

75 g / 3 oz plain flour (U.S. $\frac{3}{4}$ cup all-purpose flour)
1 teaspoon baking powder
25 g / 1 oz cocoa powder (U.S. $\frac{1}{4}$ cup unsweetened cocoa)
75 g / 3 oz (U.S. $\frac{1}{3}$ cup) butter or margarine
75 g / 3 oz caster sugar (U.S. $\frac{1}{3}$ cup granulated sugar)
1 large egg, beaten
1 tablespoon oil
2 tablespoons (U.S. 3 tablespoons) lemon curd
finely grated rind of $\frac{1}{2}$ lemon

FILLING

50 g / 2 oz (U.S. $\frac{1}{4}$ cup) butter or margarine
1 tablespoon lemon curd
100 g / 4 oz icing sugar, sifted (U.S. scant 1 cup sifted
confectioners' sugar)
1–2 teaspoons (U.S. 2–3 teaspoons) lemon juice

Heat the oven to 190°C/375°F, Gas Mark 5 and generously grease 12 deep fluted bun tins (U.S. fluted muffin pans). Alternatively, put paper cake cases in the tins and remove them from the cakes after baking, to give the fluted design.

Sift the flour with the baking powder and cocoa. Cream the butter and sugar in a bowl until light and fluffy. Gradually beat in the egg, oil, lemon curd and lemon rind. Fold in the dry ingredients. Divide among the prepared tins.

Bake for about 15 minutes, or until firm to the touch. Leave in the tins for 1 minute then gently ease out the cakes on to a wire rack to cool.

To make the lemon filling, cream the butter and lemon curd in a bowl until soft. Gradually beat in the sugar then add enough lemon juice to flavour the mixture without making it too soft. Slice off the top of each cake, spoon a little filling on the cut surfaces and press the tops back on at a jaunty angle.

VARIATIONS

Chocolate topknots Omit the lemon curd and lemon rind in the cake mixture and substitute 2 tablespoons (U.S. 3 tablespoons) grated plain chocolate (U.S. semi-sweet chocolate). Fill the buns with 150 ml / $\frac{1}{4}$ pint double cream (U.S. $\frac{2}{3}$ cup heavy cream), whipped and mixed with a further 2 tablespoons (U.S. 3 tablespoons) grated chocolate and sift the tops with icing sugar (U.S. confectioners' sugar) before serving.

Orange iced buns Use orange curd and orange rind in the cake mixture. Do not split the baked buns. While cooling, make Orange glacé icing. Combine 175 g / 6 oz icing sugar, sifted (U.S. $1\frac{1}{3}$ cups sifted confectioners' sugar) with enough orange juice to make a thick smooth mixture. Spread icing over the buns and top each with a chocolate button. Allow the icing to set before serving.

Battenburg cakes

(Illustrated opposite)

350 g / 12 oz (U.S. 1½ cups) margarine
350 g / 12 oz caster sugar (U.S. 1½ cups granulated sugar)
6 eggs
2 tablespoons cocoa powder (U.S. 3 tablespoons unsweetened cocoa), sifted
350 g / 12 oz self-raising flour (U.S. 3 cups all-purpose flour sifted with 1 tablespoon baking powder)
1 tablespoon milk
1 teaspoon vanilla essence (U.S. vanilla extract)
FILLING AND DECORATION
100 g / 4 oz plain chocolate (U.S. ⅔ cup semi-sweet chocolate pieces)
175 g / 6 oz (U.S. ¾ cup) butter or margarine
275–350 g / 10–12 oz icing sugar, sifted (U.S. 2¼–2⅔ cups sifted confectioners' sugar)
450 g / 1 lb white marzipan
about 14 sugared jelly sweets (U.S. candies)

This recipe makes 2 finished Battenburg cakes for which you need to start with 2 × 20-cm/8-inch square Victoria sandwich cakes, one flavoured chocolate and one vanilla. As the cakes must be the same size to give a good final result, it is often best to make the basic cakes separately, using the same tin.

Heat the oven to 160°C/325°F, Gas Mark 3, line a 20-cm/8-inch cake tin with greaseproof paper (U.S. waxed paper) and grease the paper.

First make the chocolate cake. Cream half the margarine and sugar in a bowl until soft and fluffy. Add 3 of the eggs, one at a time, beating well after each addition. Sift the cocoa with half the flour and fold in with the milk. Transfer to the prepared tin, level the surface then hollow out the centre slightly.

Bake for about 45 minutes, or until just firm to the touch. Turn out on a wire rack, remove the lining paper and leave to cool.

Make a vanilla-flavoured cake in exactly the same way, using the remaining margarine, sugar, eggs, flour and vanilla essence.

For the filling and decoration, melt the chocolate in a bowl over a pan of hot water. Leave to cool. Beat the butter in a bowl until soft, gradually blend in the chocolate then add enough sugar to give a spreading consistency.

Trim the cakes to the same size then cut them in half to give 4 equal-sized slabs. Cut these in half again, lengthways, giving 8 long strips. Sandwich the chocolate and vanilla pieces of cake together in pairs with buttercream. Spread a layer on top of 2 pairs and cover with the remaining pairs, alternating chocolate and vanilla each time. Cover 3 long sides of each chequered cake with buttercream.

Make sure that the marzipan is at room temperature. If too cold it will crack when handled. Take half the marzipan and roll it out between 2 sheets of non-stick baking parchment (U.S. waxed paper) to a rectangle just over 20 cm/8 inches wide and about 40 cm/16 inches long. Trim the edges with a sharp knife. Put one cake in the centre of the marzipan with the uncoated side upwards. Spread this with buttercream. Wrap the cake in marzipan, overlapping the edges. Press firmly all round so that the covering sticks to the cake, leaving the seam underneath. Then crimp the long edges. Repeat with the other cake.

Put the remaining buttercream in a piping bag fitted with a large star tube and pipe a twisted line down the centre of each cake. Spike with sweets and leave for at least 1 hour.

Layered fudge cake

225 g / 8 oz plain flour (U.S. 2 cups all-purpose flour)
25 g / 1 oz cocoa powder (U.S. ¼ cup unsweetened cocoa)
¼ teaspoon baking powder
1 teaspoon bicarbonate of soda (U.S. baking soda)
200 g / 7 oz caster sugar (U.S. scant 1 cup granulated sugar)
100 g / 4 oz (U.S. ½ cup) soft margarine
1 teaspoon vanilla essence (U.S. vanilla extract)
2 eggs
50 ml / 2 fl oz (U.S. ¼ cup) soured cream
1 tablespoon oil
icing sugar (U.S. confectioners' sugar) for sprinkling
FILLING
200 g / 7 oz icing sugar, sifted (U.S. generous 1½ cups sifted confectioners' sugar)
40 g / 1½ oz (U.S. 3 tablespoons) butter or margarine
1 tablespoon golden syrup (U.S. light corn syrup)
4 teaspoons (U.S. 2 tablespoons) milk
2 teaspoons coffee essence (U.S. 1 tablespoon sweetened concentrated coffee flavoring)

Heat the oven to 180°C/350°F, Gas Mark 4, grease 2 × 20-cm/8-inch shallow cake tins and line with greaseproof paper (U.S. waxed paper).

Sift the flour with the cocoa, baking powder and bicarbonate of soda into a bowl. Add the remaining ingredients and beat vigorously until smooth. Divide between the prepared tins.

Bake for about 25 minutes, or until just firm to the touch. Leave in the tins for 5 minutes then turn out on a wire rack, peel off the lining paper and leave to cool.

Meanwhile, make the filling. Sift the sugar into a bowl. Put the remaining ingredients in a pan and heat gently, stirring occasionally, until the butter melts. Remove from the heat, pour into the sugar and beat until smooth. Leave to cool, beating occasionally, until the mixture is thick and holds its shape. Place one cake layer on a serving dish and spread the filling over. Place the second layer on top. Sift the top lightly with icing sugar.

Battenburg cakes

Cranberry chocolate sandwich

SERVES 8

(Illustrated opposite)

150 g / 5 oz self-raising flour (U.S. 1¼ cups all-purpose flour sifted
with 1¼ teaspoons baking powder)
25 g / 1 oz cocoa powder (U.S. ¼ cup unsweetened cocoa)
¼ teaspoon baking powder
175 g / 6 oz (U.S. ¾ cup) butter or margarine
175 g / 6 oz caster sugar (U.S. ¾ cup granulated sugar)
3 eggs
2 tablespoons (U.S. 3 tablespoons) cranberry orange sauce
FILLING
100 g / 4 oz (U.S. ½ cup) butter
225 g / 8 oz icing sugar (U.S. 1¾ cups confectioners' sugar) sifted
3 tablespoons (U.S. 4 tablespoons) cranberry orange sauce
few small chocolate curls (see page 10)

Heat the oven to 190°C/375°F, Gas Mark 5, grease 2 × 20-cm/8-inch shallow cake tins and line the bases with greaseproof paper (U.S. waxed paper).

Sift the flour with the cocoa and baking powder. Cream the butter and sugar in a bowl until light and fluffy. Beat in the eggs, one at a time, adding a spoonful of the flour mixture with each. Fold in the remaining flour mixture and the cranberry sauce. Divide between the prepared tins and level the surface.

Bake for about 20 minutes, or until firm. Turn out to cool.

Next, cream the butter and sugar in a bowl then beat in the cranberry sauce. Sandwich the cakes together with one third of the filling. Use about three-quarters of the remaining filling to cover the top of the cake and mark attractively with the tip of a knife. Put the rest in a piping bag fitted with a large star tube and pipe 8 rosettes on the cake. Top each rosette with chocolate curls. Leave to stand for 30 minutes before cutting.

Cranberry chocolate buns

MAKES 12–15

(Illustrated opposite)

225 g / 8 oz self-raising flour (U.S. 2 cups all-purpose flour sifted
with 2 teaspoons baking powder)
pinch of salt
½ teaspoon ground cinnamon
100 g / 4 oz (U.S. ½ cup) butter or margarine
100 g / 4 oz caster sugar (U.S. ½ cup granulated sugar)
100 g / 4 oz chocolate dots (U.S. ⅔ cup chocolate chips)
50 g / 2 oz (U.S. ⅓ cup) chopped candied peel
2 tablespoons (U.S. 3 tablespoons) cranberry orange sauce
1 egg

Heat the oven to 200°C/400°F, Gas Mark 6 and grease 12–15 bun tins (U.S. muffin pans).

Sift the flour with the salt and cinnamon into a bowl. Rub or cut in the butter until the mixture resembles breadcrumbs. Stir in the sugar, chocolate dots and peel. Whisk the cranberry sauce and egg together, add to the dry ingredients and mix to a fairly stiff dough. Divide the mixture among the prepared tins.

Bake for about 20 minutes, or until well risen and golden.

Apple chocolate square

50 g / 2 oz (U.S. ¼ cup) butter
225 g / 8 oz caster sugar (U.S. 1 cup granulated sugar)
1 egg, beaten
200 g / 7 oz plain flour (U.S. 1¾ cup all-purpose flour)
2 teaspoons (U.S. 1 tablespoon) baking powder
½ teaspoon ground nutmeg
½ teaspoon ground cinnamon
1 teaspoon salt
25 g / 1 oz cocoa powder (U.S. ¼ cup unsweetened cocoa)
175 ml / 6 fl oz (U.S. ¾ cup) milk
2 medium-sized cooking apples (about 350 g / 12 oz (U.S. ¾ lb)
total weight)
TOPPING
25 g / 1 oz (U.S. 2 tablespoons) butter, melted
2 tablespoons caster sugar (U.S. 3 tablespoons granulated sugar)
100 ml / 4 fl oz single cream (U.S. ½ cup light cream)
DECORATION
50 g / 2 oz plain chocolate (U.S. ½ cup semi-sweet chocolate pieces)

Heat the oven to 190°C/375°F, Gas Mark 5 and generously grease a 20-cm/8-inch square loose-based cake tin.

Put the butter in a bowl and beat until creamy. Gradually add the sugar and egg, beating all the time, until the mixture is smooth. Sift the flour 3 times with the baking powder, spices, salt and cocoa. Add to the creamed mixture alternately with the milk. When smooth, spread in the prepared tin.

Peel, core and slice the apples. Arrange the slices, slightly overlapping, in rows on the cake mixture. Brush the apples with butter and sprinkle with sugar.

Bake for 30 minutes then spoon the cream evenly over the top of the cake and return it to the oven for a further 30 minutes or until a fine skewer or wooden cocktail stick (U.S. toothpick) inserted in the centre comes out clean. Cool in the tin until just warm then transfer to a serving plate, keeping the cake still on the metal base if preferred.

To decorate, melt the chocolate in a bowl over a pan of hot water. Cool slightly then place in a paper icing bag (see page 11). Snip off the end and pipe a continuous zig-zag of chocolate over the lines of apple. Leave to set before serving.

NOTE If time is short, grate the chocolate and sprinkle it over the cake as it comes hot from the oven.

Rich chocolate cakes

100 g / 4 oz plain flour (U.S. 1 cup all-purpose flour)
50 g / 2 oz cocoa powder (U.S. ½ cup unsweetened cocoa)
½ teaspoon bicarbonate of soda
¼ teaspoon baking powder
75 g / 3 oz blended white vegetable fat (U.S. ⅓ cup vegetable
shortening)
200 g / 7 oz caster sugar (U.S. scant 1 cup granulated sugar)
2 eggs, beaten
50 g / 2 oz (U.S. ½ cup) ground almonds
½ teaspoon almond essence (U.S. almond extract)
2 tablespoons (U.S. 3 tablespoons) oil
50 ml / 2 fl oz (U.S. ¼ cup) natural yogurt

Heat the oven to 180°C/350°F, Gas Mark 4, grease the shallow cake tins or the deep tin and line with greaseproof paper (U.S. waxed paper). Stand paper cake cases in bun tins (U.S. muffin pans) or on a baking sheet (U.S. cookie sheet).

Sift the flour with the cocoa, bicarbonate of soda and baking powder and set aside. Put the fat into a bowl and cream until soft. Add the sugar and continue beating until light and fluffy. Gradually add the egg, almonds, almond essence and oil, beating well after each addition. Fold in the dry ingredients alternately with the yogurt and mix well. Transfer to the chosen tin or tins, or spoon into the paper cases.

Bake until firm to the touch, allowing about 30 minutes for shallow cake layers, about 40 minutes for a deep cake and about 25 minutes for small cakes. Cool large cakes in the tins for 5 minutes then turn out on a wire rack and cool before peeling off the lining paper. Cool the small cakes, in the paper cases, on the wire rack.

NOTE Put layers together with Vanilla-flavoured butter icing as given in Chocolate butterflies (see page 16).

Syrupy chocolate cake

SERVES 6–8

1 tablespoon golden syrup (U.S. light corn syrup)
25 g / 1 oz cocoa powder (U.S. ¼ cup unsweetened cocoa), sifted
1 tablespoon hot water
175 g / 6 oz (U.S. ¾ cup) butter or margarine
175 g / 6 oz caster sugar (U.S. ¾ cup granulated sugar)
3 eggs, beaten
65 g / 2½ oz plain flour (U.S. ⅔ cup all-purpose flour)
2 teaspoons (U.S. 1 tablespoon) baking powder
65 g / 2½ oz wholemeal flour (U.S. ⅔ cup wholewheat flour)

SYRUP

4 tablespoons golden syrup (U.S. 6 tablespoons light corn syrup)
4 tablespoons (U.S. 6 tablespoons) orange juice
1 tablespoon Grand Marnier or Cointreau

Heat the oven to 180°C/350°F, Gas Mark 4, line a 20-cm/8-inch cake tin with greaseproof paper (U.S. waxed paper) and grease the paper.

Combine the syrup, cocoa and water and set aside. Cream the butter and sugar in a bowl until light and fluffy. Gradually add the egg, beating well after each addition, then blend in the cocoa mixture. Sift the white flour with the baking powder and combine with the brown flour. Fold into the creamed mixture and transfer to the prepared tin.

Bake for about 50 minutes, or until firm in the centre. Meanwhile, make the syrup. Place the golden syrup, juice and liqueur in a pan and heat gently, stirring, until the syrup has dissolved. Keep warm.

Turn the cake out of the tin, remove the paper then transfer to a serving plate. Prick the surface lightly with a fine skewer. Spoon the warm syrup over the hot cake and leave to stand for at least 2 hours before serving.

VARIATION

Mango cream cake Bake the cake as above and meanwhile drain a 425-g/15-oz can of mango or peach slices, reserving the syrup. Use 5 tablespoons (U.S. 7 tablespoons) mango syrup, 3 tablespoons golden syrup (U.S. 4 tablespoons light corn syrup) and 1 tablespoon rum to make the mixture for soaking the hot baked cake. At serving time, carefully split the cake into two layers and place the base on a plate. Whip 150 ml/¼ pint double cream (U.S. ⅔ cup heavy cream) and spread half over the cake base. Arrange most of the mango slices on this and cover with the second cake layer. Swirl the rest of the cream over the surface and decorate with the last of the mango slices. Chill briefly before serving.

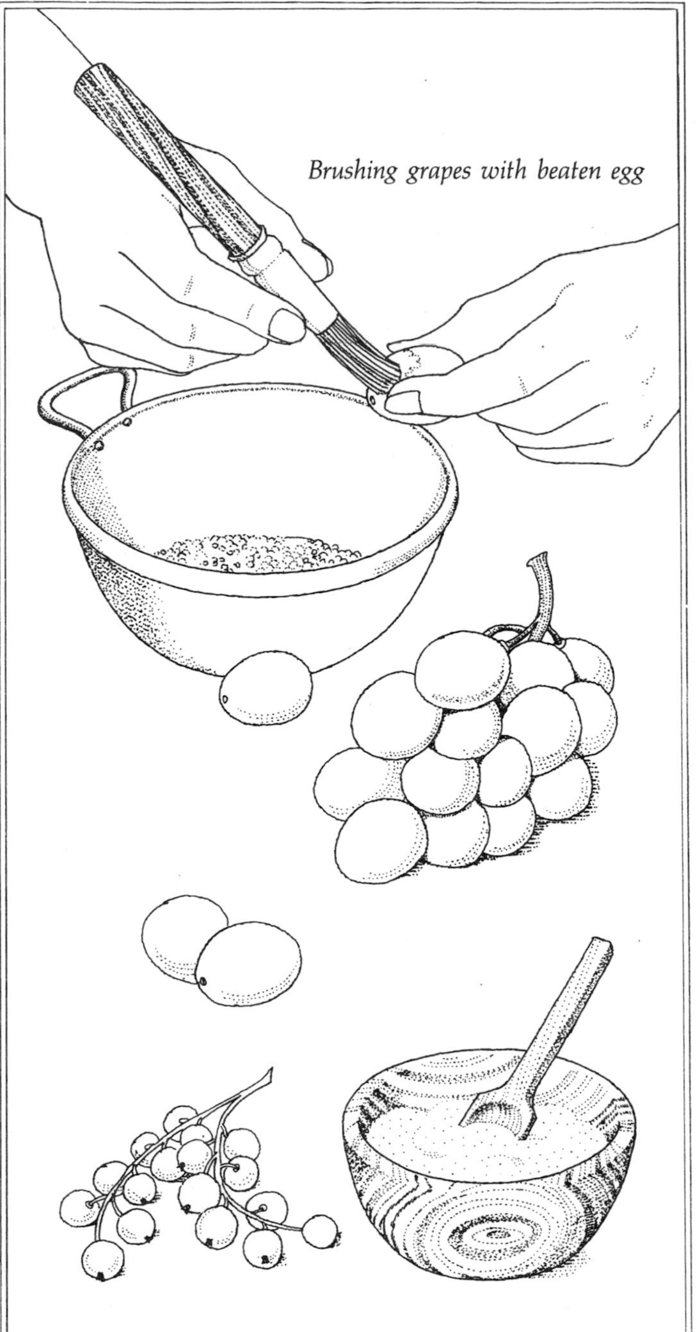

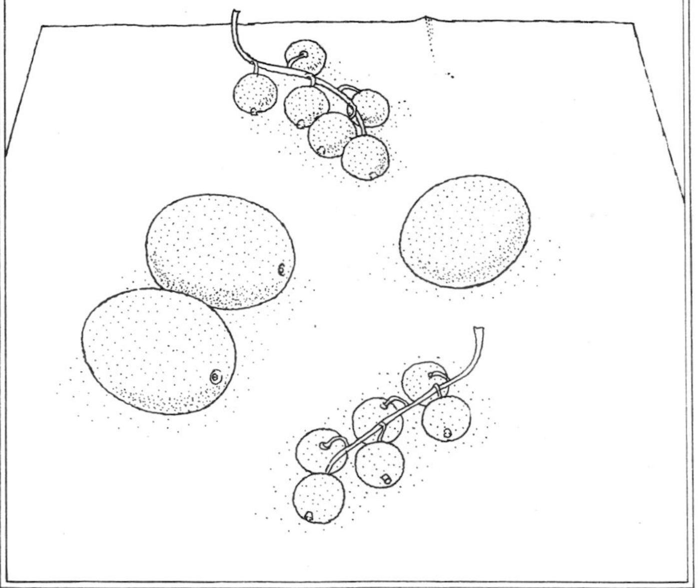

Grape cluster cake

SERVES 6

(Illustrated opposite)

75 g / 3 oz plain flour (U.S. ¾ cup all-purpose flour)
1 teaspoon baking powder
25 g / 1 oz cocoa powder (U.S. ¼ cup unsweetened cocoa)
100 g / 4 oz (U.S. ½ cup) butter or margarine
100 g / 4 oz caster sugar (U.S. ½ cup granulated sugar)
1 tablespoon oil
2 eggs
1 egg yolk
finely grated rind of 1 lime
DECORATION
15 green grapes
1 egg white
caster sugar (U.S. granulated sugar)
*150 g / 5 oz icing sugar, sifted (U.S. generous 1 cup sifted
confectioners' sugar)*
juice of 1 lime
1–2 drops green food colouring

Heat the oven to 190°C/375°F, Gas Mark 5, line a 20-cm/8-inch cake tin with greaseproof paper (U.S. waxed paper) and grease the paper.

Sift the flour with the baking powder and cocoa. Cream the butter and sugar in a bowl until light and fluffy. Add the oil, then the eggs, one at a time, beating well after each addition. Put in the egg yolk, lime rind and a little of the flour mixture and beat again. Fold in the remaining dry ingredients. Transfer to the prepared tin, level the surface, then hollow out the centre slightly so that the baked cake will be flat.

Bake for about 20 minutes, or until just firm to the touch. Turn out on a wire rack, peel off the lining paper and leave to cool.

To make the decoration, wash and dry the grapes with absorbent kitchen towel. Whisk the egg white until frothy. Brush the grapes with egg white and sprinkle generously with sugar. Place on a sheet of greaseproof paper (U.S. waxed paper). Mix the icing sugar with enough of the lime juice to make a soft spreading consistency. It will depend on the size and juiciness of the lime whether you need all the juice, or even, if the fruit is quite dry, to add a few drops of water to give the correct consistency to the icing. Tint very pale green with food colouring and spread over the top of the cake. Carefully lift the grapes and arrange them on top alternately in pairs and groups of three.

VARIATION

Currant cluster cake Substitute 6 small clusters redcurrants or blackcurrants for the grapes. Frost as for grapes. Flavour and colour the icing with 1–2 tablespoons (U.S. 2–3 tablespoons) concentrated blackcurrant fruit syrup.

Brushing grapes with beaten egg

Drying sugar-sprinkled fruit for decoration

Grape cluster cake

Chocolate mayonnaise cake

225 g / 8 oz plain flour (U.S. 2 cups all-purpose flour)
25 g / 1 oz cocoa powder (U.S. ¼ cup unsweetened cocoa)
2 teaspoons (U.S. 1 tablespoon) baking powder
½ teaspoon bicarbonate of soda (U.S. baking soda)
175 g / 6 oz caster sugar (U.S. ¾ cup granulated sugar)
3 tablespoons (U.S. 4 tablespoons) fresh egg mayonnaise
200 ml / 7 fl oz (U.S. scant 1 cup) water
1 teaspoon vanilla essence (U.S. vanilla extract)
FILLING AND DECORATION
4–5 tablespoons (U.S. 6–7 tablespoons) apricot jam
little sifted icing sugar (U.S. confectioners' sugar) for sprinkling

Heat the oven to 180°C/350°F, Gas Mark 4, grease two 17.5-cm/7-inch shallow cake tins and line the bases with greaseproof paper (U.S. waxed paper).

Sift the flour with the cocoa, baking powder and bicarbonate of soda into a bowl and stir in the sugar. Add the mayonnaise and mix with a fork, gradually adding the water, until the batter is smooth. Add the vanilla and beat for a few seconds. Divide between the prepared tins.

Bake for about 30 minutes, or until just firm to the touch. Leave in the tins to cool completely then turn out and remove the lining paper. Sandwich the cakes together with the jam and sift the top lightly with sugar before serving.

VARIATION

Spiced chocolate mayonnaise cake Add 1 teaspoon ground cinnamon, ½ teaspoon ground nutmeg and a tiny pinch of ground cloves to the dry ingredients before sifting. When cold, sandwich the cakes together with the jam and serve with whipped cream.

Chocolate coconut pyramids

2 large egg whites
175 g / 6 oz caster sugar (U.S. ¾ cup granulated sugar)
2 tablespoons drinking chocolate powder (U.S. 3 tablespoons sweetened cocoa)
½ teaspoon almond essence (U.S. almond extract)
175 g / 6 oz desiccated coconut (U.S. 2 cups shredded coconut)
about 3 glacé cherries (U.S. candied cherries), quartered
DECORATION
50 g / 2 oz plain chocolate (U.S. ⅓ cup semi-sweet chocolate pieces)

Heat the oven to 180°C/350°F, Gas Mark 4 and line 1 or 2 baking sheets (U.S. cookie sheets) with non-stick baking parchment (U.S. waxed paper) or rice paper.

Put the egg whites in a bowl and whisk until stiff. Gradually add the sugar and chocolate powder, a tablespoon at a time, whisking well after each addition until the meringue is firm and glossy. Whisk in the almond flavouring and fold in the coconut. Spoon the mixture out into 12 even sized heaps on the lined sheet and shape each into a round pyramid shape with dampened fingers. Lightly press a piece of cherry into the top of each pyramid.

Bake for about 12 minutes, or until the top of each is turning golden. Cool.

Meanwhile, melt the chocolate in a bowl over a pan of hot water and leave to cool slightly. Transfer the chocolate to a paper icing bag (see page 11). Snip off the tip of the bag and pipe a spiral of chocolate over each pyramid. Leave to set then lift off the parchment or tear away excess rice paper.

Bran fruit loaf

100 g / 4 oz (U.S. 1½ cups) All Bran or Bran Buds
100 g / 4 oz (U.S. ⅔ cup) seedless raisins
100 g / 4 oz sultanas (U.S. ⅔ cup seedless white raisins)
150 g / 5 oz soft brown sugar (U.S. ⅔ cup light brown sugar)
300 ml / ½ pint (U.S. 1¼ cups) milk
50 g / 2 oz milk chocolate (U.S. 2 squares sweet chocolate)
100 g / 4 oz self-raising flour (U.S. 1 cup all-purpose flour sifted with 1 teaspoon baking powder)
½ teaspoon ground cinnamon
1 tablespoon cocoa powder (U.S. unsweetened cocoa)

Put the cereal, raisins, sultanas and sugar in a bowl and stir to mix. Pour over the milk, stir again and leave to stand for 30 minutes.

Heat the oven to 180°C/350°F, Gas Mark 4 and generously grease a 1-kg/2-lb loaf-shaped tin.

Break up the chocolate into small pieces. Sift the flour with the cinnamon and cocoa and stir into the fruit mixture with the chocolate. Mix well, transfer to the prepared tin and level the surface.

Bake for about 1 hour, or until a fine skewer or wooden cocktail stick (U.S. toothpick) comes out clean. Cool in the tin for 10 minutes then turn out on a wire rack. When cold, slice thinly and serve with butter.

Lunchbox fruit cake

225 g/8 oz plain flour (U.S. 2 cups all-purpose flour)
1 tablespoon baking powder
1 teaspoon salt
175 g/6 oz wholemeal flour (U.S. 1½ cups wholewheat flour)
225 g/8 oz (U.S. 1 cup) butter
50 g/2 oz cocoa powder (U.S. ½ cup unsweetened cocoa)
225 g/8 oz soft brown sugar (U.S. 1 cup light brown sugar)
1 teaspoon vanilla essence (U.S. vanilla extract)
3 tablespoons (U.S. 4 tablespoons) apricot jam
225 g/8 oz (U.S. 1⅓ cups) seedless raisins
225 g/8 oz sultanas (U.S. 1⅓ cups seedless white raisins)
100 g/4 oz glacé cherries (U.S. ½ cup candied cherries), chopped
50 g/2 oz (U.S. ⅓ cup) chopped candied peel
225 ml/8 fl oz sweet stout (U.S. 1 cup dark beer)
little milk

Heat the oven to 160°C/325°F, Gas Mark 3, grease a 20-cm/8-inch square cake tin and line with greaseproof paper (U.S. waxed paper).

Sift the white flour with the baking powder and salt into a bowl and add the brown flour. Rub or cut in the butter until the mixture resembles breadcrumbs then sift in the cocoa. Add the sugar, vanilla, jam, fruit and peel and then the stout. Mix well, adding enough milk to give a soft dropping consistency. Transfer to the prepared tin and level the surface.

Bake for about 2¼ hours, or until a fine skewer or wooden cocktail stick (U.S. toothpick) inserted in the centre comes out clean. Leave in the tin for 1 hour then turn out on a wire rack and remove the lining paper. When cold, store in an airtight container and serve cut into 5-cm/2-inch squares.

Melt-and-mix refrigerator cake

100 g/4 oz plain chocolate (U.S. ⅔ cup semi-sweet chocolate pieces)
75 ml/3 fl oz golden syrup (U.S. ⅓ cup light corn syrup)
100 g/4 oz (U.S. ½ cup) butter
225 g/8 oz Rich Tea or Marie biscuits, crushed (U.S. 2⅔ cups semi-sweet cookie crumbs)
50 g/2 oz (U.S. ⅓ cup) seedless raisins
8 glacé cherries (U.S. candied cherries), quartered
25 g/1 oz (U.S. ¼ cup) chopped mixed nuts

Grease a 1-kg/2-lb loaf-shaped tin and line the base with greaseproof paper (U.S. waxed paper).

Put the chocolate, syrup and butter in a pan and heat gently, stirring, until the chocolate has melted. Remove from the heat and stir in the remaining ingredients. Mix well and press into the prepared tin.

Leave until firm then turn out on a plate and serve cut into slices.

VARIATION

Marshmallow crunchy squares Omit the raisins and nuts and substitute 16 marshmallows. Snip half of them into quarters with wet scissors and place the rest in the pan with the chocolate, syrup and butter. Stir until the marshmallows have almost completely melted before adding the crumbs, cherries and remaining marshmallows. Press into a greased 27.5-cm/11-inch by 17.5-cm/7-inch shallow tin and cut into squares when firm.

Milk chocolate bar cakes

======== MAKES 24 ========

(Illustrated opposite)

175 g/6 oz plain flour (U.S. 1½ cups all-purpose flour)
2½ teaspoons (U.S. 3½ teaspoons) baking powder
175 g/6 oz (U.S. ¾ cup) soft margarine
175 g/6 oz caster sugar (U.S. ¾ cup granulated sugar)
3 eggs
2 tablespoons coffee essence (U.S. 3 tablespoons sweetened
concentrated coffee flavoring)

DECORATION

1 (200-g/7-oz) pack milk chocolate flavour cake covering (U.S. 7-
oz pack sweet chocolate flavor cake covering)
75 g/3 oz (U.S. ⅓ cup) margarine
175 g/6 oz icing sugar, sifted (U.S. 1⅓ cups sifted confectioners'
sugar)
1 teaspoon coffee essence (U.S. sweetened concentrated coffee
flavoring)
6 glacé cherries (U.S. candied cherries), quartered
24 small pieces of angelica (U.S. candied angelica)

Heat the oven to 160°C/325°F, Gas Mark 3, line the base of a
shallow tin measuring 32.5 cm/13 inches by 22.5 cm/9 inches
with greaseproof paper (U.S. waxed paper) and grease the
paper.

Sift the flour and baking powder into a bowl and add the
margarine, sugar, eggs and coffee flavouring. Beat until well
blended. Transfer to the prepared tin and level the surface.

Bake for 30 minutes, or until firm to the touch. Leave to cool in
the tin.

Melt the cake covering and spread over the cake. Leave to set.
Divide the cake into 3 equal-sized sections lengthways.

Beat the margarine, sugar and coffee flavouring together until
fluffy. Place in a piping bag fitted with a medium-sized star
tube. Pipe a continuous wavy line of icing down the centre of
each section of cake. Work out the measurements carefully and
arrange 8 cherry quarters and pieces of angelica on each line of
icing, to give 24 bars in all. Cut into individual bars with a sharp
knife.

Milk chocolate fruit cake

======== MAKES 8–10 SLICES ========

175 g/6 oz plain flour (U.S. 1½ cups all-purpose flour)
1 teaspoon baking powder
175 g/6 oz (U.S. ¾ cup) butter or margarine
175 g/6 oz caster sugar (U.S. ¾ cup granulated sugar)
3 eggs, beaten
50 g/2 oz (U.S. ½ cup) ground almonds
finely grated rind of ½ orange
75 g/3 oz milk chocolate (U.S. 3 squares sweet chocolate)
75 g/3 oz glacé cherries (U.S. ⅓ cup candied cherries), roughly
chopped
50 g/2 oz glacé pineapple, roughly chopped (U.S. ¼ cup roughly
chopped candied pineapple)
50 g/2 oz sultanas (U.S. ⅓ cup seedless white raisins)
50 g/2 oz (U.S. ⅓ cup) chopped candied peel

Heat the oven to 180°C/350°F, Gas Mark 4, grease a 17.5-
cm/7-inch round cake tin, line with a double thickness of
greaseproof paper (U.S. waxed paper) and grease the paper.
Stand the cake tin on a baking sheet (U.S. cookie sheet).

Sift the flour with the baking powder. Cream the butter and
sugar in a bowl until light and fluffy. Gradually add the egg,
beating well after each addition. Fold in the dry ingredients,
almonds and orange rind. Quarter each square of chocolate (U.S.
quarter each square of chocolate then quarter the smaller
squares). Add the chocolate, fruit and peel to the bowl and mix
well. Transfer to the prepared tin, level the surface then hollow
out the centre slightly.

Bake for about 1¼ hours, or until a fine skewer inserted in the
cake comes out clean. Lay a sheet of foil on the cake after 1 hour
to prevent over-browning. Leave to stand in the tin for 15
minutes then turn out on a wire rack, peel off the lining paper
and allow to cool. If time permits, wrap the cake tightly and
store for 2 days before cutting.

======== VARIATION ========

Flaky fruit cake Bake the cake as above. When ready to serve,
make a Vanilla butter icing. Cream 100 g/4 oz (U.S. ½ cup) butter
or margarine with 225 g/8 oz icing sugar, sifted (U.S. 1¾ cups
sifted confectioners' sugar) and 1 teaspoon vanilla essence (U.S.
vanilla extract). Put the cake on a serving dish and use the icing
to cover the sides thinly and the top generously. Mark the top
surface with a fork, drawing the prongs repeatedly from the
outside edge of the cake to the centre point. Take 3 large
chocolate flakes and cut into lengths the same size as the depth
of the side of the cake. Split each short length of flake into
several thinner pieces with a sharp knife. Arrange these close
together all round the sides of the cake, pressing them into the
icing so that they adhere. Finish with a glacé cherry (U.S.
candied cherry) placed in the centre of the cake.

Milk chocolate bar cakes

Ginger iced buns

===== MAKES 12 =====

(Illustrated below)

25 g / 1 oz cocoa powder (U.S. ¼ cup unsweetened cocoa), sifted
1 tablespoon boiling water
2 tablespoons (U.S. 3 tablespoons) ginger syrup from jar
75 g / 3 oz (U.S. ⅓ cup) butter or margarine
75 g / 3 oz caster sugar (U.S. ⅓ cup granulated sugar)
1 egg, beaten
1 egg yolk
3 pieces preserved ginger, chopped
100 g / 4 oz self-raising flour, sifted (U.S. 1 cup all-purpose flour
sifted with 1 teaspoon baking powder)
DECORATION
150 g / 5 oz icing sugar, sifted (U.S. generous 1 cup sifted
confectioners' sugar)
1 tablespoon ginger syrup from jar
little hot water
24 pieces crystallized ginger cake toppings (U.S. candied ginger
cake toppings)

Heat the oven to 200°C / 400°F, Gas Mark 6 and place 12 paper cake cases in bun tins (U.S. muffin pans).

Put the cocoa powder in a bowl and stir in the hot water and ginger syrup. Set aside. Cream the butter and sugar in a bowl until light and fluffy. Add the egg, then the egg yolk, beating all the time. Stir in the chopped ginger and the cocoa mixture.

When well blended, fold in the flour. Using a teaspoon, divide the mixture among the paper cases.

Bake for about 12 minutes, or until firm to the touch. Turn on to a wire rack to cool.

To make the decoration, put the sugar and ginger syrup in a bowl and gradually add just enough water to make a thick smooth mixture. Put a cap of icing on each bun and top with pieces of ginger topping. Allow the icing to set before serving.

===== VARIATIONS =====

Pineapple iced buns Omit the ginger and ginger syrup and substitute 40 g / 1½ oz glacé pineapple, chopped (U.S. scant ¼ cup chopped candied pineapple) and 2 tablespoons (U.S. 3 tablespoons) pineapple juice in the cake mixture. Make the icing with pineapple juice and top each bun with a small piece of glacé pineapple (U.S. candied pineapple).

Walnut iced buns Omit the ginger and ginger syrup and substitute 40 g / 1½ oz (U.S. ⅓ cup) chopped walnuts, 2 tablespoons (U.S. 3 tablespoons) milk and 1 teaspoon vanilla essence (U.S. vanilla extract) in the cake mixture. Make the icing with milk and top each bun with a large piece of walnut.

Pan-mix chocolate loaf

MAKES ABOUT 10 SLICES

(Illustrated below)

150 g / 5 oz (U.S. ⅔ cup) soft margarine
2 tablespoons golden syrup (U.S. 3 tablespoons light corn syrup)
50 g / 2 oz cocoa powder (U.S. ½ cup unsweetened cocoa), sifted
175 g / 6 oz caster sugar (U.S. ¾ cup granulated sugar)
½ teaspoon salt
150 ml / ¼ pint (U.S. ⅔ cup) milk
3 eggs, beaten
225 g / 8 oz plain flour (U.S. 2 cups all-purpose flour)
2½ teaspoons (U.S. 3½ teaspoons) baking powder

Heat the oven to 160°C/325°F, Gas Mark 3 and grease a 1-kg/2-lb loaf-shaped tin.

Put the margarine, syrup and cocoa in a large SilverStone pan and heat gently, stirring with a wooden spoon, until smooth. Add the sugar and salt and stir until again smooth. Blend in the milk and remove the pan from the heat. Put in the egg, beating all the time. Sift the flour and baking powder together straight into the pan and beat until well blended. Transfer to the prepared tin.

Bake for about 50 minutes, or until firm to the touch in the centre. Leave in the tin for 10 minutes then turn out on a wire rack to cool. The texture of this loaf improves if allowed to mature, sealed in a plastic bag, for at least 1 day before cutting. Serve sliced.

Date and chocolate teabread

MAKES ABOUT 10 SLICES

200 g / 7 oz plain flour (U.S. 1¾ cups all-purpose flour)
½ teaspoon baking powder
1 teaspoon bicarbonate of soda (U.S. baking soda)
225 g / 8 oz stoned dates (U.S. 1¼ cups pitted dates), chopped
150 ml / ¼ pint (U.S. ⅔ cup) water
75 g / 3 oz (U.S. ⅓ cup) butter or margarine
1 egg
75 g / 3 oz plain chocolate (U.S. 3 squares semi-sweet chocolate), grated

Heat the oven to 150°C/300°F, Gas Mark 2, grease a 1-kg/2-lb loaf-shaped tin and line with greaseproof paper (U.S. waxed paper).

Sift the flour with the baking powder and bicarbonate of soda. Put the dates in a pan and pour the water over. Cook gently, stirring, until the fruit is soft. Do not allow to boil. Remove from the heat, mix in the butter and beat until the mixture is almost smooth. Leave to cool until just warm. Beat in the egg then add the dry ingredients and beat lightly until well blended. Fold in the chocolate. Transfer to the prepared tin.

Bake for about 1¼ hours, or until springy to the touch. Cool on a wire rack and when cold, peel off the lining paper. Store, sealed in a plastic bag, for 1 day before cutting. Serve sliced and lightly buttered.

Lemon lattice cakes

(Illustrated below)

175 g / 6 oz plain flour (U.S. 1½ cups all-purpose flour)
2½ teaspoons (U.S. 3½ teaspoons) baking powder
175 g / 6 oz (U.S. ¾ cup) soft margarine
175 g / 6 oz caster sugar (U.S. ¾ cup granulated sugar)
3 eggs
finely grated rind of 2 small lemons
2 tablespoons (U.S. 3 tablespoons) lemon juice
FILLING AND DECORATION
225 ml / 8 fl oz (U.S. 1 cup) lemon curd
2 large milk chocolate flakes

Heat the oven to 160°C / 325°F, Gas Mark 3, line the base of a shallow tin measuring 32.5 cm / 13 inches by 22.5 cm / 9 inches with greaseproof paper (U.S. waxed paper) and grease the paper.

Sift the flour and baking powder into a bowl and add the margarine, sugar, eggs, lemon rind and juice. Beat well until smooth, transfer to the prepared tin and level the surface.

Bake for 30 minutes, or until firm to the touch. Leave in the tin for 5 minutes then turn out on a wire rack and remove the lining paper. Allow to cool. Spread the lemon curd over the cake then cut it in half across. Split the flakes with a sharp knife to make little 'logs' and sprinkle any flake crumbs over the lemon curd on one section of cake. Put the second piece of cake on top. Decorate with the flake 'logs', arranging them in a lattice pattern. Cut into individual cakes with a sharp knife.

Banana chocolate chip muffins

200 g / 7 oz plain flour (U.S. 1¾ cups all-purpose flour)
1½ teaspoons (U.S. 2 teaspoons) baking powder
½ teaspoon salt
½ teaspoon bicarbonate of soda (U.S. baking soda)
50 g / 2 oz (U.S. ¼ cup) lard
75 g / 3 oz caster sugar (U.S. ⅓ cup granulated sugar)
1 egg, beaten
2 bananas, mashed
50 g / 2 oz plain chocolate dots (U.S. ⅓ cup semi-sweet chocolate chips)

Heat the oven to 200°C / 400°F, Gas Mark 6 and generously grease about 16 deep bun tins (U.S. muffin pans).

Sift the flour with the baking powder, salt and bicarbonate of soda and set aside. Put the lard in a bowl and beat until creamy. Add the sugar and continue beating until the mixture is smooth and fluffy. Gradually add the egg, beating well after each addition. Start adding the dry ingredients alternately with the banana, stirring until the mixture is just smooth. Fold in the chocolate dots. Divide the mixture among the prepared tins, filling them two-thirds full.

Bake for about 20 minutes, or until firm to the touch. Serve warm.

Family fudge cake

150 g / 5 oz plain flour (U.S. 1¼ cups all-purpose flour)
2¼ teaspoons (U.S. 3½ teaspoons) baking powder
40 g / 1¼ oz cocoa powder (U.S. ⅓ cup unsweetened cocoa)
175 g / 6 oz (U.S. ¾ cup) soft margarine
175 g / 6 oz caster sugar (U.S. ¾ cup granulated sugar)
100 g / 4 oz ground toasted hazelnuts (U.S. 1 cup ground toasted filberts)
3 eggs

ICING AND DECORATION
350 g / 12 oz icing sugar, sifted (U.S. 2⅔ cups sifted confectioners' sugar)
2 tablespoons cocoa powder (U.S. 3 tablespoons unsweetened cocoa)
75 g / 3 oz (U.S. ⅓ cup) soft margarine
2 tablespoons (U.S. 3 tablespoons) milk
25 g / 1 oz chopped toasted hazelnuts (U.S. ¼ cup chopped toasted filberts)

Heat the oven to 160°C/325°F, Gas Mark 3, grease a 20-cm/8-inch cake tin and line with greaseproof paper (U.S. waxed paper).

Sift the flour with the baking powder and cocoa into a bowl, add the remaining cake ingredients and beat with a wooden spoon until smooth. Transfer to the prepared tin and level the surface.

Bake for about 1 hour, or until just firm to the touch. Leave in the tin for 5 minutes then turn out on a wire rack and cool before removing the lining paper.

To make the icing, sift the sugar and cocoa into a bowl and add the margarine and milk. Stand the bowl over a pan of hot water and stir until the icing is smooth, dark and glossy. Remove from the heat and cool, beating occasionally, until the icing is thick enough to spread.

Split the cake into two layers and sandwich together with one third of the icing. Place on a serving dish. Use the remaining icing to mask the cake completely then sprinkle the nuts evenly over the top and press down lightly with a palette knife (U.S. metal spatula) so that they adhere to the icing.

Orange ring cake

175 g / 6 oz plain flour (U.S. 1½ cups all-purpose flour)
½ teaspoon baking powder
175 g / 6 oz (U.S. ¾ cup) soft margarine
175 g / 6 oz caster sugar (U.S. ¾ cup granulated sugar)
3 eggs
50 g / 2 oz plain chocolate dots (U.S. ⅓ cup semi-sweet chocolate chips)
100 g / 4 oz sultanas (U.S. ⅔ cups seedless white raisins)
finely grated rind of ½ orange
2 tablespoons (U.S. 3 tablespoons) orange juice

ICING
100 g / 4 oz icing sugar, sifted (U.S. scant 1 cup sifted confectioners' sugar)
finely grated rind of ½ orange
about 2 tablespoons orange juice

Heat the oven to 160°C/325°F, Gas Mark 3 and grease and flour a 20-cm/8-inch plain ring tin. Place it on a baking sheet (U.S. cookie sheet).

Sift the flour with the baking powder into a bowl, add the remaining ingredients and beat with a wooden spoon until well blended. Spoon into the prepared tin and level the surface.

Bake for about 1¼ hours, or until just firm to the touch. Cool in the tin then turn out on a serving plate.

To make the icing, mix the sugar with the orange rind and enough juice to make an icing which is quite thick but will just run off the spoon. Spoon it over the ring so that it trickles down inside and out but does not cover the cake completely.

VARIATION

Whiskey fruit ring cake Omit the orange juice from the cake and substitute 2 tablespoons (U.S. 3 tablespoons) Irish whiskey.

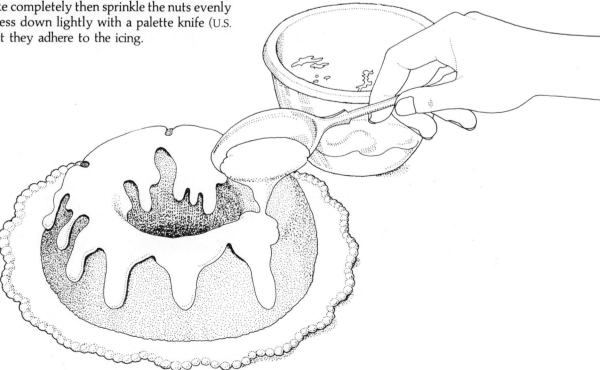

Toffee peanut fingers

MAKES 24

100 g/4 oz plain flour (U.S. 1 cup all-purpose flour)
40 g/1½ oz cornflour (U.S. ⅓ cup cornstarch)
2 tablespoons cocoa powder (U.S. 3 tablespoons unsweetened cocoa)
50 g/2 oz caster sugar (U.S. ¼ cup granulated sugar)
150 g/5 oz (U.S. ⅔ cup) butter or margarine
TOPPING
100 g/4 oz (U.S. ½ cup) butter or margarine
100 g/4 oz caster sugar (U.S. ½ cup granulated sugar)
2 tablespoons golden syrup (U.S. 3 tablespoons light corn syrup)
1 (198-g/7-oz) can sweetened condensed milk
50 g/2 oz (U.S. ½ cup) finely chopped roasted peanuts
1 (200-g/7-oz) pack milk chocolate flavour cake covering (U.S. 7-oz pack sweet chocolate flavor cake covering)

Heat the oven to 180°C/350°F, Gas Mark 4 and grease a shallow tin measuring about 27.5 cm/11 inches by 17.5 cm/7 inches.

Sift the flour with the cornflour and cocoa into a bowl and stir in the sugar. Rub or cut in the butter then mix until you can gather the dough together into a ball. Press it into the prepared tin and bake for 20 minutes, or until very pale golden.

Meanwhile, make the topping. Put the butter, sugar, syrup and condensed milk into a pan and heat gently, stirring, until the sugar has dissolved, then boil slowly without stirring, for 7 minutes. Stir in the nuts and pour immediately over the shortbread. Leave to set. Melt the cake covering as directed and spread over the caramel. Mark into 24 fingers before the covering has completely set.

VARIATIONS

Toffee raisin bars Omit the peanuts and substitute 50 g/2 oz (U.S. ⅓ cup) seedless raisins, adding them to the pan of topping before it comes to the boil.
Coconut squares Make up the shortbread base and cover with toffee as in the main recipe, omitting the peanuts. Spread 75 g/3 oz tenderized shredded coconut (U.S. 1 cup shredded coconut) on a sheet of foil and toast under a moderately hot grill (U.S. broiler) until turning golden, stirring occasionally. Take care at this point as the coconut scorches easily. Melt the cake covering, spread over the toffee and scatter the coconut on top before it sets. Press in lightly and cut into 15 squares.
Krispie fingers Make the base and toffee topping as in the main recipe and immediately it is spread over the base, sprinkle on 25 g/1 oz (U.S. 1¼ cups) crisp rice cereal and use a rolling pin to flatten it into the setting toffee. Shake off any loose cereal, then cover with chocolate cake covering in the usual way.

Frozen biscuit cake

SERVES 6–8

(Illustrated opposite)

175 g/6 oz plain chocolate (U.S. 1 cup semi-sweet chocolate pieces)
1 tablespoon golden syrup (U.S. light corn syrup)
100 g/4 oz (U.S. ½ cup) butter or margarine
100 g/4 oz digestive biscuits, roughly crumbled (U.S. 1½ cups roughly crumbled graham crackers)
1 tablespoon seedless raisins
4 glacé cherries (U.S. candied cherries), halved
50 g/2 oz flaked almonds (U.S. ½ cup slivered almonds)
1 (35-g/1¼-oz) sachet cream topping mix
150 ml/¼ pint (U.S. ⅔ cup) cold milk
6 large crystallized rose petals (U.S. candied rose petals)

Grease a 450-g/1-lb loaf-shaped tin and draw a rectangle measuring 15 cm/6 inches by 5 cm/2 inches on a sheet of non-stick baking parchment (U.S. waxed paper).

Melt the chocolate in a bowl over a pan of hot water. Take about a third of it to make the chocolate triangles (see page 10). Spread the chocolate thinly inside the marked rectangle. Leave to set.

Add the syrup and butter to the remaining chocolate and leave the bowl over the heat until the butter has melted. Stir to blend and remove from the heat. Leave to cool slightly. Mix in the biscuits, fruit and nuts. Make up the topping mix with the milk.

Spread half the chocolate mixture in the prepared tin. Top with about two-thirds of the topping, then cover with the rest of the chocolate mixture and level the surface. Cover and freeze for 2 hours. Meanwhile, trim the sheet of chocolate with a sharp knife, cut it into 5-cm/2-inch squares then divide the squares in half to give 6 triangles.

Turn the frozen cake out on a serving dish. Put the reserved topping in a piping bag fitted with a large star tube and pipe rosettes along the top of the cake. Decorate the topping with rose petals and the chocolate triangles. Serve at once.

Frozen biscuit cake

Brownies

MAKES 9

(Illustrated below)

175 g/6 oz (U.S. ¾ cup) margarine
2 tablespoons cocoa powder (U.S. 3 tablespoons unsweetened cocoa), sifted
175 g/6 oz soft brown sugar (U.S. ¾ cup light brown sugar)
2 eggs, beaten
50 g/2 oz self-raising flour, sifted (U.S. ½ cup all-purpose flour sifted with ½ teaspoon baking powder)
50 g/2 oz (U.S. ½ cup) chopped walnuts
SAUCE
100 g/4 oz (U.S. ½ cup) butter
175 g/6 oz soft brown sugar (U.S. ¾ cup light brown sugar)
4 tablespoons golden syrup (U.S. 6 tablespoons light corn syrup)
few drops lemon juice

Heat the oven to 180°C/350°F, Gas Mark 4, grease a 17.5-cm/7-inch square shallow cake tin and line the base with greaseproof paper (U.S. waxed paper).

Melt 50 g/2 oz of the margarine in a pan, stir in the cocoa and leave to cool. Place the remaining margarine and the sugar in a bowl and beat until light and fluffy. Gradually add the egg then the cocoa mixture. Finally, fold in the flour and nuts. Transfer to the prepared tin and level the surface.

Bake for about 35 minutes, or until just firm to the touch. Meanwhile, make the sauce. Put the butter, sugar and syrup in a pan and heat gently, stirring, until the sugar has dissolved. Bring to the boil and cook for 1 minute, then blend in the lemon juice. Use a SilverStone pan to prevent sticking.

Serve the brownies straight from the oven, cut into 9 squares, with the hot butterscotch sauce. Or, cool in the tin and serve plain, cut into squares.

VARIATION

Fudge brownies Bake the brownies as in the main recipe and leave to cool then cover with this Fudge icing. Put 25 g/1 oz (U.S. 2 tablespoons) butter or margarine in a pan with 75 g/3 oz plain chocolate dots (U.S. ½ cup semi-sweet chocolate chips), 75 g/3 oz caster sugar (U.S. ⅓ cup granulated sugar) and 3 tablespoons (U.S. 4 tablespoons) milk. Heat very gently, stirring all the time, until the chocolate has melted and the sugar dissolved. Bring to the boil then cook over low heat for 3 minutes. Remove from the heat, add 100 g/4 oz icing sugar, sifted (U.S. scant 1 cup sifted confectioners' sugar) and ½ teaspoon vanilla essence (U.S. vanilla extract) and beat until smooth. Spread over the brownies and leave to set. Cut into 9 squares. If wished, press a walnut or pecan half into the icing on each portion before it sets.

Pistachio cake

SERVES ABOUT 8

(Illustrated below)

*225 g / 8 oz self-raising flour (U.S. 2 cups all-purpose flour sifted
with 2 teaspoons baking powder)
pinch of salt
225 g / 8 oz (U.S. 1 cup) butter or margarine
225 g / 8 oz caster sugar (U.S. 1 cup granulated sugar)
4 eggs
1½ teaspoons pistachio or almond essence (U.S. extract)
few drops green food colouring*

FILLING AND DECORATION

*little boiling water
4 tablespoons cocoa powder (U.S. 6 tablespoons unsweetened
cocoa), sifted
175 g / 6 oz (U.S. ¾ cup) butter or margarine
350 g / 12 oz icing sugar, sifted (U.S. 2⅔ cups sifted confectioners'
sugar)
2 tablespoons (U.S. 3 tablespoons) chopped blanched pistachio
nuts
2 tablespoons (U.S. 3 tablespoons) grated chocolate
8 chocolate dots (U.S. chocolate chips)*

Heat the oven to 180°C/350°F, Gas Mark 4, grease a 20-cm/8-inch square non-stick cake tin. Line other tins with greaseproof paper (U.S. waxed paper) and grease the paper lightly.

Sift the flour with the salt and set aside. Cream the butter and sugar in a bowl until light and fluffy. Add the eggs, one at a time, beating well after each addition and sprinkling in a little of the dry ingredients with the last egg. Beat in the pistachio essence then fold in the rest of the flour mixture. Tint pale green with food colouring. Transfer to the prepared tin, level the surface then hollow out the centre slightly so that the baked cake will be flat.

Bake for about 55 minutes, or until firm to the touch. Turn out on a wire rack and leave to cool.

Meanwhile, make the filling and decoration. Mix just enough boiling water into the cocoa to make a thick smooth cream. Cool. Cream the butter and sugar in a bowl until light and fluffy. Gradually beat in the cocoa mixture.

Split the cake into 2 layers and sandwich it together with about one third of the buttercream. Spread another one third on the top of the cake and put the remainder in a piping bag fitted with a large star tube. Pipe a border of shells and rosettes around the top edge of the cake. Sprinkle the centre with chopped pistachios and then grated chocolate. Press a pair of chocolate dots at each corner.

Coffee iced Swiss roll

(Illustrated opposite)

50 g / 2 oz plain flour (U.S. ½ cup all-purpose flour)
25 g / 1 oz cocoa powder (U.S. ¼ cup unsweetened cocoa)
pinch of salt
3 large eggs
75 g / 3 oz caster sugar (U.S. ⅓ cup granulated sugar)
extra caster sugar (U.S. granulated sugar)
FILLING AND DECORATION
175 g / 6 oz (U.S. ¾ cup) butter or margarine
250 g / 9 oz icing sugar, sifted (U.S. 2 cups sifted confectioners'
sugar)
1 tablespoon coffee essence (U.S. sweetened concentrated coffee
flavoring) or 1 teaspoon instant coffee powder dissolved in
1 tablespoon hot water

Heat the oven to 200°C/400°F, Gas mark 6, line a shallow tin measuring about 32.5 cm/13 inches by 22.5 cm/9 inches with greaseproof paper (U.S. waxed paper), then grease the paper.

Sift the flour with the cocoa powder and salt and set aside. Put the eggs and sugar in a large bowl and stand this over a pan of simmering water, without allowing the base of the bowl to touch the water. Whisk steadily, using an electric mixer if possible, until thick. When ready, the mixture should fall back on itself in a firm ribbon when the beaters are lifted. Remove the bowl from the heat and continue whisking until cool. Fold in the dry ingredients lightly but thoroughly. Transfer to the prepared tin and tilt this until the mixture forms an even layer.

Bake for about 10 minutes, or until the centre of the cake springs back when lightly pressed. While the cake is in the oven, lay a clean damp tea-towel on a working surface and cover this with a sheet of greaseproof paper (U.S. waxed paper). Sprinkle sugar over the paper.

Turn the cake out on the sugared surface, remove the lining paper and trim off the crusty cake edges with a sharp knife. Cut a shallow groove in the cake about 2 cm/¾ inch from one short end then tightly roll up the cake with the paper inside. Place on a wire rack with the end underneath and leave to cool for just 30 minutes. Meanwhile, make the icing. Cream the butter until soft then gradually beat in the sugar and coffee flavouring.

Unroll the cake, spread it thinly with icing and roll up again. Set the cake on a serving dish and put the rest of the butter icing in a piping bag fitted with a medium-sized star tube. Cover the sides and top of the cake with parallel lines of icing, piping it in continuous twisting ropes.

Peppermint sandwich crunchies

100 g / 4 oz (U.S. ½ cup) butter or margarine
225 g / 8 oz golden syrup (U.S. ⅔ cup light corn syrup)
100 g / 4 oz drinking chocolate powder (U.S. 1 cup sweetened
cocoa)
100 g / 4 oz (U.S. 5 cups) bran or wheat flakes
FILLING
350 g / 12 oz icing sugar, sifted (U.S. 2⅔ cups sifted confectioners'
sugar)
75 g / 3 oz (U.S. ⅓ cup) butter or margarine
3 tablespoons (U.S. 4 tablespoons) milk
few drops peppermint essence (U.S. peppermint extract)
few drops green food colouring

Lightly grease a 20-cm/8-inch square loose-based cake tin.

Put the butter and syrup in a large pan and heat gently until the fat melts. Stir in the drinking chocolate powder and the flakes.

To make the filling, put the sugar into a bowl. Place the butter and milk in a pan and heat gently until the fat melts. Pour into the sugar, add the essence and food colouring and beat until smooth.

Press half the flake mixture into the prepared tin to make an even layer. Cover with the peppermint filling and then the rest of the flake mixture. Press down all over with the back of a spoon. Chill until firm then cut into 5-cm/2-inch squares.

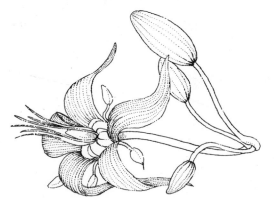
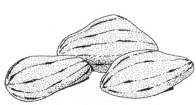

Coffee iced Swiss roll

Confectionery

Those tempting boxes of petits fours and hand-made chocolates once considered acceptable small gifts have now soared dramatically in price. When you buy them the ingredients are not always of the finest, and however pretty the box, its contents may prove disappointing. Making your own sweetmeats is well worth while, and is really much easier than it appears. Even simple fudge, fondants and truffles are expensive to buy. The cost, if you make your own confectionery, is probably halved, and you can be sure only the finest ingredients are used. Presentation is extremely important so don't stint on decorative paper sweet cases. Fortunately, each tiny pack holds dozens. Cardboard gift boxes do cost more than one expects, but are not strictly necessary. Pack your gift in a plastic container that will have a secondary use for storage in the kitchen when it is empty, as it soon will be with such delicious contents. Or cover boxes that come your way in the course of food shopping with gift paper and a ribbon bow. Squat glass jars with their own stoppers are fine for truffles and fudge. Dressing up the container to a professional standard is a great part of the fun in sweet-making. And what delightful presents they make, especially as you can custom-tailor the contents to suit individual tastes.

The art of chocolate-making was once considered quite beyond the amateur's scope. In fact, it requires no special expertize or tools. I have found the warnings given in many books on the importance of gauging the exact temperature of the liquid chocolate used for dipping or the humidity of the atmosphere unnecessarily off-putting. Nothing could be simpler. The method is very fully described on page 51, including ways to decorate, even using gold leaf as the most refined experts do.

Petits fours are sometimes moulded, or piped while the mixture is still warm. That too is relatively easy. The Schokaladen Fisch could be finished in any small mould not necessarily a fish mould, or in the base of a larger mould as it turns out with very little persuasion. This, and the hazelnut mixture, can be more simply finished by forming into balls, rolling these in cocoa powder or very finely chopped nuts.

Clockwise from top right: Jigsaw roll (see page 56). Flake treats (recipe page 56). Swirled mallow fudge (recipe page 44). Miniature florentines (recipe page 47)

Date and cherry chews

50 g / 2 oz (U.S. ¼ cup) butter or margarine
75 g / 3 oz drained maraschino cherries (U.S. ⅓ cup drained cocktail cherries), roughly chopped
225 g / 8 oz stoned dates (U.S. ½ lb pitted dates), roughly chopped
75 g / 3 oz caster sugar (U.S. ⅓ cup granulated sugar)
40 g / 1½ oz (U.S. 1½ cups) cornflakes
75 g / 3 oz (U.S. ¾ cup) chopped walnuts
50 g / 2 oz plain chocolate dots (U.S. ⅓ cup semi-sweet chocolate chips)
COATING
sifted drinking chocolate powder (U.S. sweetened cocoa)

Put the butter in a pan and heat very gently until melted. Add the cherries, dates and sugar and stir until the date pieces are soft. Cool until just warm then stir in the cornflakes, nuts and chocolate dots and mix well.

Shape the mixture into balls, each about the size of a walnut, and roll in chocolate powder. Serve in small paper cases.

VARIATION

Coconut chocolate chews Add an extra 25 g / 1 oz (U.S. 2 tablespoons) butter. Omit the cherries and add 25 g / 1 oz desiccated coconut (U.S. ⅓ cup shredded coconut) with the flakes, nuts and chocolate dots. Roll the shaped balls in more coconut if preferred.

Coconut petits fours

175 g / 6 oz tenderized desiccated coconut (U.S. 2 cups shredded coconut)
225 g / 8 oz icing sugar, sifted (U.S. 1¾ cups sifted confectioners' sugar)
1 tablespoon orange flower water or orange juice
4 tablespoons (U.S. 6 tablespoons) rum
¼ teaspoon coconut essence (U.S. coconut extract)
COATING
about 225 g / 8 oz plain chocolate (U.S. 1⅓ cups semi-sweet chocolate pieces)

Combine the coconut, sugar, orange flower water, rum and coconut essence in a bowl working with a wooden spoon until the mixture sticks together. Place a sheet of non-stick baking parchment (U.S. waxed paper) on a baking sheet (U.S. cookie sheet).

Form the coconut mixture into even-sized balls, each about the size of a large cherry. Arrange on the parchment and chill for 30 minutes.

Melt the chocolate in a bowl over a pan of hot water.

Using a wooden cocktail stick (U.S. toothpick) to lift each ball, dip in the chocolate then allow excess to drip off and use another stick to remove any drips and to push the coated ball off the spike on to the parchment again. When all are coated, leave to set. Serve in small paper cases if wished. (Use any leftover chocolate to make Nutty clusters, see page 52.)

Chocolate fudge variations

(Illustrated opposite)

450 g / 1 lb granulated sugar
50 g / 2 oz (U.S. ¼ cup) butter
25 g / 1 oz cocoa powder (U.S. ¼ cup unsweetened cocoa), sifted
2 tablespoons (U.S. 3 tablespoons) clear honey
1 (198-g / 7-oz) can sweetened condensed milk
4 tablespoons (U.S. 6 tablespoons) water

Grease a 17.5-cm / 7-inch square shallow cake tin.

Put all the ingredients into a large heavy-based pan. Stir constantly over very gentle heat until the sugar has completely dissolved. Bring slowly to the boil then cook steadily, stirring occasionally to prevent the mixture burning on the base, until it reaches a temperature of 114°C / 238°F. To test without using a thermometer, drop a little of the mixture into cold water. If you can lift it out and mould it into a soft ball with your fingers, it is ready. Remove the pan from the heat and immediately beat the mixture vigorously with a wooden spoon until it thickens and is smooth without being grainy. Pour the plain chocolate fudge into the prepared tin or add the chosen flavouring ingredients. Leave to set for at least 6 hours then cut into 2.5-cm / 1-inch squares.

VARIATIONS

Swirled mallow fudge (Illustrated on pages 42 and 45) Add 100 g / 4 oz (U.S. ¼ lb) marshmallows to the hot fudge in the pan and pour into the prepared tin. As the marshmallows melt slightly, swirl a knife blade through the fudge a couple of times but do not over-mix. The fudge will have a very interesting pattern when cut.

Nutty fudge Stir 50 g / 2 oz (U.S. ½ cup) chopped pecans, walnuts, peanuts or hazelnuts (U.S. filberts) into the fudge in the pan.

Rum and raisin fudge Soak 100 g / 4 oz (U.S. ⅔ cup) seedless raisins in 2 tablespoons (U.S. 3 tablespoons) rum for 2 hours. Add to the fudge mixture before pouring it into the tin.

Chocolate cherry fudge Quarter 100 g / 4 oz glacé cherries (U.S. ½ cup candied cherries) and scatter over the fudge mixture as soon as it is poured into the tin. Press the cherries into the surface with the back of a spoon before the fudge sets.

Orange chocolate fudge Add the finely grated rind of 1 orange and also, if wished, 40 g / 1½ oz (U.S. ¼ cup) finely chopped candied peel to the fudge in the pan.

Chocolate fudge variations

Hazelnut petits fours

(Illustrated opposite)

100 g/4 oz marzipan (U.S. ¼ lb almond marzipan)
few drops green food colouring
200 g/7 oz plain chocolate (U.S. generous 1 cup semi-sweet
chocolate pieces)
100 g/4 oz (U.S. ½ cup) unsalted butter
175 g/6 oz icing sugar, sifted (U.S. 1¼ cups sifted confectioners'
sugar)
50 g/2 oz ground hazelnuts (U.S. ⅓ cup ground filberts)
about 3 tablespoons chocolate vermicelli (U.S. 4 tablespoons
chocolate sprinkles or finely grated chocolate)
few small lemon slice and mimosa ball cake decorations

Have ready about 24 small paper cases. Take half the marzipan and tint green with food colouring. Roll out thinly and trim to a 12.5-cm/5-inch square then divide into 4 × 6.5-cm/2½-inch squares. Repeat with the yellow marzipan.

Put the chocolate and butter in a pan over very gentle heat, stirring frequently, until the chocolate melts. Remove from the heat and work in the sugar and nuts. Transfer to a piping bag fitted with a large star tube. While the mixture is still warm and pliable, pipe rosettes into about 15 of the paper cases. When it becomes too firm to pipe, form the remainder into small balls, about the same size as the rosettes. There will be between 15 and 18.

Place a ball of chocolate mixture in the centre of each marzipan square, bring up all 4 corners into the centre and pinch the folded sides to hold the ball in place. Open back the top points like flower petals. Coat the remaining balls of chocolate mixture with vermicelli and serve in paper cases. Decorate each piped petit four with a tiny cake decoration.

Uncooked chocolate nougat

Line a 17.5-cm/7-inch square shallow tin with non-stick baking parchment (U.S. waxed paper). Melt 75 g/3 oz plain chocolate (U.S. ½ cup semi-sweet chocolate pieces) in a bowl over a pan of hot water. Whisk 2 egg whites in a clean bowl until stiff and gradually blend in 225 g/8 oz icing sugar, sifted (U.S. 1¾ cups sifted confectioners' sugar), 50 g/2 oz (U.S. ½ cup) finely chopped almonds, 6 glacé cherries (U.S. candied cherries), quartered and 50 g/2 oz (U.S. ⅓ cup) seedless raisins. When well combined, add the melted chocolate and mix thoroughly. Press into the prepared tin and level the surface. Leave to set for 24 hours then cut into 2.5-cm/1-inch squares.

Nougat and marzipan candies Make the nougat as above but do not cut up. Roll out 225 g/8 oz marzipan (U.S. ½ lb almond marzipan) and trim to a rectangle measuring 35 cm/14 inches by 17.5 cm/7 inches. Cut in half to give 2 squares. lay one on a sheet of non-stick baking parchment (U.S. waxed paper). Turn the nougat out on top, remove the lining parchment and lay the second square of marzipan over the nougat. Put the same piece of lining parchment over the surface and press with the base of the tin to make the layers adhere to each other. Cut into pieces measuring 4 cm/1½ inches by 2 cm/¾ inch with a sharp knife.

Hazelnut petits fours

Miniature florentines

(Illustrated on page 42)

50 g/2 oz (U.S. ¼ cup) butter
50 g/2 oz caster sugar (U.S. ¼ cup granulated sugar)
4 glacé cherries (U.S. candied cherries), chopped
25 g/1 oz (U.S. scant ¼ cup) chopped candied peel
15 g/½ oz flaked almonds (U.S. ⅛ cup slivered almonds)
50 g/2 oz blanched hazelnuts, chopped (U.S. ½ cup chopped
blanched filberts)
1 tablespoon whipped cream
175 g/6 oz plain chocolate (U.S. 1 cup semi-sweet chocolate
pieces)

Heat the oven to 180°C/350°F, Gas Mark 4 and line 2 baking sheets (U.S. cookie sheets) with non-stick baking parchment (U.S. waxed paper).

Melt the butter in a pan, add the sugar and stir over gentle heat until it has dissolved. Bring slowly to the boil. Remove from the heat, stir in the cherries, peel and nuts then fold in the cream. Put 18 small heaps of the mixture on the lined sheets, spacing them out well, and flatten each one slightly.

Bake for about 8 minutes or until the mixture has spread and turned golden brown. After 5 minutes, draw the edges of the florentines into a neat round shape using a plain biscuit cutter (U.S. cookie cutter).

Leave to stand for a few minutes, then transfer with a spatula to a wire rack and allow to cool completely.

Melt the chocolate in a bowl over a pan of hot water, spread generously over the flat side of each florentine and mark with a fork into wavy lines. Leave to set before serving.

Ginger and almond florentines *(Illustrated on page 9)* Omit the hazelnuts and peel and substitute a total of 65 g/2½ oz flaked almonds (U.S. generous ½ cup slivered almonds) and 25 g/1 oz (U.S. scant ¼ cup) chopped preserved ginger. Increase the whipped cream to 3 tablespoons (U.S. 4 tablespoons) and add 2 tablespoons plain flour (U.S. 3 tablespoons all-purpose flour) with the fruit and nuts to the pan. Spoon out into 12 heaps, flatten and bake for about 10 minutes, or until golden brown. Coat the biscuits with chocolate as above.

Apricot and coconut florentines *(Illustrated on page 102)* Substitute 40 g/1½ oz (U.S. ¼ cup) chopped dried apricots for the peel, reduce the almonds to 25 g/1 oz (U.S. ¼ cup) and add 25 g/1 oz desiccated coconut (U.S. ⅓ cup shredded coconut, chopped). Spoon out and bake as for Ginger and almond florentines. Use 1 (200-g/7-oz) pack milk chocolate flavour cake covering (U.S. 7-oz pack sweet chocolate flavor cake covering) to coat the biscuits.

Marzipan targets

=============== MAKES 12 ===============

225 g / 8 oz marzipan (U.S. ½ lb almond marzipan)
few drops orange food colouring
few drops green food colouring
100 g / 4 oz plain chocolate (U.S. ⅔ cup semi-sweet chocolate pieces)

Take half the marzipan and tint orange with food colouring. Take two-thirds of the remaining marzipan and tint this green with food colouring.

Form the yellow marzipan into a roll 17.5 cm / 7 inches long. Roll out the green marzipan to an oblong the same length and just wide enough to enclose the roll (about 6.5 cm / 2½ inches). Roll out the orange marzipan to an oblong, again the same length but about 9 cm / 3½ inches wide.

Wrap the green marzipan around the roll, smoothing out all air bubbles and easing the cut edges together to make a neat seam. Roll lightly along the length with the palm of your hand to encourage the layers of marzipan to adhere to each other. Repeat with the orange marzipan. If time permits, leave to dry out slightly at room temperature for 30 minutes.

Melt the chocolate in a bowl over a pan of hot water and brush over the roll. Before it sets, score the surface with the tip of a pointed knife to make the roll look more like a log.

Trim off one end at an angle then cut 12 diagonal slices.

=============== VARIATIONS ===============

Marzipan plaits Divide the marzipan into 3 equal portions and tint one green and one orange as above. Tint the remaining portion by kneading in ½ teaspoon cocoa powder (U.S. unsweetened cocoa). Roll out each piece separately to a thin rope about 30 cm / 12 inches long. Place the ropes side by side on a board and plait them (U.S. braid them) evenly from one end to the other. Cut into 12 equal-sized pieces, then coat each with chocolate and leave to set on non-stick baking parchment (U.S. waxed paper). Serve in paper cases if wished.

Cherry marzipan delights Tint the whole of the marzipan pale green with food colouring and roll out to a thickness of about 6 mm / ¼ inch. Stamp out rounds using a small fluted cutter (about 4 cm / 1½ inches in diameter is ideal). Gather up the trimmings and re-roll to make more rounds. Place the rounds on a sheet of non-stick baking parchment (U.S. waxed paper) and leave to dry for 8 hours. Drain maraschino cherries (U.S. cocktail cherries) and cut in half. Place one on each marzipan round, cut surface downwards. Melt the chocolate and use to coat the cherry and marzipan shapes. When set, serve in small paper cases.

Marzipan basket

To make a centrepiece that is edible, roll 225 g / 8 oz marzipan (U.S. ½ lb almond marzipan) out 1.25-cm / ½-inch thick, cut round a 15-cm / 6-inch plate to form a neat circle and place on a loose cake tin base. Gather up the trimmings, add to a further 225 g / 8 oz marzipan and roll out thinly. Cut into narrow strips and form these into thin rolls, and twist 2 evenly to form a coiled rope long enough to edge the circle neatly. Brush the rope with beaten egg and press into place. Form another coiled

rope a little longer than the first, brush with egg and press on to the first rope, so that the top of the basket is a little more open. Brush all sides with egg and bake at 180°C/350°F, Gas Mark 4 for 10 minutes, or until just beginning to turn golden. Loosen while still warm and transfer very carefully to a flat serving plate using 2 palette knives (U.S. metal spatulas). Serve filled with miniature Easter eggs.

Stages in making Marzipan targets

Chocolate covered fondants

(Illustrated opposite)

450 g/1 lb granulated sugar
1 teaspoon lemon juice
100 ml/4 fl oz (U.S. ½ cup) water
large pinch of cream of tartar
few drops peppermint, orange, lemon and vanilla essences (U.S.
peppermint, orange, lemon and vanilla extracts)
few drops green, yellow and orange food colourings
icing sugar (U.S. confectioners' sugar) for sprinkling
225 g/8 oz couverture, bitter or plain chocolate (U.S. ½ lb
unsweetened or semi-sweet chocolate)
1 teaspoon corn oil
DECORATION
pieces of walnut or pecan
gold leaf flake

Prepare the fondant and shape the centres, then allow them to dry out for 24 hours before coating with chocolate.

Put the sugar, lemon juice and water in a large pan and stir over gentle heat until the sugar has completely dissolved. Bring to the boil, add the cream of tartar and cook steadily, without stirring, until the syrup reaches a temperature of 116°C/240°F. To test without using a thermometer, drop a little of the syrup into cold water. If you can lift it out and form it into a soft ball with your fingertips, it has reached the correct temperature. Draw the pan off the heat and leave to stand for 5 minutes.

Meanwhile, have ready a marble slab, a clean working surface or a heavy mixing bowl. If using a bowl, rinse this with water. Pour the syrup on to the chosen surface, or into the bowl, and leave to stand for about 10 minutes, or until it begins to form a skin round the edges. Then start to 'work' the fondant with a wooden spoon or spatula. Scrape around half the circle of fondant and turn the edges into the centre, then do the same on the other side, working in a continuous figure of 8 shape all the time. The fondant will thicken and become opaque. When it is too thick to work with the spoon or spatula, continue the movement with your hands until it is smooth and satiny and will hold its shape firmly. The longer you work, the finer the texture of the fondant will be.

Divide the fondant into 4 portions and colour and flavour them as follows. Flavour one with peppermint essence and tint it pale green, another with orange essence and tint pale orange, a third with lemon essence and tint pale yellow. Flavour the last portion with vanilla essence and leave it white. Add both colourings and flavourings sparingly and knead into the fondant until it is no longer streaky.

Sprinkle a surface with icing sugar and roll out the fondant to a thickness of about 8 mm/⅓ inch. Stamp out small round, diamond or square shapes using cutters or a sharp knife. Arrange the shapes on a sheet of non-stick baking parchment (U.S. waxed paper) and leave to dry overnight.

To coat the fondant centres, put the chocolate and oil in a bowl over a pan of hot water and leave until the chocolate has melted. Stir until experiment shows that the mixture coats well then dip the fondant centres in the chocolate, one at a time, using a two-tined dipping fork or fondue fork if possible, with a cocktail stick (U.S. toothpick) to whisk away excess chocolate before transferring the coated shapes again to the parchment. When the chocolate coating is almost set, decorate the surface with the tines of the dipping fork, or brush with soft chocolate and top with a piece of nut or a flake of gold leaf. Tweezers are the best method of transferring these tiny flakes from the tube to the chocolate. Or, put some melted chocolate in a paper icing bag (see page 11), snip off the end and pipe lines across the finished chocolates. Leave to set. When all the centres have been dipped, use up remaining melted chocolate to make Nutty clusters (see note below). If necessary, neaten the bases of the chocolates by trimming off any 'frill' before placing in paper cases or packing in gift boxes.

NOTE: To make Nutty clusters, stir chopped nuts into the left-over melted chocolate and spoon out in little heaps on the non-stick baking parchment to set.

=========== VARIATIONS ===========

Chocolate covered marzipan Substitute 1 lb marzipan (U.S. almond marzipan) for the fondant. Divide into 3 portions, leave one plain, work 2 teaspoons (U.S. 1 tablespoon) toasted sesame seeds into one and a few drops of pistachio essence (U.S. pistachio extract) and a little green food colouring into the other. Shape and coat as for fondant.
Chocolate covered candied orange peel Buy candied peel in large pieces and cut into long narrow strips with a sharp knife before coating with chocolate as above. You will need about 100 g/4 oz plain chocolate (U.S. $\frac{2}{3}$ cup semi-sweet chocolate pieces) to coat 100 g/4 oz (U.S. $\frac{1}{4}$ lb) candied peel.

Brandy truffles

=========== MAKES 16 ===========

(Illustrated below)

175 g/6 oz plain chocolate (U.S. 6 squares semi-sweet chocolate)
2 tablespoons (U.S. 3 tablespoons) brandy
10 glacé cherries (U.S. candied cherries)
40 g/1½ oz (U.S. 3 tablespoons) unsalted butter, softened
50 g/2 oz icing sugar, sifted (U.S. scant ½ cup sifted confectioners' sugar)
50 g/2 oz (U.S. ½ cup) ground almonds

Place two-thirds of the chocolate and the brandy in a bowl and stand this over a pan of hot water until the chocolate has melted. Meanwhile, chop 6 of the cherries and quarter the remainder. Add the butter, sugar, almonds and chopped cherries to the bowl and mix well. Leave in a cool place until firm enough to shape.

Divide the mixture into 16 equal pieces and form each into a ball. Grate the remaining chocolate and place in a plastic bag. Drop the truffles in, one at a time, and shake the bag until coated with chocolate. Decorate each with a piece of cherry, and serve in paper sweet cases.

Rum delights

(Illustrated below)

100 g/4 oz left-over chocolate cake, crumbled (U.S. 2 cups chocolate cake crumbs)
100 g/4 oz caster sugar (U.S. ½ cup granulated sugar)
100 g/4 oz (U.S. 1 cup) ground almonds
100 g/4 oz (U.S. ⅓ cup) apricot jam
2 tablespoons (U.S. 3 tablespoons) rum

COATING AND DECORATION

50 g/2 oz plain chocolate (U.S. ⅓ cup semi-sweet chocolate pieces)
50 g/2 oz (U.S. ½ cup) chopped blanched pistachio nuts
3 tablespoons chocolate vermicelli (U.S. 4 tablespoons chocolate sprinkles or finely grated chocolate)
3 tablespoons drinking chocolate powder (U.S. 4 tablespoons sweetened cocoa)

Mix together all the truffle ingredients and leave in a cool place for 30 minutes.

Melt the chocolate in a bowl over a pan of hot water. Put the nuts and vermicelli on separate plates and the drinking chocolate in a plastic bag. Set about 30 small paper cases on a tray.

Pinch off pieces of the truffle mixture and form into balls about 2.5 cm/1 inch in diameter. Brush the balls sparingly with melted chocolate, then roll in nuts or vermicelli, or drop into the bag of drinking chocolate powder and shake the bag until coated. Transfer at once to the paper cases.

Cherry-topped rum swirls

(Illustrated below)

275 g/10 oz plain chocolate (U.S. 1⅔ cups semi-sweet chocolate pieces)
4 tablespoons (U.S. 6 tablespoons) sweetened condensed milk
1 tablespoon rum
1 tablespoon boiling water
about 4 glacé cherries (U.S. candied cherries), cut into small pieces

Put the chocolate and condensed milk in a bowl and stand this over a pan of hot water, stirring occasionally, until the chocolate has melted. Blend in the rum and water and leave to cool, stirring occasionally, until the mixture holds its shape.

Have ready about 24 small paper cases. Put the rum mixture into a piping bag fitted with a large star tube and pipe a swirl into each paper case. Top each swirl with a small piece of cherry.

VARIATION

Almond-topped cherry swirls Use 1 tablespoon Cherry Marnier in place of the rum and top each swirl with a toasted almond flake (U.S. toasted almond sliver).

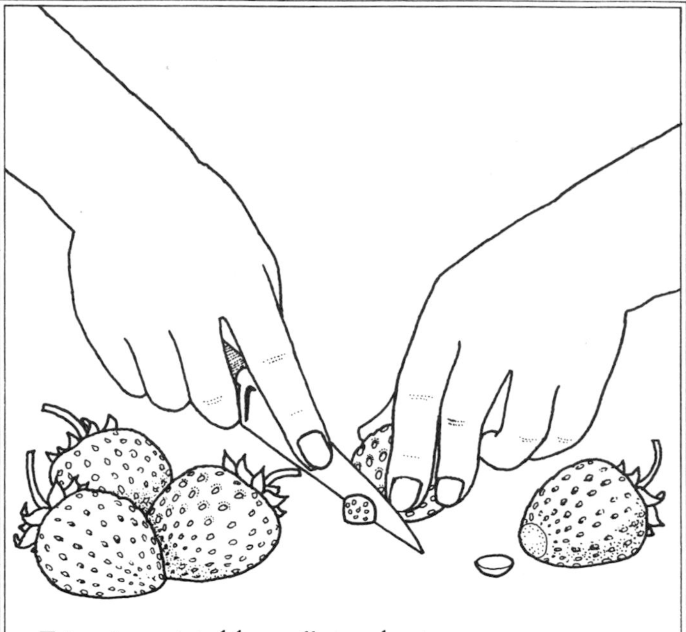

Chocolate dipped strawberries

SERVES 4

100 g/4 oz plain chocolate (U.S. ⅔ cup semi-sweet chocolate pieces)
100 g/4 oz white chocolate (U.S. ¼ lb or 4 squares white chocolate)
8 very large or 16 large strawberries, with hulls, chilled

Have ready a sheet of non-stick baking parchment (U.S. waxed paper).

Put the dark and white chocolate into separate small bowls. Stand these over hot water until the chocolate has melted. Make sure the strawberries are clean and dry. Do not wash them unless absolutely necessary. Trim a small piece off the point of each berry just before dipping, so that it will stand upright.

Holding one strawberry by the hull, dip it into dark chocolate until it is half coated. Whisk off excess chocolate with a cocktail stick (U.S. toothpick) then stand the coated berry on the parchment. Repeat with half the berries, then coat the remainder with white chocolate in the same way. Chill until set. Use up left-over melted chocolate to make Nutty clusters (see page 52).

Serve the strawberries in paper cases, giving each person fruit coated in both white and dark chocolate. Best eaten on the same day as making.

VARIATION

Chocolate dipped cherries Use 225 g/8 oz (U.S. ½ lb) ripe red cherries instead of the strawberries. Leave the stalks on and coat the cherries completely with chocolate.

Uncooked mocha fudge

MAKES ABOUT 64 PIECES

50 g/2 oz (U.S. ¼ cup) soft margarine
100 g/4 oz plain chocolate (U.S. ⅔ cup semi-sweet chocolate pieces)
2 teaspoons (U.S. 1 tablespoon) instant coffee powder
3 tablespoons single cream (U.S. 4 tablespoons light cream)
450 g/1 lb icing sugar (U.S. confectioners' sugar), sifted
DECORATION
100 g/4 oz plain chocolate (U.S. ⅔ cup semi-sweet chocolate pieces)

Grease a 20-cm/8-inch square loose-based cake tin and line the bottom with non-stick baking parchment (U.S. waxed paper).

Put the margarine and chocolate in a bowl and stand this over a pan of hot water until the chocolate has melted. Stir in the coffee, cream and sugar and mix well. Press into the prepared tin to make an even layer. Chill until firm.

Remove the sides of the cake tin and leave the fudge on the base. Melt the chocolate in a bowl as above, spread over the fudge and swirl the surface diagonally with the tip of a round-bladed knife. When set, cut into 2.5-cm/1-inch squares with a sharp knife.

Trimming pointed base off strawberries

Dipping fruit into melted chocolate

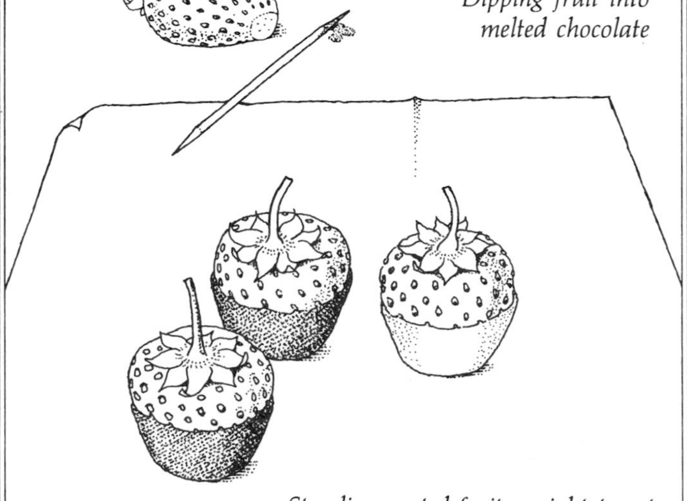

Standing coated fruit upright to set

Chocolate walnut tartlets

(Illustrated on page 97)

1½ (200-g/7-oz) packs plain chocolate flavour cake covering (U.S.
1½ × 7-oz packs semi-sweet chocolate flavor cake covering)
100 g/4 oz (U.S. ½ cup) butter or margarine
100 g/4 oz icing sugar, sifted (U.S. scant 1 cup sifted
confectioners' sugar)
50 g/2 oz chocolate cake, crumbled (U.S. 1 cup chocolate cake
crumbs)
2 tablespoons (U.S. 3 tablespoons) sweet sherry
50 g/2 oz (U.S. ½ cup) finely chopped walnuts

Melt the cake covering as directed and use two-thirds of it to
make 12 chocolate cups (see page 11). Keep the remainder
warm. Chill the chocolate cups until firm.

Cream the butter and sugar in a bowl until light and fluffy.
Gradually add the remaining cake covering and leave until the
mixture holds its shape. Transfer to a piping bag fitted with a
large star tube.

Remove the paper cases from the chocolate cups and place on
serving dishes. Moisten the cake crumbs with the sherry and
spoon into the cups. Sprinkle with almost all the nuts. Pipe a
large swirl of chocolate butter icing to cover the filling in each
tartlet and sprinkle half of them with the remaining nuts.

VARIATIONS

Ginger cream tartlets Use all the chocolate to make tartlet
cases. Fill with ginger cake crumbs mixed with the sherry and 4
pieces of preserved ginger, finely chopped, instead of the nuts.
Whip 150 ml/¼ pint double cream (U.S. ⅔ cup heavy cream) with
2 tablespoons (U.S. 3 tablespoons) syrup from the jar of ginger
and place in a piping bag fitted with a large star tube. Pipe a big
whirl of ginger cream into each tartlet case and spike the whirls
with thin slices of preserved ginger.
Mandarin chocolate tartlets Make chocolate tartlets as in the
main recipe and fill each with 3 drained mandarin orange
segments before piping the chocolate mixture on top.
Ice cream chocolate tartlets Use all the chocolate to make
tartlet cases and when ready to serve, spoon a small ball of
chocolate ice cream into each one. Press half a glacé cherry (U.S.
candied cherry) on top and serve at once.
Strawberry dessert cups Use all the chocolate to make tartlet
cases. When set, spoon a little strawberry jam into the base of
each case. Make up a 64-g/2¼-oz Sachet strawberry flavour
whipped dessert mix with just 225 ml/8 fl oz (U.S. 1 cup) milk.
As soon as it thickens, place in a piping bag fitted with a large
star tube. Pipe a rosette of strawberry dessert into each tartlet
and chill briefly before serving.

Sesame chocolate toffee

150 ml/¼ pint (U.S. ⅔ cup) clear honey
225 g/8 oz soft brown sugar (U.S. 1 cup light brown sugar)
50 g/2 oz (U.S. ¼ cup) butter or margarine
175 g/6 oz (U.S. ¾ cup) sesame seeds
25 g/1 oz cocoa powder (U.S. ¼ cup unsweetened cocoa), sifted

Grease a shallow cake tin measuring about 27.5 cm/11 inches
by 17.5 cm/7 inches.

Place all the ingredients in a pan and stir over gentle heat until
the sugar has completely dissolved. Boil steadily until the
mixture reaches a temperature of 145°C/295°F. To test
without a sugar thermometer, drop a little of the syrup into
cold water. If it separates into brittle strands, the toffee is ready.
Pour into the prepared tin, leave to cool slightly but mark into
48 squares before the toffee sets.

When completely cold, wrap closely in foil or cling film and
break off squares as required. Alternatively, break up the toffee
and wrap each piece individually in cling film.

VARIATION

Chocolate coated sesame toffee Make the toffee as above,
omitting the cocoa powder. When set, break into squares and
coat each in melted chocolate using a small pair of tongs. It
would take about 225 g/8 oz plain chocolate (U.S. 1⅓ cups semi-
sweet chocolate pieces) to coat all the toffee squares. Leave to
set on non-stick baking parchment (U.S. waxed paper) then
store in an airtight container.

After dinner cups

(Illustrated on page 9)

100 g/4 oz plain chocolate (U.S. 4 squares semi-sweet chocolate)
FILLING
150 ml/¼ pint double cream (U.S. ⅔ cup heavy cream)
few drops of coffee essence (U.S. sweetened concentrated coffee
flavoring)
1–2 drops peppermint essence (U.S. peppermint extract)
1–2 drops green food colouring
DECORATION
4 whole hazelnuts (U.S. filberts)
2 canned mandarin segments
2 canned pineapple pieces

Grate about 2 teaspoons of chocolate and reserve for the
decoration. Melt the remainder. Use to coat the insides of 12
small paper cases (see page 11). Chill until firm.

Whip the cream until just stiff and divide into 3 portions.
Flavour one with coffee essence and another with peppermint
essence, tinting it pale green with food colouring. Leave the
remaining portion unflavoured.

Carefully peel the paper cases away from the chocolate cups
and pipe or spoon in the different creams. Top each coffee cup
with a hazelnut, each peppermint cup with grated chocolate
and each plain cream cup with a small piece of fruit. Chill until
required. Serve on the day of preparation.

Peanut butter oaties

MAKES 64

100 g / 4 oz plain chocolate (U.S. $\frac{2}{3}$ cup semi-sweet chocolate pieces)
100 g / 4 oz (U.S. $\frac{1}{2}$ cup) butter or margarine
150 ml / $\frac{1}{4}$ pint evaporated milk (U.S. $\frac{2}{3}$ cup unsweetened evaporated milk)
3 tablespoons cocoa powder (U.S. 4 tablespoons unsweetened cocoa), sifted
400 g / 14 oz (U.S. $1\frac{3}{4}$ cups) granulated sugar
100 g / 4 oz (U.S. $\frac{1}{2}$ cup) crunchy peanut butter
175 g / 6 oz (U.S. $1\frac{3}{4}$ cups) rolled oats
1 teaspoon vanilla essence (U.S. vanilla extract)

Grease a 20-cm / 8-inch square loose-based cake tin and line the bottom with non-stick baking parchment (U.S. waxed paper).

Melt the chocolate in a bowl over a pan of hot water. Set aside to cool slightly. Put the butter, evaporated milk, cocoa and sugar in a pan and stir over low heat until the sugar has dissolved. Bring to the boil then cook gently for 2 minutes. Remove from the heat and add the peanut butter, oats and vanilla essence. Mix well.

Spread the chocolate in the base of the prepared tin and leave to set just until no longer sticky. Immediately spoon the peanut butter mixture on top and press down well to make an even layer. Chill for 4 hours.

Remove the tin and leave the mixture on the metal base at room temperature for 30 minutes. Using a sharp knife, cut into 2.5-cm / 1-inch squares and lift off the parchment. Serve in small paper cases if wished.

Flake treats

MAKES 18

(Illustrated on page 42)

225 g / 8 oz marzipan (U.S. $\frac{1}{2}$ lb almond marzipan)
few drops red food colouring
caster sugar (U.S. granulated sugar) for sprinkling
few drops green food colouring
18 small milk chocolate flakes

Take a quarter of the marzipan, pinch off about a third of this piece and colour bright red with food colouring. Form into 54 tiny balls and roll in sugar. These are the holly 'berries'. Colour the rest of this small piece of marzipan bright green and roll out very thinly. Using a special cutter if possible, stamp out 18 miniature holly 'leaves', or cut out diamonds with a small pointed knife then, using a round cutter, remove 2 opposite corners. Gather up the green trimmings to make more leaves. Mark veins on the leaves with the tip of the knife and sprinkle them with sugar.

Roll out the rest of the marzipan thinly and trim to a rectangle measuring 37.5 cm / 15 inches by 19 cm / 7$\frac{1}{2}$ inches. Cut this into 18 × 6.5-cm / 2$\frac{1}{2}$-inch squares with a sharp knife.

Place a flake diagonally across each square of marzipan, bring up 2 opposite corners to meet over the centre and pinch together to seal. Top each treat with a holly leaf and 3 berries.

Stuffed dates

MAKES 16

(Illustrated opposite)

16 fresh dates
225 g / 8 oz white marzipan (U.S. $\frac{1}{2}$ lb white almond marzipan)
few drops red food colouring
50 g / 2 oz plain chocolate (U.S. $\frac{1}{3}$ cup semi-sweet chocolate pieces)

Using a sharp pointed knife, slit each date and remove the stone (U.S. pit). Take half the marzipan and tint pink with food colouring. Divide each portion of marzipan into 8 equal pieces and form into sausage shapes to fit into the dates. Insert the filling in the dates and press the fruit back into shape neatly.

Melt the chocolate in a bowl over a pan of hot water. Dip the stuffed dates into the chocolate until they are about one third covered then brush off any excess. Leave to set on a sheet of non-stick baking parchment (U.S. waxed paper). Serve in small paper cases.

Jigsaw roll

MAKES ABOUT 25 SLICES

(Illustrated on page 42)

100 g / 4 oz (U.S. $\frac{1}{4}$ lb) marshmallows
75 g / 3 oz (U.S. $\frac{1}{3}$ cup) butter or margarine
75 g / 3 oz caster sugar (U.S. $\frac{1}{3}$ cup granulated sugar)
1 tablespoon cocoa powder (U.S. unsweetened cocoa), sifted
1 (150-g / 5-oz) pack Shorties – chocolate butter shortcake biscuits (U.S. 5-oz pack chocolate-coated shortcake cookies), roughly crumbled
1 egg, beaten
icing sugar (U.S. confectioners' sugar) for sprinkling

Reserve a few marshmallows to serve with the roll or, if preferred, snip them all into quarters. Put the butter in a large pan and heat gently until melted. Stir in the sugar and cocoa. When blended, add the biscuits and egg and mix well. Fold in the marshmallows.

Place a double thickness of greaseproof paper (U.S. waxed paper) on a board and sprinkle generously with sugar. Turn the biscuit mixture out on the paper and form into a roll about 20 cm / 8 inches long, using the paper to help you. Chill, wrapped in the sugared paper, for at least 6 hours.

Cut into thin slices with a sharp knife and arrange, overlapping, on a plate. Serve with any reserved marshmallows in the centre.

Stuffed dates

Schokoladen fisch

(Illustrated opposite)

3 tablespoons (U.S. 4 tablespoons) water
3 tablespoons (U.S. 4 tablespoons) sugar
1 tablespoon instant coffee powder
100 g/4 oz plain chocolate (U.S. 4 squares semi-sweet chocolate),
grated
100 g/4 oz (U.S. 1 cup) ground almonds
100 g/4 oz (U.S. ⅔ cup) chopped candied peel

Lightly oil a small decorative mould, the traditional shape being a fish.

Put the water in a pan and add the sugar and coffee. Stir over gentle heat until the sugar has dissolved then add the chocolate, almonds and peel and simmer for 5 minutes, stirring very frequently. Press into the prepared mould. Cool and chill for at least 8 hours.

Turn the mould out on a serving dish and cut into slices.

Boiled chocolate coconut ice

Put 150 ml/¼ pint (U.S. ⅔ cup) water in a heavy-based pan with 450 g/1 lb (U.S. 2 cups) granulated sugar. Heat gently, stirring, until the sugar has dissolved then add a pinch of cream of tartar and boil steadily to a temperature of 114°C/238°F, or until a little syrup dropped into cold water forms a soft ball. Add 75 g/3 oz drinking chocolate powder (U.S. ¾ cup sweetened cocoa) and stir over the heat for 1 minute. Remove and mix in 100 g/4 oz desiccated coconut (U.S. 1⅓ cups shredded coconut) and 2 tablespoons double cream (U.S. 3 tablespoons heavy cream). Beat with a wooden spoon until the mixture turns cloudy then pour into a greased 17.5-cm/7-inch square cake tin, base-lined with non-stick baking parchment (U.S. waxed paper). Leave to set then cut into 2.5-cm/1-inch squares.

Chocolate-topped coconut ice Omit the drinking chocolate (U.S. sweetened cocoa) from the recipe. Pour half the white mixture into the tin then tint the remainder pink with food colouring. Pour over the white mixture and leave to set. Melt 100 g/4 oz plain chocolate (U.S. ⅔ cup semi-sweet chocolate pieces) in a bowl over a pan of hot water. Spread evenly on the coconut ice and leave to set. Cut into 2.5-cm/1-inch squares.

Mint chocolate creams

50 g/2 oz plain chocolate (U.S. ⅓ cup semi-sweet chocolate pieces)
450 g/1 lb icing sugar (U.S. confectioners' sugar)
50 g/2 oz (U.S. ¼ cup) soft margarine
2 tablespoons (U.S. 3 tablespoons) milk
few drops peppermint essence (U.S. peppermint extract)
few drops green food colouring
icing sugar (U.S. confectioners' sugar) for sprinkling
DECORATION
75 g/3 oz plain chocolate (U.S. ½ cup semi-sweet chocolate pieces)

Melt the chocolate in a bowl over a pan of hot water. Have ready 2 bowls and sift half the sugar into each. Put half the margarine and half the milk in a pan and heat gently until the margarine has melted. Remove from the heat and add to one bowl of sugar with the chocolate. Mix with a wooden spoon until evenly combined then leave in a cool place until firm.

Melt the remaining margarine in the rest of the milk as above and add to the second bowl of sugar with 2–3 drops of peppermint essence. Mix until a ball of fondant forms. Tint this pale green with food colouring. Add more peppermint essence, a drop at a time, until flavoured to taste, kneading the paste constantly to get the colour and flavour even.

Turn the 2 balls of paste on to a surface lightly sprinkled with icing sugar and press the colours together but do not over-mix or the swirled effect will be lost. Roll out and trim to a 20-cm/8-inch square. Cut into 2.5-cm/1-inch squares with a sharp knife. Transfer the squares with a spatula on to a sheet of non-stick baking parchment (U.S. waxed paper) and leave to dry out for 8 hours.

Melt the remaining chocolate in a bowl as above. Carefully dip each square diagonally into the chocolate so that half is coated, ending up with a chocolate-covered triangle and an uncovered triangle on each square. Brush off excess chocolate and leave the squares on the parchment until set.

Uncooked ginger coconut candy

Place 100 g/4 oz plain chocolate (U.S. ⅔ cup semi-sweet chocolate pieces) and 75 ml/3 fl oz (U.S. ⅓ cup) sweetened condensed milk in a bowl and stand this over a pan of hot water until the chocolate has melted. Remove from the heat and mix in 175 g/6 oz desiccated coconut (U.S. 2 cups shredded coconut), 6 pieces preserved ginger, chopped and 275 g/10 oz icing sugar, sifted (U.S. 2¼ cups sifted confectioners' sugar). Press into a 17.5-cm/7-inch square shallow cake tin, base-lined with non-stick baking parchment (U.S. waxed paper). When firm, cut into 2.5-cm/1-inch squares.

Schokoladen fisch

Fancy Baking

Variety is endless in this department of the good cook's repertoire. It includes crisp shortbreads, delicate choux pastries, iced sweet biscuits, cookies, not to speak of costly French, Swiss and Austrian specialities which one tends to admire reverently on a display shelf behind glass, and could quite easily make up at home. Why not try your hand at some of my more exotic recipes? Begin with the simple ones first, such as Choc 'n cherry shortbread, or Date, chocolate and walnut crunch. These are recommended when you need to bake quickly, and produce plenty of the delicious results to store away so that the cookie jar or sweet biscuit tin is not empty overnight.

When small items are baked on a greased or oiled sheet, prepare it carefully, to avoid breaking when removing them from the sheet. A metal surface, even non-stick, does sometimes adhere to the underside. Check the directions carefully and, unless indicated to cool completely first, ease off the sheet while still warm. Many items which are soft at this stage will harden up and become crisp when cold, but can't be moved safely then.

Some basic items store so well, in fact, that they warrant the slightly more elaborate preparation required. Take chocolate meringues, for example. Although they can be spooned out on to non-stick baking parchment (U.S. waxed paper), from which you can easily remove them even if it has not been oiled, they look so much prettier piped with a large piping bag and a fancy tube. The long, slow, drying out process requires to be planned ahead, so that you are not in a hurry to use the oven for something else. If they are not quite dry, the centre is delightfully chewy in texture, and some people prefer them this way. Put together with sweetened whipped cream, or coffee flavoured cream, they are infinitely more sophisticated than the classic white and rather flavourless meringue. Mandel confeckt has a crisp, meringue-like surface, achieved by brushing with whipped egg white and a little sugar. Chocolate shorties, piped out on sheets, are quick to bake and quite economical, for they need very little cocoa powder added to simple basic ingredients, yet they look so pretty and taste so delicious. For daily offerings, serve them as they come; for parties, put two together with a rich orange buttercream, well flavoured and tinted pale orange.

Marie Louise tartlets and Fresh fruit chocolate tartlets (recipe page 69)

Chocolate walnut boxes

(Illustrated on the cover)

100 g/4 oz (U.S. ½ cup) butter or margarine
100 g/4 oz caster sugar (U.S. ½ cup granulated sugar)
2 eggs, beaten
100 g/4 oz self-raising flour, sifted (U.S. 1 cup all-purpose flour
sifted with 1 teaspoon baking powder)
1 tablespoon milk
DECORATION
225 g/8 oz plain chocolate (U.S. 1⅓ cups semi-sweet chocolate
pieces)
225 g/8 oz (U.S. ⅔ cup) apricot jam, sieved
50 g/2 oz (U.S. ¼ cup) sugar
75 ml/3 fl oz (U.S. ⅓ cup) water
1 tablespoon Tia Maria
½ teaspoon instant coffee powder
150 ml/¼ pint double cream (U.S. ⅔ cup heavy cream), whipped
12 walnut or pecan halves

Heat the oven to 190°C/375°F, Gas Mark 5, line a shallow tin measuring 27.5 cm/11 inches by 17.5 cm/7 inches with greaseproof paper (U.S. waxed paper) and grease the paper.

Cream the butter and sugar in a bowl until light and fluffy. Gradually add the egg, beating well after each addition. Fold in the flour and then the milk. Transfer to the prepared tin and level the surface.

Bake for about 20 minutes, or until just firm to the touch. Turn out on a wire rack and remove the lining paper. Leave to cool.

Meanwhile, make the chocolate squares (see page 10). Melt the chocolate in a bowl over hot water. Draw a rectangle 30 cm/12 inches by 22.5 cm/9 inches on a sheet of non-stick baking parchment (U.S. waxed paper). Spread the melted chocolate inside the marked shape, keeping the thickness as even as possible. Leave to set. Trim the edges.

Cut the cake in half crossways, spread one half with two-thirds of the jam and place the second half on top. Put the sugar and water in a pan and heat gently, stirring, until the sugar has dissolved. Boil rapidly for 1 minute, remove from the heat and stir in the liqueur. Spoon the syrup slowly over the cake and leave to stand for 1 hour.

Cut the cake into 12 × 4-cm/1½-inch squares. Warm the remaining jam with 1 tablespoon water. Use to brush the sides of the cakes. Cut the chocolate into 4-cm/1½-inch squares.

To assemble the cakes, press squares of chocolate firmly against the sides of the cakes. Dissolve the coffee in ½ teaspoon hot water. Fold into the cream, then spoon into a piping bag fitted with a small star tube. Pipe lines of coffee cream on top of the cakes and decorate each with a walnut half. Best served on the day of making.

NOTE A time-saving alternative is to use thin square chocolate mints or bought chocolate square 'leaves' instead of making your own.

Crunchy chocolate parcels

(Illustrated opposite)

100 g/4 oz (U.S. ½ cup) margarine
100 g/4 oz caster sugar (U.S. ½ cup granulated sugar)
2 eggs, beaten
100 g/4 oz self-raising flour, sifted (U.S. 1 cup all-purpose flour
sifted with 1 teaspoon baking powder)
2 tablespoons (U.S. 3 tablespoons) milk
50 g/2 oz (U.S. 1½ cups) crunchy honey and nut-coated cornflakes
finely grated rind of ½ orange
DECORATION
350 g/12 oz plain chocolate (U.S. 2 cups semi-sweet chocolate
pieces)
100 g/4 oz (U.S. ½ cup) butter or margarine
275 g/10 oz icing sugar, sifted (U.S. 2¼ cups sifted confectioners'
sugar)
1 tablespoon orange juice
little water

Heat the oven to 180°C/350°F, Gas Mark 4, line a 17.5-cm/7-inch square cake tin with greaseproof paper (U.S. waxed paper) and grease the paper.

Cream the margarine and sugar in a bowl until light and fluffy. Gradually beat in the egg. Fold in half the flour, then add the milk and the rest of the flour. When well blended, stir in the cereal and orange rind. Transfer to the prepared tin and smooth the top.

Bake for about 40 minutes, or until firm to the touch.

Meanwhile, make the chocolate squares (see page 10). Mark a rectangle measuring 45 cm/18 inches by 25 cm/10 inches on a sheet of non-stick baking parchment (U.S. waxed paper). Melt the chocolate and spread it inside the marked area, keeping it an even thickness. When set, trim the edges neatly and cut the sheet of chocolate into 9 × 5-cm/2-inch squares with a sharp knife.

Cream the butter in a bowl until soft then beat in 225 g/8 oz (U.S. 1¾ cups) of the sugar and the orange juice.

Turn the cake out on a wire rack and peel off the lining paper. Leave to cool. Trim the edges and cut the cake into 9 × 5-cm/2-inch squares. Spread butter icing on the 4 sides and top of each piece of cake. Press chocolate squares over the icing.

Mix the remaining sugar with a small quantity of water to make a stiff glacé icing. Place in an icing bag or syringe fitted with a writing tube. Pipe lines of 'string' and a 'bow' to decorate each cake 'parcel'. Leave to set and transfer to a serving plate using a cake slice.

Crunchy chocolate parcels

Dominoes

MAKES ABOUT 48

(Illustrated below)

150 g/5 oz plain flour (U.S. 1¼ cups all-purpose flour)
2½ teaspoons (U.S. 3½ teaspoons) baking powder
25 g/1 oz cocoa powder (U.S. ¼ cup unsweetened cocoa)
2 teaspoons (U.S. 1 tablespoon) instant coffee powder
1 teaspoon warm water
3 eggs, beaten
175 g/6 oz caster sugar (U.S. ¾ cup granulated sugar)
175 g/6 oz (U.S. ¾ cup) soft margarine
1 (200-g/7-oz) pack milk chocolate flavour cake covering (U.S. 7-
oz pack sweet chocolate flavor cake covering)
little water
100 g/4 oz icing sugar, sifted (U.S. scant 1 cup sifted
confectioners' sugar)

Heat the oven to 160°C/325°F, Gas Mark 3, grease a shallow tin measuring about 32.5 cm/13 inches by 22.5 cm/9 inches, line the base with greaseproof paper (U.S. waxed paper) and grease the paper.

Sift the flour with the baking powder and cocoa into a bowl. Dissolve the coffee in the water and add to the bowl with the egg, sugar and margarine. Beat with a wooden spoon for about 2 minutes, or for 1 minute with an electric mixer, until well blended. Transfer to the prepared tin and level the surface.

Bake for about 30 minutes, or until firm to the touch. Leave to cool in the tin.

Melt the cake covering in a bowl over a pan of hot water and spread over the cake. Mark into bars measuring 5 cm/2 inches by 2.5 cm/1 inch before the covering sets. Cut up the cake with a sharp knife.

Gradually mix enough water into the icing sugar to give a thick smooth consistency. Place in a paper icing bag (see page 11). Snip off the end and pipe a centre line and the required number of dots on each cake to make the dominoes. Leave to set.

VARIATION

Pineapple meringue squares Make up the cake mixture as above and spread in a greased and lined 30-cm/12-inch by 20-cm/8-inch tin at least 3 cm/1¼ inches deep. Drain a 382-g/13½-oz can crushed pineapple and spread over the cake mixture. Whisk 2 egg whites in a clean bowl until stiff. Gradually add 100 g/4 oz caster sugar (U.S. ½ cup granulated sugar), a tablespoon at a time, whisking well after each addition until the meringue is firm and glossy. Fold in 50 g/2 oz (U.S. ¼ cup) melted margarine, 175 g/6 oz desiccated coconut (U.S. 2 cups shredded coconut) and 50 g/2 oz plain chocolate (U.S. 2 squares semi-sweet chocolate), grated. Spread over the pineapple and bake for about 50 minutes, or until golden brown all over. Cool in the tin and serve cut into squares.

Choc 'n cherry shortbread

(Illustrated on pages 64–65)

100 g/4 oz (U.S. ½ cup) butter or margarine
50 g/2 oz caster sugar (U.S. ¼ cup granulated sugar)
175 g/6 oz plain flour (U.S. 1½ cups all-purpose flour), sifted
50 g/2 oz chocolate dots (U.S. ⅓ cup chocolate chips)
6 glacé cherries (U.S. candied cherries), quartered

Heat the oven to 160°C/325°F, Gas Mark 3 and lightly grease 2 × 17.5-cm/7-inch shallow cake tins.

Cream the butter and sugar in a bowl until light and fluffy. Gradually add the flour, chocolate dots and cherries. Mix well. Divide between the prepared tins and press firmly to the shape of the tin, levelling the surface.

Bake for 25 minutes, or until pale golden. Cut each shortbread into 8 portions and leave in the tin until cold.

Spiced crunchy cookies

MAKES ABOUT 24

(Illustrated on pages 64–65)

75 g/3 oz (U.S. ⅓ cup) butter or margarine
75 g/3 oz caster sugar (U.S. ⅓ cup granulated sugar)
1 egg, beaten
1 teaspoon lemon juice
1 teaspoon ground mixed spice
175 g/6 oz self-raising flour, sifted (U.S. 1½ cups all-purpose flour sifted with 1½ teaspoons baking powder)
1 (113-g/4-oz) packet chocolate dots (U.S. ⅔ cup chocolate chips)

Heat the oven to 180°C/350°F, Gas Mark 4 and grease 2 baking sheets (U.S. cookie sheets).

Cream the butter and sugar in a bowl until light and fluffy. Gradually add the egg, lemon juice and spice, beating well after each addition. Stir in the flour and chocolate dots. Pinch off pieces of dough and shape into balls, each about the size of a walnut. Arrange, well apart, on the prepared sheets and flatten each ball with a fork.

Bake for about 15 minutes, or until the edges are golden. Leave on the tins for about 2 minutes, then transfer to a wire rack to cool. When cold, store in an airtight container.

Chocolate macaroons

MAKES 24

175 g/6 oz (U.S. 1½ cups) ground almonds
75 g/3 oz plain chocolate (U.S. 3 squares semi-sweet chocolate), grated
150 g/5 oz caster sugar (U.S. ⅔ cup granulated sugar)
3 egg whites
¼ teaspoon almond essence (U.S. almond extract)
pinch of ground mace

Heat the oven to 180°C/350°F, Gas Mark 4 and line 2 baking sheets (U.S. cookie sheets) with rice paper or non-stick baking parchment (U.S. waxed paper).

Mix the almonds with the chocolate and 1 tablespoon of the sugar. Set aside. Put the egg whites in a bowl and whisk until stiff. Gradually add the remaining sugar, a tablespoon at a time, whisking vigorously after each addition until the meringue is firm and glossy. Whisk in the almond flavouring and spice, then fold in the chocolate mixture. Spoon out into 24 small heaps on the lined sheets, leaving room between each.

Bake for about 15 minutes, or until the surface is crusty all over. The centres will still be quite soft. Leave to cool on the paper. Cut round each macaroon if using rice paper, which is edible.

Fudgy squares

MAKES 16

(Illustrated on pages 64–65)

100 g/4 oz (U.S. ½ cup) margarine
100 g/4 oz (U.S. ½ cup) granulated sugar
200 g/7 oz Rich Tea biscuits, crushed (U.S. 2⅓ cups semi-sweet cookie crumbs)
50 g/2 oz (U.S. ½ cup) chopped walnuts or pecans
50 g/2 oz (U.S. ⅓ cup) seedless raisins
1 egg, beaten
1 teaspoon vanilla essence (U.S. vanilla extract)
1 (113-g/4-oz) packet chocolate dots (U.S. ⅔ cup chocolate chips)

Generously grease a 20-cm/8-inch square shallow cake tin.

Place the margarine in a pan and heat gently until melted. Add the sugar and heat, stirring, until it has dissolved. Remove from the heat and put in the biscuit crumbs, nuts, raisins, egg and vanilla essence. Mix well.

Press into the prepared tin and level the surface. Scatter the chocolate dots over the top and press them in firmly. Chill for 1 hour then cut into 16 squares.

Photographed on pages 64/65. Above: Choc 'n cherry shortbread (recipe page 67). Below left: Spiced crunchy cookies (recipe page 67). Below right: Fudgy squares (recipe page 67)

Profiteroles with liqueur filling

SERVES 6

(Illustrated on pages 2–3)

50 g / 2 oz (U.S. ¼ cup) butter or margarine
150 ml / ¼ pint (U.S. ⅔ cup) water
65 g / 2½ oz plain flour (U.S. ⅔ cup all-purpose flour), sifted
pinch of salt
2 eggs, beaten
SAUCE
100 g / 4 oz plain chocolate (U.S. ⅔ cup semi-sweet chocolate pieces)
100 ml / 4 fl oz golden syrup (U.S. ½ cup light corn syrup)
25 g / 1 oz (U.S. 2 tablespoons) butter or margarine
FILLING
3 egg yolks
50 g / 2 oz caster sugar (U.S. ¼ cup granulated sugar)
25 g / 1 oz plain flour (U.S. ¼ cup all-purpose flour), sifted
300 ml / ½ pint (U.S. 1¼ cups) milk
1–2 tablespoons Grand Marnier

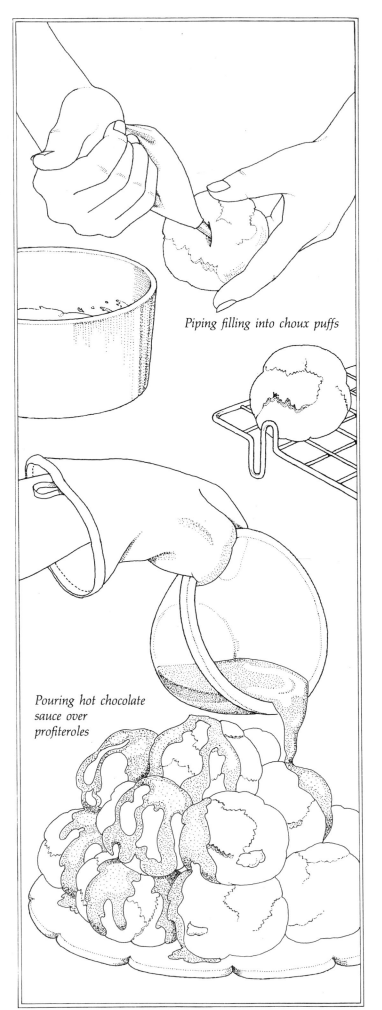

Piping filling into choux puffs

Pouring hot chocolate sauce over profiteroles

Place the butter and water in a pan and heat gently until the fat melts. Bring to the boil, remove from the heat and immediately add all the flour and the salt and beat with a wooden spoon until smooth. Gradually add the egg, beating vigorously after each addition, until the paste looks glossy and leaves the sides of the pan clean. Allow to cool. Meanwhile, heat the oven to 220°C/425°F, Gas Mark 7 and grease and flour a baking sheet (U.S. cookie sheet).

Place the choux paste in a piping bag fitted with a 2-cm/¾-inch plain tube. Pipe out 24 balls of paste, each about the size of a walnut, keeping them well apart.

Bake for about 15 minutes, or until well risen, golden and crisp. If the profiteroles are still slightly soft after this time, reduce the oven temperature to 180°C/350°F, Gas Mark 4 and continue cooking for a further 5 minutes, or until quite dry. Make a slit in the side of each puff to allow steam to escape and leave to cool on a wire rack.

To make the sauce, place the chocolate in a bowl with the syrup and butter. Stand the bowl over a pan of simmering water and leave until the chocolate melts. Stir the ingredients briskly until smooth. Keep warm.

To make the liqueur filling, whisk the egg yolks and sugar until creamy, then stir in the flour. Bring the milk to the boil in a pan, then whisk a little of it into the egg yolk mixture. Pour back into the remainder of the boiling milk and stir briskly until boiling again. Leave until cold then add the liqueur. Place in a piping bag fitted with a small nozzle and pipe a little into each profiterole. Pile them up in a dish. Pour a third of the warm chocolate sauce over the profiteroles and hand the rest separately in a jug.

Chocolate-dipped Viennese fingers

MAKES ABOUT 40

75 g/3 oz (U.S. ⅓ cup) butter
100 g/4 oz (U.S. ½ cup) margarine
75 g/3 oz icing sugar, sifted (U.S. ¾ cup sifted confectioners' sugar)
grated rind of 2 oranges
1 tablespoon cornflour (U.S. cornstarch)
225 g/8 oz plain flour (U.S. 2 cups all-purpose flour)
1 teaspoon baking powder
1 tablespoon milk
DECORATION
175 g/6 oz plain chocolate (U.S. 1 cup semi-sweet chocolate pieces)

Heat the oven to 180°C/350°F, Gas Mark 4 and grease several baking sheets (U.S. cookie sheets).

Cream the butter, margarine and sugar in a bowl until light and fluffy. Beat in the orange rind and cornflour. Sift the flour with the baking powder and add to the bowl with the milk. Mix well.

Transfer to a piping bag fitted with a large star tube. Pipe 7.5-cm/3-inch lengths of mixture on to the prepared sheets. If time permits, chill for 10 minutes.

Bake for about 15 minutes, or until the edges are pale golden. Leave to cool on the trays for 5 minutes, then transfer to a wire rack.

Melt the chocolate in a small bowl over a pan of hot water. Dip the ends of each finger in chocolate. Allow a moment for excess chocolate to drip off, and place on a wire rack to set.

VARIATIONS

Chocolate shorties Omit the orange rind and reduce the quantity of flour to 200 g/7 oz (U.S. 1¾ cups). Add 25 g/1 oz cocoa powder (U.S. ¼ cup unsweetened cocoa), sifting this with the flour and baking powder. Pipe the mixture into stars and bake as above for about 12 minutes. Sandwich the stars together in pairs with vanilla-flavoured buttercream (see page 16).

Wreath cookies Instead of piping the mixture into stars, pipe into wreaths with a very small hole in the centre. Bake for about 15 minutes. When cold, melt 100 g/4 oz (U.S. 4 squares) white chocolate and, using a paper icing bag (see page 13), pipe a zig-zag pattern of chocolate on each cookie. This shape is suitable for making with either the plain or chocolate dough.

Marie Louise tartlets

MAKES 8

(Illustrated on page 60)

115 g/4½ oz plain flour (U.S. 1⅛ cups all-purpose flour)
pinch of salt
40 g/1½ oz caster sugar (U.S. scant ¼ cup granulated sugar)
50 g/2 oz (U.S. ¼ cup) butter, chilled and diced
2 large egg yolks
100 g/4 oz plain chocolate (U.S. ⅔ cup semi-sweet chocolate pieces)
2 tablespoons (U.S. 3 tablespoons) sweet sherry
75 g/3 oz (U.S. 1½ cups) crumbled plain or chocolate sponge cake
1 (35-g/1¼-oz) sachet cream topping mix
100 ml/4 fl oz (U.S. ½ cup) cold milk
small pieces of fruit, such as halved and deseeded (U.S. pitted)
grapes, slices of strawberry, glacé cherries (U.S. candied cherries)

Sift the flour and salt into a bowl. Add the sugar, butter and egg yolks and mix to a dough with your fingertips. Knead lightly until smooth then wrap and chill for 30 minutes. Meanwhile, heat the oven to 200°C/400°F, Gas Mark 6 and have ready 8 deep plain or fluted tartlet cases and a baking sheet (U.S. cookie sheet).

Divide the dough into 8 equal portions and roll each out to a circle a little larger than the top of a tartlet tin. Put in the tins and very gently ease to fit. Do not stretch the pastry. Trim the edges with a sharp knife and prick the bases several times. Stand the tartlet tins on the sheet.

Bake for about 10 minutes, or until cooked through and just turning golden. Leave in the tins for 5 minutes then ease out on to a wire rack to cool.

Mark a 10-cm/4-inch square on a sheet of non-stick baking parchment (U.S. waxed paper). Melt the chocolate in a bowl over a pan of hot water. Spread about one third of it inside the marked shape. Use the rest to coat the insides of the tartlet cases, using a brush to help you. Leave to set. Trim the chocolate to the marked square with a sharp knife, then cut into 4 smaller squares and finally into 8 triangles. Stand the tartlet cases on a serving dish. Pour the sherry over the cake. Make up the topping mix with the milk and place in a piping bag fitted with a large star tube.

Spoon the moistened cake into the tartlets and pipe a generous swirl of topping over this. Decorate each tartlet with a chocolate triangle and a piece of fruit.

VARIATION

Fresh fruit chocolate tartlets Omit the pastry and use all the chocolate to coat 8 paper cake cases (see page 11). Chill then remove the paper cases and fill with sponge, topping and fruit, as above.

Chocolate cream meringues

MAKES ABOUT 9

(Illustrated opposite)

2 tablespoons cocoa powder (U.S. 3 tablespoons unsweetened cocoa)
50 g / 2 oz icing sugar (U.S. ½ cup sifted confectioners' sugar)
50 g / 2 oz caster sugar (U.S. ¼ cup granulated sugar)
2 large egg whites
FILLING
150 ml / ¼ pint double cream (U.S. ⅔ cup heavy cream), whipped
crystallized violet petals (U.S. candied violet petals)

Heat the oven to 130°C/250°F, Gas Mark ½ and line 2 baking sheets (U.S. cookie sheets) with non-stick baking parchment (U.S. waxed paper).

Sift the cocoa with the icing sugar and stir in the caster sugar. Place the egg whites in a large bowl and whisk until stiff. Add the sugar mixture, a tablespoon at a time, whisking vigorously after each addition until the meringue is thick and glossy. Transfer to a piping bag fitted with a large star tube. If you find it easier to manage, put only half the mixture into the bag at one time. Pipe about 18 shells on to the prepared sheets.

Bake for about 1 hour then reduce the heat to the lowest possible and leave the meringues to dry out for a further 2 hours. Cool on a wire rack.

Place the cream in a piping bag fitted with a medium-sized star tube. Pipe a swirl of cream on one meringue shell and top with a second. Arrange on a serving dish and decorate with violet petals.

VARIATION

Brown sugar meringues Omit the cocoa and substitute ½ teaspoon ground ginger. Use 50 g / 2 oz soft brown sugar (U.S. ¼ cup light brown sugar) instead of the caster sugar (U.S. granulated sugar). Put the meringue shells together with Chocolate crème (see page 73) and use slivers of preserved ginger to decorate in place of the violet petals.

NOTE The unfilled meringues can be stored in an airtight container at room temperature for about 5 days, or for a longer period in the freezer, but they remain fragile even when frozen.

Stages in making Chocolate cream meringues

Milky Way stars

MAKES ABOUT 18, DEPENDING ON SIZE

225 g/8 oz plain flour (U.S. 2 cups all-purpose flour)
2 tablespoons cocoa powder (U.S. 3 tablespoons unsweetened cocoa)
1 teaspoon instant coffee powder
¼ teaspoon baking powder
100 g/4 oz (U.S. ½ cup) butter or block margarine
100 g/4 oz caster sugar (U.S. ½ cup granulated sugar)
1 egg
1 tablespoon milk
DECORATION
50 g/2 oz (U.S. 2 squares) white chocolate
silver balls

Sift the flour with the cocoa, coffee and baking powder and set aside. Cream the butter until soft then add the sugar and beat until soft and fluffy. Add the egg and beat in well then fold in the dry ingredients and milk and mix to a dough. Knead until smooth then wrap and chill for 45 minutes. Meanwhile, heat the oven to 190°C/375°F, Gas Mark 5 and have ready 2 baking sheets (U.S. cookie sheets).

Roll out the dough on a floured surface and stamp out with a star-shaped cutter. Gather up the trimmings and re-roll to make more biscuits. Arrange on the sheets, allowing room between each.

Bake for about 8 minutes for medium-sized stars, or until surface looks dry. Large stars will take a little longer than this and small stars less time. Leave on the sheets until firm then transfer to a wire rack and cool.

To decorate the biscuits, melt the chocolate in a bowl over a pan of hot water. Place in a paper icing bag (see page 11) and snip off the tip. Pipe random lines of chocolate across each biscuit and decorate with silver balls occasionally where 2 lines cross. Allow chocolate to set.

Chocolate cup cakes

MAKES 24

100 g/4 oz self-raising flour (U.S. 1 cup all-purpose flour sifted with 1 teaspoon baking powder)
2 tablespoons cocoa powder (U.S. 3 tablespoons unsweetened cocoa)
100 g/4 oz (U.S. ½ cup) soft margarine
100 g/4 oz light soft brown sugar (U.S. ½ cup light brown sugar)
75 ml/3 fl oz golden syrup (U.S. ⅓ cup light corn syrup)
3 tablespoons (U.S. 4 tablespoons) milk
2 large eggs
ICING
175 g/6 oz plain chocolate (U.S. 1 cup semi-sweet chocolate pieces)
400 g/14 oz icing sugar, sifted (U.S. 3 cups sifted confectioners' sugar)
90 ml/3½ fl oz (U.S. ⅓ cup) warm water

Heat the oven to 180°C/350°F, Gas Mark 4 and stand 24 paper cake cases on 2 baking sheets (U.S. cookie sheets).

Sift the flour with the cocoa into a bowl and add the remaining cake ingredients. Beat with a wooden spoon until just smooth.

Spoon the mixture evenly into the paper cases.

Bake for about 15 minutes or until just firm to the touch. Cool on the sheets.

To make the icing, melt the chocolate in a bowl over a pan of hot water. Put the sugar in another bowl and mix in the water to give a smooth consistency. Add the warm chocolate and stir quickly until the icing thickens.

Spoon icing generously over each cake until it almost fills the paper case. Leave to set.

VARIATION

Chocolate cherry cup cakes Add 50 g/2 oz chopped glacé cherries (U.S. ¼ cup chopped candied cherries) to the mixture before spooning into the paper cases. When the cakes have been iced, top each with half a cherry.

Fruit and chocolate chip scones

MAKES ABOUT 10

225 g/8 oz plain flour (U.S. 2 cups all-purpose flour)
½ teaspoon salt
1 teaspoon bicarbonate of soda (U.S. baking soda)
2 teaspoons (U.S. 1 tablespoon) cream of tartar
½ teaspoon ground cinnamon
50 g/2 oz (U.S. ¼ cup) butter or margarine
50 g/2 oz (U.S. ⅓ cup) seedless raisins
50 g/2 oz plain chocolate, chopped (U.S. ⅓ cup semi-sweet chocolate chips)
1 egg, separated
about 150 ml/¼ pint (U.S. ⅔ cup) milk
little caster sugar (U.S. granulated sugar) for sprinkling

Heat the oven to 230°C/450°F, Gas Mark 8 and grease a baking sheet (U.S. cookie sheet).

Sift the flour with the salt, bicarbonate of soda, cream of tartar and cinnamon into a bowl and rub or cut in the fat until the mixture resembles breadcrumbs. Stir in the raisins and chocolate pieces and add the egg yolk and enough milk to make a fairly soft dough.

Turn on to a floured surface and pat out to a thickness of about 2 cm/¾ inch. Stamp out rounds using a 5-cm/2-inch plain cutter and transfer to the prepared sheet. Gather up the trimmings and re-roll to make more scones. Whisk the egg white lightly and use to brush the tops of the scones. Sprinkle them lightly with sugar.

Bake for about 8 minutes, or until well risen and golden brown on top. Cool on a wire rack until warm and serve split and generously buttered.

VARIATION

Speckly nut scones Grate the chocolate instead of chopping it and use 50 g/2 oz (U.S. ½ cup) finely chopped walnuts for the raisins.

Special occasion chocolate scones Split the freshly baked scones, spoon a little chocolate or chocolate hazelnut spread on each half and top with whipped cream.

Golden squares

(Illustrated below)

175 g/6 oz (U.S. ¾ cup) butter or margarine
75 g/3 oz caster sugar (U.S. ⅓ cup granulated sugar)
finely grated rind of 1 lemon or 1 small orange
2 eggs, beaten
50 g/2 oz desiccated coconut (U.S. ⅔ cup shredded coconut,
chopped)
100 g/4 oz self-raising flour, sifted (U.S. 1 cup all-purpose flour
sifted with 1 teaspoon baking powder)
50 g/2 oz (U.S. 2½ cups) crisp rice cereal
about 2 tablespoons (U.S. 3 tablespoons) milk
ICING
175 g/6 oz icing sugar, sifted (U.S. 1⅓ cups sifted confectioners'
sugar)
2 tablespoons custard powder (U.S. 3 tablespoons Bird's English
dessert mix)
juice of 1 lemon or 1 small orange
1 (51-g/1¾-oz) pack milk chocolate buttons

Heat the oven to 180°C/350°F, Gas Mark 4 and grease a shallow tin measuring about 30 cm/12 inches by 17.5 cm/ 7 inches.

Cream the butter and sugar in a bowl until soft and fluffy. Gradually beat in the fruit rind, egg and coconut. Fold in the flour and cereal, adding enough milk to give a soft dropping consistency. Spread the mixture in the prepared tin.

Bake for about 30 minutes, or until firm to the touch. Leave to cool in the tin.

Meanwhile, making the icing. Sift the icing sugar and custard powder into a bowl and add enough juice to give a smooth flowing mixture. Use to cover the cake and when almost set, cut into 18 squares with a sharp knife. Smooth the buttons lightly with the tip of a finger to make them shine, then cut each in half. Press 4 pieces into the icing on each cake, arranging them to look like flower petals.

Minty button bars Make and bake the cake mixture as above. When cool, make a Peppermint icing. Cream 100 g/4 oz (U.S. ½ cup) butter or margarine until soft and beat in 200 g/7 oz icing sugar (U.S. generous 1½ cups sifted confectioners' sugar) and a few drops of peppermint essence (U.S. peppermint extract). Add this carefully, a drop at a time, until flavoured to taste. Tint the icing pale green with food colouring and spread over the cake in the tin. mark and then cut into 16 bars measuring 9 cm/3½ inches by 4 cm/1½ inches and decorate each bar with 3 chocolate buttons, polishing them with your finger as directed above.

Chocolate éclairs

(Illustrated below)

50 g/2 oz (U.S. ¼ cup) butter or margarine
150 ml/¼ pint (U.S. ⅔ cup) water
65 g/2½ oz plain flour (U.S. ⅔ cup all-purpose flour)
pinch of salt
2 eggs, beaten

FILLING AND DECORATION

150 ml/¼ pint double cream (U.S. ⅔ cup heavy cream), whipped
65 g/2½ oz plain chocolate (U.S. scant ½ cup semi-sweet chocolate pieces)
15 g/½ oz (U.S. 1 tablespoon) butter or margarine
1 tablespoon hot water
25 g/1 oz icing sugar, sifted (U.S. ¼ cup sifted confectioners' sugar)

Heat the oven to 190°C/375°F, Gas Mark 5 and grease and flour 2 baking sheets (U.S. cookie sheets).

Make up the choux paste as directed in recipe for Profiteroles with liqueur filling (see page 68). Place it in a piping bag fitted with a 2-cm/¾-inch plain tube. Pipe about 12 × 7.5-cm/3-inch lengths of paste on to the prepared sheets, cutting each one off neatly at the end of the tube, using a sharp knife dipped in hot water.

Bake for 30 minutes, or until golden brown. Split the éclairs while still hot and scoop out any soft filling. Return the shapes to the oven for a further 2 minutes then cool on a wire rack.

Put the cream in a piping bag fitted with a medium-sized star tube. For the icing, place the chocolate, butter, water and icing sugar in a bowl and stand this over a pan of hot water until the chocolate has melted. Beat until smooth then leave to cool until the icing thickens. Fill the éclairs with cream and cover the tops with chocolate icing. Leave to set before serving.

VARIATIONS

Banana cream éclairs Omit the whipped cream filling and use this Banana cream instead. Mash 2 ripe but firm bananas until smooth with 1 tablespoon icing sugar (U.S. confectioners' sugar). Whip 150 ml/¼ pint double cream (U.S. ⅔ cup heavy cream) until thick. Mix in the bananas and 1 tablespoon Tia Maria. Use to fill the éclairs then top with the chocolate icing and allow to set. These are best eaten within 2 hours of filling.

Mocha éclairs Omit the whipped cream filling and chocolate icing and use this Chocolate crème and coffee icing instead. To make the filling, melt 50 g/2 oz plain chocolate (U.S. ⅓ cup semi-sweet chocolate pieces) in a bowl over a pan of hot water. Cool. Whip 150 ml/¼ pint double cream (U.S. ⅔ cup heavy cream) and gradually mix in the chocolate. Use to fill the éclairs. Sift 75 g/3 oz icing sugar (U.S. scant ¾ cup sifted confectioners' sugar) and mix in enough strong black coffee to make a thick smooth icing. Coat the tops of the éclairs and leave to set.

Petits pains au chocolat

25 g/1 oz fresh yeast (U.S. 1 cake compressed yeast) or 15 g/½ oz
dried yeast (U.S. 1 package active dried yeast)
1 teaspoon caster sugar (U.S. granulated sugar)
225 ml/8 fl oz (U.S. 1 cup) lukewarm water
450 g/1 lb strong white flour (U.S. white bread flour), sifted
1 teaspoon salt
25 g/1 oz (U.S. 2 tablespoons) lard
1 egg, beaten
175 g/6 oz (U.S. ¾ cup) butter
225 g/8 oz plain chocolate (U.S. ½-lb bar semi-sweet chocolate)
GLAZE
1 egg yolk, beaten
1 teaspoon water
pinch of caster sugar (U.S. granulated sugar)

Cream the fresh yeast with the sugar and gradually add the water. Or, if using dried yeast, dissolve the sugar in the water and sprinkle the yeast over the surface. Leave in a warm place for about 10 minutes, or until frothy.

Put the flour and salt in a bowl and rub in the lard. Add the yeast liquid and egg and mix to a dough. Turn out on a floured surface and knead for 10 minutes, or until the dough is smooth. Roll out lightly to a strip measuring 50 cm/20 inches by 20 cm/8 inches, keeping the edges straight and the corners square. Have one short side towards you.

Soften the butter and divide into 3 portions. Dot one portion over the two thirds of the dough nearest to you, leaving a narrow border round the edges. Fold the unbuttered dough down over the centre third, then fold up the last third over the centre third. Seal the edges with the rolling pin. Give the dough a quarter turn and reshape into a long strip by gently pressing at intervals with the rolling pin. Repeat the rolling, dotting, folding, sealing, turning and pressing processes twice more, using up all the butter. Wrap and chill for 30 minutes.

Roll the dough out again and fold, seal and turn 3 times more. Wrap and chill for 1 hour.

Have ready 2 greased baking sheets (U.S. cookie sheets). Roll out the dough to a strip measuring 52.5 cm/21 inches by 25 cm/10 inches then divide into 12 rectangles measuring 12.5 cm/5 inches by 9 cm/3½ inches. Have the chocolate at room temperature and cut it into 12 strips across the width. Lay a strip of chocolate across the narrow edge of one piece of dough and roll up loosely. Do not close the rolled ends. Dampen the last narrow edge, press to seal and place the roll on the prepared sheet, with this seam underneath. Cover lightly with greased cling film and leave in a warm place until double in size.

Meanwhile, heat the oven to 230°C/450°F, Gas Mark 8. Beat the egg yolk with the water and sugar. Uncover the rolls, brush with glaze and bake for about 15 minutes, or until golden brown. Serve warm or cold.

Mandel confeckt

(Illustrated opposite)

200 g/7 oz caster sugar (U.S. generous ¾ cup granulated sugar)
2 eggs
150 g/5 oz plain chocolate (U.S. 5 squares semi-sweet chocolate),
grated
200 g/7 oz (U.S. 1¾ cups) ground almonds
2 tablespoons cornflour (U.S. 3 tablespoons cornstarch)
DECORATION
1 egg white
1 tablespoon icing sugar, sifted (U.S. sifted confectioners' sugar)
50 g/2 oz plain chocolate (U.S. 2 squares semi-sweet chocolate or
⅓ cup semi-sweet chocolate pieces)
1 tablespoon chocolate vermicelli (U.S. chocolate sprinkles or finely
grated chocolate)

Prepare the cookies one day for baking the next. Have ready several baking sheets (U.S. cookie sheets).

Place the sugar and eggs in a bowl and whisk until foamy. Add the chocolate, almonds and cornflour and mix well. Turn out on a surface dusted with more cornflour and roll out to a thickness of about 6 mm/¼ inch. Stamp out shapes with biscuit cutters (U.S. cookie cutters). Transfer to the prepared sheets, gather up the dough trimmings and re-roll to make more biscuits. Leave uncovered on the trays overnight at room temperature to dry.

The next day, heat the oven to 160°C/325°F, Gas Mark 3. Bake for about 25 minutes. Remove the sheets from the oven and slip a palette knife or spatula under each biscuit to release it. When quite cool, transfer to a wire rack. Lightly whisk the egg white and sugar together in a bowl and brush this over the biscuits. Leave to dry.

Melt the chocolate in a bowl over a pan of hot water. Place in a paper icing bag (see page 11). Snip off the end of the bag and decorate each biscuit with a curving zig-zag line of chocolate. Sprinkle with vermicelli and allow to set.

Mandel confeckt

Scrumptious slice

SERVES 8

(Illustrated opposite)

1 (370-g/13-oz) pack puff pastry (U.S. ¾-lb pack prepared flaky pastry)
225 g/8 oz marzipan (U.S. ½ lb almond marzipan)
2 egg whites
75 g/3 oz desiccated coconut (U.S. 1 cup shredded coconut)
75 g/3 oz glacé cherries (U.S. ⅓ cup candied cherries), chopped
8 small milk chocolate flakes
little caster sugar (U.S. granulated sugar)

Heat the oven to 230°C/450°F, Gas Mark 8 and grease a baking sheet (U.S. cookie sheet).

Roll out the pastry on a lightly floured surface and trim to a rectangle measuring 30 cm/12 inches by 25 cm/10 inches. Roll out the marzipan and trim to a rectangle measuring 25 cm/10 inches by 20 cm/8 inches. Place the marzipan on the pastry, leaving an even border all round.

Whip the egg whites just until frothy. Put the coconut and cherries in a bowl and add enough egg white to bind them together. Spread down the centre of the marzipan in a strip about 10 cm/4 inches wide. Lay the flakes on top in pairs.

Brush the exposed pastry edges with egg white, bring up both long sides and seal them together over the filling. Press the ends together well. Transfer to the prepared sheet with the seal underneath. Brush the top with egg white and sprinkle with sugar. Mark diagonally with a sharp knife without piercing the pastry.

Bake for about 15 minutes, or until well risen and golden brown. Trim off one end corner then cut into diagonal slices. Serve hot or cold.

Southern magic pecan pie

SERVES 6

175 g/6 oz plain flour (U.S. 1½ cups all-purpose flour)
40 g/1½ oz (U.S. 3 tablespoons) lard
40 g/1½ oz (U.S. 3 tablespoons) butter or block margarine
1–2 tablespoons (U.S. 2–3 tablespoons) water
FILLING
175 g/6 oz (U.S. ¾ cup) butter
40 g/1½ oz cocoa powder (U.S. ⅓ cup unsweetened cocoa), sifted
225 g/8 oz soft brown sugar (U.S. 1 cup light brown sugar)
3 eggs, beaten
finely grated rind and juice of 2 small oranges
225 g/8 oz (U.S. ½ lb) pecan halves

Heat the oven to 180°C/350°F, Gas Mark 4 and have ready a 20-cm/8-inch flan tin or a shallow cake tin, or a flan ring standing on a baking sheet (U.S. cookie sheet).

Sift the flour into a bowl and rub or cut in the lard and butter until the mixture resembles breadcrumbs. Add enough water to make a firm dough. Roll out on a lightly floured surface and use to line the prepared tin.

To make the filling, melt one third of the butter and mix with the cocoa powder. Set aside. Cream the remaining butter with the sugar in a bowl until soft and fluffy. Gradually add the egg, beating well after each addition. Beat in the blended cocoa and the orange rind and juice. Stir in the nuts and transfer to the pastry case.

Bake for about 45 minutes, or until the filling is brown and firm to the touch. Serve warm or cold with scoops of ice cream.

Scrumptious slice

Date, chocolate and walnut crunch

(Illustrated below)

75 g/3 oz (U.S. ⅓ cup) butter or margarine
75 g/3 oz light soft brown sugar (U.S. ⅓ cup light brown sugar)
2 tablespoons golden syrup (U.S. 3 tablespoons light corn syrup)
100 g/4 oz (U.S. 1 cup) wholewheat flour
50 g/2 oz (U.S. generous ½ cup) rolled oats
100 g/4 oz stoned dates (U.S. ½ cup pitted dates), chopped
50 g/2 oz plain chocolate dots (U.S. ⅓ cup semi-sweet chocolate chips)
50 g/2 oz (U.S. ½ cup) chopped walnuts or pecans
1 tablespoon lemon juice

Heat the oven to 180°C/350°F, Gas Mark 4 and grease a 17.5-cm/7-inch square shallow cake tin.

Put the butter, sugar and syrup in a pan and heat gently until the fat has melted. Stir in the flour and oats. Press half the mixture to the base of the prepared tin. Combine the dates, chocolate, nuts and lemon juice and spread over the top. Cover with the rest of the oat mixture and press down firmly with a fork to level the surface.

Bake for about 25 minutes, or until golden brown. Cut into 10 pieces and cool in the tin.

Chocolate filled shortbread

100 g/4 oz plain chocolate (U.S. ⅔ cup semi-sweet chocolate pieces)
150 g/5 oz plain flour (U.S. 1¼ cups all-purpose flour)
25 g/1 oz cornflour (U.S. ¼ cup cornstarch)
1½ teaspoons (U.S. 2 teaspoons) baking powder
100 g/4 oz (U.S. ½ cup) butter
75 g/3 oz caster sugar (U.S. ⅓ cup granulated sugar)
1 egg, beaten
little caster sugar (U.S. granulated sugar) for sprinkling

Heat the oven to 160°C/325°F, Gas Mark 3, grease a shallow 17.5-cm/7-inch cake tin and line with greaseproof paper (U.S. waxed paper). Melt the chocolate in a bowl over a pan of hot water. Set aside.

Sift the flour with the cornflour and baking powder. Cream the butter and sugar in a bowl until light and fluffy. Gradually beat in the egg then add the dry ingredients and mix to a dough. Take half the dough and press it into the prepared tin. Level the surface. Cover with the chocolate, spreading it almost to the edges. Leave until the chocolate is firm but not hard then spread the remaining dough over the top. Level the surface.

Bake for 1 hour, or until pale golden. Mark into 8 portions with a sharp knife. Leave in the tin for 10 minutes, then turn out on to a wire rack to cool. Serve lightly sprinkled with sugar.

Chocolate sandwich drops

=====MAKES ABOUT 12=====

(Illustrated below)

100 g / 4 oz (U.S. ½ cup) butter or margarine
50 g / 2 oz caster sugar (U.S. ¼ cup granulated sugar)
100 g / 4 oz self-raising flour, sifted (U.S. 1 cup all-purpose flour
sifted with 1 teaspoon baking powder)
25 g / 1 oz drinking chocolate (U.S. ¼ cup sweetened cocoa)
25 g / 1 oz cocoa powder (U.S. ¼ cup unsweetened cocoa), sifted
few drops vanilla essence (U.S. vanilla extract)
little icing sugar (U.S. confectioners' sugar)
FILLING
25 g / 1 oz plain chocolate (U.S. 1 square semi-sweet
chocolate, grated)
2 teaspoons (U.S. 1 tablespoon) hot milk
50 g / 2 oz (U.S. ¼ cup) butter or margarine
100 g / 4 oz icing sugar, sifted (U.S. scant 1 cup sifted
confectioners' sugar)

Heat the oven to 190°C / 375°F, Gas Mark 5 and grease baking sheets (U.S. cookie sheets).

Cream the butter and sugar in a bowl until light and fluffy. Add the flour, drinking chocolate, cocoa and vanilla essence and mix to a stiff paste. Pinch off pieces and roll into balls about the size of a small walnut. Place well apart on the prepared sheets and flatten each ball with a fork dipped into cold water.

Bake for 10 minutes, or until dry to the touch. Leave on the tins for 5 minutes, then remove to a wire rack

Meanwhile, make the filling. Stir the chocolate into the milk until melted. Cool. Beat the butter in a bowl until soft then beat in the sugar and the chocolate mixture. Transfer to a piping bag fitted with a small star tube and if necessary chill briefly until firm.

When the drops are cold, sandwich them together with a piped swirl of the filling. Sift the tops lightly with sugar before serving.

Surprise orange slices

25 g / 1 oz plain chocolate (U.S. scant $\frac{1}{4}$ cup semi-sweet chocolate
pieces)
200 g / 7 oz plain flour (U.S. 1$\frac{3}{4}$ cups all-purpose flour)
25 g / 1 oz cocoa powder (U.S. $\frac{1}{4}$ cup unsweetened cocoa)
pinch of salt
100 g / 4 oz (U.S. $\frac{1}{2}$ cup) unsalted butter
100 g / 4 oz (U.S. $\frac{1}{2}$ cup) cream cheese
100 g / 4 oz caster sugar (U.S. $\frac{1}{2}$ cup granulated sugar)
1 teaspoon vanilla essence (U.S. vanilla extract)
finely grated rind of 1 orange
ICING
225 g / 8 oz icing sugar, sifted (U.S. 1$\frac{3}{4}$ cups sifted confectioners'
sugar)
juice of 1 orange
1–2 drops orange food colouring

Melt the chocolate in a bowl over a pan of hot water. Cool. Sift the flour with the cocoa and salt. Put the butter and cheese in a bowl and beat until smooth and soft. Add the chocolate, sugar, vanilla and orange rind and beat well until pale and fluffy. Mix in the dry ingredients to make a dough. Cover and chill for at least 2 hours, or until firm enough to roll out. Meanwhile, heat the oven to 180°C/350°F, Gas Mark 4 and have ready several ungreased baking sheets (U.S. cookie sheets).

Roll out the dough on a floured surface to a thickness of about 6 mm/$\frac{1}{4}$ inch. Stamp into 7.5-cm/3-inch plain rounds then cut each round in half to make 2 half-circles. Transfer to the sheets, allowing room for spreading. Gather up the trimmings and re-roll to make more cookies but do not allow the dough to become warm or it is too sticky to roll out easily. Re-chill the dough if necessary.

Bake for about 10 minutes, or until the edges are turning light brown. Leave on the sheets until firm then cool on a wire rack.

To make the icing, mix the sugar with enough orange juice to make a smooth mixture, adding a few drops of water if necessary. The icing should thickly coat the back of a spoon. Tint orange with food colouring and place some in a paper piping bag (see page 11). Snip off the end of the bag and pipe 5 lines of icing from points around the curved edge of each cookie to meet at the centre point on the straight side, like the spokes of a wheel. Finish by piping an outline around the curved edge, to make the cookies look like halved orange slices.

======= VARIATIONS =======

Surprise lemon slices Omit the orange and use the finely grated rind of 1 lemon in the cookie dough and the juice of 1 lemon plus 1–2 drops of yellow food colouring to make the icing. Decorate in the same way as for Surprise orange slices.
Surprise lime slices Omit the orange and use the finely grated rind of 1 lime in the cookie dough and the juice of 1 lime and a drop or 2 of green food colouring to make the icing. Cut the dough into 5-cm/2-inch plain rounds and do not divide in half. Bake as for Surprise orange slices and decorate by piping 4 lines of icing right across the circle, cutting through the central point each time, then by piping in a circular outline.

Teatime fancies

(Illustrated opposite)

225 g / 8 oz (U.S. 1 cup) butter or margarine
225 g / 8 oz caster sugar (U.S. 1 cup granulated sugar)
4 eggs, beaten
175 g / 6 oz self-raising flour (U.S. 1$\frac{1}{2}$ cups all-purpose flour sifted
with 1$\frac{1}{2}$ teaspoons baking powder)
50 g / 2 oz cocoa powder (U.S. $\frac{1}{2}$ cup unsweetened cocoa)
2 tablespoons (U.S. 3 tablespoons) milk
ICING
100 g / 4 oz (U.S. $\frac{1}{2}$ cup) butter or margarine
225 g / 8 oz icing sugar, sifted (U.S. 1$\frac{3}{4}$ cups sifted confectioners'
sugar)
little hot milk
few drops vanilla essence (U.S. vanilla extract)
25 g / 1 oz plain chocolate (U.S. 1 square semi-sweet chocolate),
grated
very finely grated rind of $\frac{1}{2}$ orange
few drops orange food colouring

Heat the oven to 190°C/375°F, Gas Mark 5, grease a 17.5-cm/7-inch square cake tin and line the base with greaseproof paper (U.S. waxed paper), then stand 8 small paper cake cases in bun tins (U.S. muffin pans).

Cream the butter and sugar in a bowl until light and fluffy. Gradually add the egg, beating well after each addition. Sift the flour and cocoa together and fold into the creamed mixture with the milk. Spread half the mixture in the prepared cake tin, then spoon the rest into the paper cases.

Bake the small cakes for about 10 minutes, and the large cake for about 25 minutes, or until firm to the touch. Turn the square layer out on a wire rack and cool before removing the lining paper.

To make the butter icings, cream the butter and sugar in a bowl until soft and creamy. Divide the mixture into 3 equal portions then take an extra tablespoon from one to another. Beat 2 teaspoons (U.S. 1 tablespoon) hot milk into the smallest portion and flavour with a few drops of vanilla essence. Stir the chocolate into a further 2 teaspoons (U.S. 1 tablespoon) of the milk until melted, then add to the largest portion of icing. Finally beat 1 teaspoon milk, the orange rind and a few drops of orange colouring into the last portion of icing.

Using a sharp knife, divide the cake to give 4 oblong and 4 diamond shapes. However, if you cut only oblongs, you will manage to get more cakes. Decorate the cakes as follows.

Teatime fancies

Orange and almond delights Spread orange butter icing around the sides of the cake oblongs and cover with 50 g/2 oz (U.S. ½ cup) chopped almonds, toasted. Spread a little icing over the tops of the cakes then place the remainder in a piping bag fitted with a small star tube. Pipe a zig-zag line down each long edge and overlap small orange and lemon jelly cake decorations down the centre.

Chocolate diamonds Spread chocolate butter icing around the sides of the cake diamonds and cover with about 3 tablespoons chocolate vermicelli (U.S. 4 tablespoons chocolate sprinkles or 2 squares semi-sweet chocolate, finely grated). Coat the tops of the cakes with more butter icing. Put the rest in a piping bag fitted with a small star tube and pipe a shell border around the edge of each cake. Leave the remaining icing in the bag for decorating the cup cakes.

Vanilla and chocolate cup cakes Pipe small rosettes of chocolate icing to half-cover the tops of 4 small cakes. Fill in with rosettes of vanilla butter icing in the same way.

Redcurrant fancies Put 2 tablespoons (U.S. 3 tablespoons) redcurrant jelly in a very small pan with 1 teaspoon water. Heat gently, stirring constantly, until smooth. Cool then spoon over the remaining 4 cakes. When set, pipe small rosettes of vanilla butter icing in a ring round the edge.

Mocha flapjacks

MAKES 12

50 g/2 oz (U.S. ¼ cup) butter or margarine
3 tablespoons golden syrup (U.S. 4 tablespoons light corn syrup)
2 teaspoons coffee essence (U.S. 1 tablespoon sweetened concentrated coffee flavoring)
50 g/2 oz plain chocolate (U.S. ⅓ cup semi-sweet chocolate pieces), roughly chopped
50 g/2 oz (U.S. ½ cup) chopped walnuts or pecans
100 g/4 oz (U.S. generous 1 cup) rolled oats

Heat the oven to 160°C/325°F, Gas Mark 3 and lightly grease a 17.5-cm/7-inch square shallow cake tin.

Put the butter, syrup and coffee essence in a pan and heat gently until the butter has melted. Remove from the heat and stir in the chocolate, nuts and oats. Press the mixture into the prepared tin and level the surface.

Bake for 25 minutes, or until pale golden. Cut into 12 bars but leave in the tin until cold.

Gâteaux

When you enter the wonderful world of gâteaux you attain the peak of the *pâtissier's* art. You are also investing time, trouble, and the cost of ingredients which may add up to quite an impressive sum. The result, if successful, more than justifies your investment, so take extra care to ensure producing a confection that you'll be proud to set on the table.

Begin with the cake base you intend to build up into a glorious gâteau. The more delicate the mixture, the more care it requires to turn out absolutely perfect in texture. For instance, when the recipe says fold in beaten egg whites, have them peaky and firm but not overbeaten to the consistency of cotton wool. Use a metal spoon or spatula to lift and gently combine the mixture, retaining as much air in it as possible. Some recipes may require tin sizes you don't possess; or you may wish to make a square cake when it is intended for a round one. Here's a hint to ensure that you don't upset baking time or texture by spreading the mixture too thin or too deep. A 22.5-cm/9-inch round tin roughly equates in volume to a 20-cm/8-inch square one. The same volume of mixture will fill a shallow rectangular tin to make a cake 2.5 cm/1 inch high. If you have no square tins, block off the extra space in this kind of tin with a firm folded strip of foil. Here's where you can use your imagination to change the toppings suggested for others you fancy trying out. A cake with a chocolate cone trim can be topped with triangles, leaves or piped shapes instead. On pages 10 to 11 you can see how easy it is to make these eye-catching decorations.

Fortunately all cakes store well, and this includes gâteaux. Put them in airtight tins, or plastic containers. For short storage, cover lightly with a foil dome, so as not to damage the decorations, and put in the refrigerator. For longer storage, open-freeze for 2 hours, enclose in foil, and put in a freezer position where weighty items cannot harm it. Remember that when it emerges, the cake should be unwrapped while still firmly frozen, and allowed to defrost at room temperature. A word of warning: cakes that have been frozen tend to go dry in a few days and need to be eaten up quickly. But you'll find such delicious treats as the gâteaux in this section will disappear quickly.

Above: Rich chocolate button cake (recipe page 84).
Below: Easter chocolate cake (recipe page 89)

Rich chocolate button cake

(Illustrated on page 82)

175 g/6 oz self-raising flour (U.S. 1½ cups all-purpose flour sifted
with 1½ teaspoons baking powder)
25 g/1 oz cocoa powder (U.S. ¼ cup unsweetened cocoa)
175 g/6 oz (U.S. ¾ cup) butter or margarine
175 g/6 oz caster sugar (U.S. ¾ cup granulated sugar)
3 eggs, beaten
1 teaspoon vanilla essence (U.S. vanilla extract)
2 tablespoons (U.S. 3 tablespoons) milk
FILLING AND DECORATION
175 g/6 oz icing sugar, sifted (U.S. 1⅓ cups sifted confectioners'
sugar)
50 g/2 oz cocoa powder (U.S. ½ cup unsweetened cocoa)
100 g/4 oz (U.S. ½ cup) butter or margarine
2 large milk chocolate flakes, crumbled
75 g/3 oz plain chocolate (U.S. ½ cup semi-sweet chocolate pieces)
30 milk chocolate buttons

Heat the oven to 180°C/350°F, Gas Mark 4, grease a 20-cm/8-inch cake tin and line with greaseproof paper (U.S. waxed paper).

Sift the flour with the cocoa. Cream the butter and sugar in a bowl until light and fluffy. Gradually add the egg and vanilla essence, beating well after each addition and adding a little of the dry ingredients with the last of the egg. Fold in the remaining flour mixture and the milk. Transfer to the prepared tin and level the surface.

Bake for about 50 minutes, or until firm to the touch. Leave in the tin for 5 minutes then turn out on a wire rack, peel off the lining paper and allow to cool.

Meanwhile, make the filling. Sift the sugar with the cocoa into a bowl. Add the butter and beat until soft and fluffy.

Split the cake into 2 layers and sandwich these together again with half the butter icing. Sprinkle the crushed flake on a sheet of greaseproof paper (U.S. waxed paper). Spread the remaining icing around the sides of the cake and roll in the crushed flake to cover evenly. Set the cake on a serving dish.

Melt the chocolate in a bowl over a pan of hot water. Cool until it thickens slightly, then spread over the cake. Before the chocolate sets, mark it with a fork into a zig-zag pattern. Finish with a border of buttons, overlapping, round the edge of the cake.

Cranberry Black Forest cake

(Illustrated opposite)

75 g/3 oz plain flour (U.S. ¾ cup all-purpose flour)
2 tablespoons cocoa powder (U.S. 3 tablespoons unsweetened
cocoa)
3 large eggs
115 g/4½ oz caster sugar (U.S. generous ½ cup granulated sugar)
FILLING AND DECORATION
150 g/5 oz plain chocolate (U.S. 5 squares semi-sweet chocolate)
450 ml/¾ pint (U.S. 2 cups) whipping cream
150 ml/¼ pint double cream (U.S. ⅔ cup heavy cream)
4 tablespoons (U.S. 6 tablespoons) Kirsch or rum
2 (185-g/6.5-oz) jars cranberry sauce

Heat the oven to 190°C/375°F, Gas Mark 5, grease a 22.5-cm/9-inch cake tin, line with greaseproof paper (U.S. waxed paper) and grease the paper.

Sift the flour with the cocoa twice then set aside. Place the eggs and sugar in a large bowl, stand this over a pan of simmering water but do not let the base of the pan touch the water. Whisk steadily, if possible with an electric beater, until thick. If ready, the mixture will fall back on itself in a firm ribbon when the beaters are lifted. Remove from the heat and whisk until cool. Fold in the dry ingredients quickly and evenly. Transfer to the prepared tin.

Bake for about 30 minutes, or until just firm to the touch. Turn out on a wire rack to cool, then remove the lining paper.

Make the chocolate into small curls (see page 10). Place the creams together in a bowl and whip until just stiff. Spoon about one quarter of the cream into a piping bag fitted with a large star tube. Split the cake into 2 even layers, place one on a serving plate and sprinkle with half the liqueur. Reserve about 2 tablespoons (U.S. 3 tablespoons) of the cranberry sauce and spread the rest over the cake. Cover with about one third of the remaining cream then the second layer of cake, sprinkling this also with liqueur. Mask the cake completely, using the last of the cream. Press chocolate curls against the sides evenly all round. Pipe a 7.5-cm/3-inch circle of small rosettes in the centre of the cake, then 8 large rosettes around the edge. Top each large rosette with a single chocolate curl and spoon the reserved cranberry sauce into the centre of the cake.

Cranberry Black Forest cake

Almond mandarin gâteau

(Illustrated opposite)

250 g / 9 oz self-raising flour (U.S. 2¼ cups all-purpose flour sifted with 2¼ teaspoons baking powder)
25 g / 1 oz cocoa powder (U.S. ¼ cup unsweetened cocoa)
275 g / 10 oz (U.S. 1¼ cups) butter or margarine
275 g / 10 oz caster sugar (U.S. 1¼ cups granulated sugar)
4 eggs
1½ teaspoons almond essence (U.S. 2 teaspoons almond extract)
FILLING AND DECORATION
2 (35-g / 1¼-oz) sachets cream topping mix
225 ml / 8 fl oz (U.S. 1 cup) cold milk
about 6 tablespoons (U.S. 9 tablespoons) apricot jam
100 g / 4 oz flaked almonds (U.S. 1 cup slivered almonds), toasted
1 (311-g / 11-oz) can mandarin orange segments, drained
few plain chocolate curls (U.S. semi-sweet chocolate curls)
(see page 10)

Heat the oven to 190°C/375°F, Gas Mark 5, line a 22.5-cm/9-inch square cake tin with greaseproof paper (U.S. waxed paper) and grease the paper.

Sift the flour with the cocoa and set aside. Cream the butter and sugar in a bowl until light and fluffy. Beat in the eggs, one at a time, adding a little of the flour mixture between each addition. Stir in the almond flavouring and fold in the remaining flour mixture. Transfer to the prepared tin and level the surface.

Bake for about 35 minutes, or until springy to the touch. Turn out on a wire rack, remove the lining paper and leave to cool.

Make up the cream topping mixes with the specified quantity of milk to give a firm piping consistency. Stir the jam so that it is easy to spread and chop any large lumps. Sprinkle the almonds on a board.

Split the cake into 2 layers and sandwich these together again with jam. Cover the sides of the cake with cream topping, then with almonds. Transfer to a serving dish. Carefully arrange 4 rows of mandarin segments diagonally across the cake. Put the remaining topping in a piping bag fitted with a large star tube and pipe in zig-zag lines between the oranges. Press a few chocolate curls lightly on each corner.

Sachertorte

SERVES 8–10

(Illustrated below)

225 g/8 oz plain chocolate (U.S. 1⅓ cups semi-sweet chocolate pieces)
100 g/4 oz (U.S. ½ cup) unsalted butter, softened
190 g/6½ oz caster sugar (U.S. generous ¾ cup granulated sugar)
5 eggs, separated
50 g/2 oz self-raising flour, sifted (U.S. ½ cup all-purpose flour sifted with ½ teaspoon baking powder)
75 g/3 oz ground hazelnuts or almonds (U.S. ¾ cup ground filberts or almonds)

FILLING
100 g/4 oz (U.S. ⅓ cup) apricot jam
150 ml/¼ pint double cream (U.S. ⅔ cup heavy cream), whipped

DECORATION
3 tablespoons (U.S. 4 tablespoons) apricot jam, sieved
175 g/6 oz plain chocolate (U.S. 1 cup semi-sweet chocolate pieces)
65 g/2½ oz (U.S. ⅓ cup) unsalted butter, diced

Heat the oven to 180°C/350°F, Gas Mark 4, line the bases of 3 × 20-cm/8-inch shallow cake tins with greaseproof paper (U.S. waxed paper) and grease the paper.

Melt the chocolate in a large bowl over a pan of hot water. Remove from the heat, add the butter, sugar and egg yolks and beat until smooth. Place the egg whites in a clean bowl and whisk until stiff. Fold into the chocolate mixture with the flour and nuts. Divide among the prepared tins.

Bake for about 15 minutes, or until firm to the touch. Leave in the tins for 10 minutes then turn out on a wire rack, remove the lining paper and leave to cool.

If the jam has large lumps in it, break them up lightly with a spoon but do not sieve the jam. Fold into the cream. Sandwich the cold cakes together with the apricot cream and place on a wire rack over a tray.

To decorate the cake, warm the jam and brush it over the top and sides. Melt 150 g/5 oz (U.S. scant 1 cup) of the chocolate in a bowl, remove from the heat and beat in the butter a little at a time. Pour over the cake and ease down over the sides with the back of a metal spoon to give a smooth coating. Leave to set for 10 minutes. Melt the remaining chocolate and place in a small paper icing bag (see page 11). Snip off the end of the bag and pipe the word 'Sacher' in the centre of the cake and a simple flowing scroll design round the top edge. Leave to set. Transfer the cake carefully to a serving plate.

Fudgy peanut cake

50 g/2 oz plain chocolate (U.S. ⅓ cup semi-sweet chocolate pieces)
225 g/8 oz plain flour (U.S. 2 cups all-purpose flour)
¼ teaspoon bicarbonate of soda (U.S. baking soda)
pinch of salt
50 g/2 oz (U.S. ¼ cup) soft margarine
100 g/4 oz (U.S. ½ cup) smooth peanut butter
225 g/8 oz caster sugar (U.S. 1 cup granulated sugar)
2 eggs, beaten
½ teaspoon almond essence (U.S. almond extract)
100 ml/4 fl oz (U.S. ½ cup) water
FILLING AND TOPPING
150 ml/¼ pint single cream (U.S. ⅔ cup light cream)
75 g/3 oz (U.S. ⅓ cup) smooth peanut butter
50 g/2 oz plain chocolate (U.S. ⅓ cup semi-sweet chocolate pieces),
roughly chopped
225 g/8 oz caster sugar (U.S. 1 cup granulated sugar)
50 g/2 oz (U.S. ½ cup) chopped roasted peanuts

Heat the oven to 180°C/350°F, Gas Mark 4 and grease and flour 2 shallow 20-cm/8-inch cake tins.

Melt the chocolate in a bowl over a pan of hot water. Sift the flour with the bicarbonate of soda and salt. Cream the margarine, peanut butter and sugar in a bowl until soft and fluffy. Gradually add the egg, chocolate and almond essence, beating well after each addition. Fold in the dry ingredients alternately with the water. Divide between the prepared tins.

Bake for about 30 minutes, or until firm to the touch. Leave to stand for 5 minutes then turn out on a wire rack to cool.

To make the fudge frosting, put half the cream in a pan with the peanut butter and chocolate. Stir over very gentle heat until the chocolate has melted, then blend in the remaining cream and finally the sugar. Continue to heat gently, stirring all the time, until the sugar has dissolved, then boil steadily, stirring occasionally, to a temperature of 116°C/240°F. To test without a thermometer, drop a little of the mixture into cold water. If you can lift it out and form it into a soft ball with your fingers, it is ready. Remove the pan from the heat, leave to cool slightly then beat until thick enough to spread.

Sandwich the cakes together with about one third of the fudge filling. Spread the rest over the top and sides of the cake. Sprinkle with the chopped peanuts before the frosting sets.

Easter chocolate cake

(Illustrated on page 82)

350 g/12 oz plain chocolate (U.S. 2 cups semi-sweet chocolate
pieces)
350 g/12 oz (U.S. 1½ cups) butter
3 eggs, beaten
2 teaspoons rum essence (U.S. rum flavoring)
1 teaspoon ground cinnamon
350 g/12 oz gingernut biscuits, crushed (U.S. 4 cups gingersnap
cookie crumbs)
10 glacé cherries (U.S. candied cherries), quartered
50 g/2 oz (U.S. ½ cup) chopped mixed nuts
DECORATION
25 g/1 oz icing sugar, sifted (U.S. ¼ cup sifted confectioners' sugar)
few drops milk
2 'Easter bunny' cake decorations

Grease a 17.5-cm/7-inch loose-based cake tin and line the sides only with non-stick baking parchment (U.S. waxed paper).

Put the chocolate and butter in a large bowl and stand this over a pan of simmering water until the chocolate melts. Stir lightly to mix then gradually add the egg, rum essence and cinnamon. When evenly combined, put in the biscuit crumbs, cherries and nuts and mix well. Transfer to the prepared tin and level the surface. Chill until firm.

Remove the tin and transfer the cake, still on the metal base, to a serving dish. Peel off the lining parchment. Mix the icing sugar with enough milk to give a thick smooth consistency. Transfer to a paper icing bag (see page 11). Snip off the end, pipe the greeting across the centre of the cake and finish with the Easter bunnies.

Making your own Easter eggs
To track down Easter egg moulds, you may have to visit a shop which sells cake decorating supplies, or send for them by mail order. Before use, polish the insides of the moulds carefully with wadded absorbent kitchen towel, but do not oil them. Brush inside the moulds with at least 2 layers of melted chocolate, 3 if you wish, letting each layer dry before adding the next. Trim off to a clean edge before the chocolate finally sets. When the chocolate is hard, the shapes will slip easily out of the moulds. Run a little melted chocolate round the edge of one half of the egg then gently but firmly press the two halves together. lay the egg down very carefully so that the join does not touch a hard surface. For children, place a fluffy chick toy inside one half before sealing it to the other. Decorate either by tying a ribbon round the egg, or by piping rosettes of Royal icing (see page 156) round the join, and an Easter greeting or child's name on one side. If you have a breakage, melt the chocolate down and start again, polishing the moulds each time you use them.

Luscious frosted layer cake

200 g / 7 oz plain flour (U.S. 1¾ cups all-purpose flour)
25 g / 1 oz cocoa powder (U.S. ¼ cup unsweetened cocoa)
2 teaspoons (U.S. 1 tablespoon) instant coffee powder
2 teaspoons (U.S. 1 tablespoon) baking powder
1 teaspoon bicarbonate of soda (U.S. baking soda)
1 tablespoon lemon juice
about 200 ml / 7 fl oz (U.S. about scant 1 cup) milk
100 g / 4 oz (U.S. ½ cup) butter, softened
175 g / 6 oz caster sugar (U.S. ¾ cup granulated sugar)
2 large eggs, beaten
½ teaspoon vanilla essence (U.S. vanilla extract)
SYRUP
2 tablespoons (U.S. 3 tablespoons) apricot jam, sieved
2 tablespoons (U.S. 3 tablespoons) lemon juice
2 tablespoons golden syrup (U.S. 3 tablespoons light corn syrup)
1 tablespoon rum
FILLING
100 g / 4 oz plain chocolate (U.S. ⅔ cup semi-sweet chocolate pieces)
50 g / 2 oz (U.S. ¼ cup) butter, unsalted if possible
*100 g / 4 oz icing sugar, sifted (U.S. scant 1 cup sifted
confectioners' sugar)*
1 large egg yolk
FROSTING
2 egg whites
450 g / 1 lb (U.S. 2 cups) granulated sugar
150 ml / ¼ pint (U.S. ⅔ cup) water
pinch of cream of tartar

Heat the oven to 190°C/375°F, Gas Mark 5, grease 2 × 20-cm/8-inch shallow cake tins and line the bases with greaseproof paper (U.S. waxed paper).

Sift the flour with the cocoa, coffee, baking powder and bicarbonate of soda, set aside. Stir the lemon juice and milk together. Put the butter and sugar in a bowl and beat until soft and fluffy. Gradually add the egg and vanilla, beating well after each addition. Fold in the dry ingredients, alternately with the milk liquid. Stop adding milk when the mixture is of a stiff dropping consistency. Divide between the prepared tins and level the surface.

Bake for about 20 minutes, or until just firm to the touch. Leave to stand for 5 minutes then turn out on a wire rack and cool the cakes with the bases upwards.

Meanwhile, put the ingredients for the syrup in a small pan and heat, stirring, until smooth. Remove from the heat and leave until just warm. Prick the bases of the cakes all over with a fine skewer or cocktail stick (U.S. toothpick) and spoon over the syrup. Leave for at least 30 minutes.

To make the filling, melt the chocolate in a bowl over a pan of hot water then allow to cool. Beat the butter and sugar together until creamy then add the egg yolk and finally the chocolate and beat until smooth. Use to sandwich the cake layers together on a serving plate.

For the frosting, have the egg whites ready in a clean bowl and put the sugar and water in a pan. Heat gently, stirring, until the sugar has dissolved. Add the cream of tartar and boil to 116°C/240°F, or until a little syrup dropped into cold water

Pricking cakes with fine skewer

Pouring syrup mixture over cakes

forms a soft ball. While the syrup is boiling, whisk the egg whites until stiff. Gradually add the syrup, in a thin stream, whisking constantly until the frosting holds its shape. Swirl immediately over the cake to cover it completely. Leave to set before serving.

Rum gâteau

SERVES 10

150 g / 5 oz self-raising flour (U.S. 1¼ cups all-purpose flour sifted with 1¼ teaspoons baking powder)
25 g / 1 oz cocoa powder (U.S. ¼ cup unsweetened cocoa)
175 g / 6 oz (U.S. ¾ cup) butter
175 g / 6 oz caster sugar (U.S. ¾ cup granulated sugar)
3 large eggs, separated
3 tablespoons (U.S. 4 tablespoons) milk
SYRUP
150 ml / ¼ pint (U.S. ⅔ cup) water
100 g / 4 oz caster sugar (U.S. ½ cup granulated sugar)
3 tablespoons (U.S. 4 tablespoons) rum
FILLING
300 ml / ½ pint double cream (U.S. 1¼ cups heavy cream)
2 tablespoons (U.S. 3 tablespoons) milk
ICING
2 tablespoons (U.S. 3 tablespoons) water
50 g / 2 oz (U.S. ¼ cup) butter
1 tablespoon rum
225 g / 8 oz icing sugar, sifted (U.S. 1¾ cups sifted confectioners' sugar)
50 g / 2 oz cocoa powder (U.S. ½ cup unsweetened cocoa), sifted
DECORATION
50 g / 2 oz plain chocolate (U.S. 2 squares semi-sweet chocolate), made into curls (see page 10)

Heat the oven to 180°C/350°F, Gas Mark 4, grease a 20-cm/8-inch cake tin and line with greaseproof paper (U.S. waxed paper).

Sift the flour with the cocoa and set aside. Cream the butter and sugar together until soft and fluffy. Beat in the egg yolks, one at a time, then fold in about half the dry ingredients and the milk. Whisk the egg whites in a clean bowl until stiff and fold into the cake batter with the remaining dry ingredients. Transfer to the prepared tin and level the surface.

Bake for about 50 minutes, or until just firm to the touch. Leave in the tin for 5 minutes then turn out on a wire rack, remove the lining paper and allow to cool. Cut the cake into 3 even layers with a sharp knife and spread them out on a board.

To make the syrup, put the water and sugar in a pan and heat gently until the sugar has dissolved. Remove from the heat and add the rum. When the syrup is just warm, spoon it over the cake layers.

Whip the cream with the milk and use to sandwich the cake layers carefully together on a serving plate. Put the water and butter in a pan for the icing and heat gently until the butter has melted. Remove from the heat, add the rum, sugar and cocoa and beat until smooth. Spread over the top of the cake and leave to set. Pile the chocolate curls in the centre before serving.

Tipsy mocha cream cake

SERVES 6–8

175 g / 6 oz (U.S. ¾ cup) butter or margarine
175 g / 6 oz caster sugar (U.S. ¾ cup granulated sugar)
3 eggs, lightly beaten
150 g / 5 oz plain flour (U.S. 1¼ cups all-purpose flour)
25 g / 1 oz cocoa powder (U.S. ¼ cup unsweetened cocoa)
SYRUP
175 ml / 6 fl oz (U.S. ¾ cup) water
175 g / 6 oz (U.S. ¾ cup) sugar
1 tablespoon instant coffee powder
2 tablespoons (U.S. 3 tablespoons) Tia Maria
DECORATION
150 ml / ¼ pint double cream (U.S. ⅔ cup heavy cream), whipped
few chocolate curls (see page 10)

Heat the oven to 180°C/350°F, Gas Mark 4, grease a 20-cm/8-inch cake tin and line the base with greaseproof paper (U.S. waxed paper).

Cream the butter and sugar in a bowl until light and fluffy. Gradually beat in the egg. Sift the flour with the cocoa and fold into the creamed mixture. Transfer to the prepared tin and level the surface.

Bake for about 40 minutes, or until firm to the touch.

Meanwhile, make the syrup. Place the water and sugar in a pan and heat gently until the sugar has dissolved. Boil for 2 minutes, remove from the heat and stir in the coffee and liqueur.

Leave the cake in the tin for 2 minutes, then turn out on a wire rack and remove the lining paper. Immediately transfer the cake to a serving plate and prick the top lightly with a fine skewer. Spoon the hot syrup slowly over the warm cake and leave to stand for at least 4 hours.

Pipe or spread the cream over the top of the cake and sprinkle with the chocolate curls.

Mocha wedge gâteau

(Illustrated opposite)

100 g/4 oz plain flour (U.S. 1 cup all-purpose flour)
25 g/1 oz cornflour (U.S. ¼ cup cornstarch)
2 teaspoons (U.S. 1 tablespoon) baking powder
½ teaspoon salt
25 g/1 oz cocoa powder (U.S. ¼ cup unsweetened cocoa)
275 g/10 oz caster sugar (U.S. 1¼ cups granulated sugar)
100 ml/4 fl oz (U.S. ½ cup) corn oil
75 ml/3 fl oz (U.S. ⅓ cup) water
2 eggs, separated
FILLING AND DECORATION
2 egg yolks
75 g/3 oz caster sugar (U.S. ⅓ cup granulated sugar)
4 tablespoons (U.S. 6 tablespoons) water
1 teaspoon instant coffee powder
175 g/6 oz (U.S. ¾ cup) butter
5 chocolate triangles (see page 10) or use thin mint chocolate squares, halved
little icing sugar (U.S. confectioners' sugar) for sprinkling

Heat the oven to 190°C/375°F, Gas Mark 5, grease 2 × 17.5-cm/7-inch shallow cake tins, line the bases with greaseproof paper (U.S. waxed paper) and grease the paper.

Sift the flour, cornflour, baking powder, salt and cocoa into a bowl and stir in the sugar. Put the oil, water and egg yolks in a jug and whisk lightly. Add to the dry ingredients and beat until smooth. Place the egg whites in a clean bowl and whisk until stiff. Fold evenly into the batter. Divide between the prepared tins.

Bake for about 25 minutes, or until firm to the touch. Turn out on a wire rack, peel off the paper and leave to cool.

Meanwhile, make the coffee filling. Put the egg yolks in a large bowl. Place the sugar and water in a pan and heat gently, stirring, until the sugar has dissolved. Then boil without stirring until the syrup reaches a temperature of 107°C/225°F. To test the syrup without a thermometer, take 2 teaspoons and place them back to back. Dip in the syrup then pull apart. If ready, the syrup will form a short thread between the 2 spoons. Remove from the heat, add the coffee and stir once. Whisk the egg yolks, if possible with an electric mixer, and add the syrup in a thin stream, whisking constantly. Place the butter in another bowl and beat until soft and creamy. Gradually add the egg mousse, beating vigorously all the time. Leave until cold and thick. Transfer to a piping bag fitted with a large star tube.

Make a template from greaseproof paper (U.S. waxed paper), with the base of one cake tin as a guide. Fold this in half, then into thirds. Use the triangular shape to mark out and then cut 6 sections from one layer of cake.

Place the uncut cake layer on a serving plate and pipe concentric circles of coffee filling on top. Pipe more cream in the centre to support the top layer of cake. Discarding one, arrange 5 cake wedges on the filling, propping them up slightly in the middle. Pipe shells of filling between the wedges, a rosette on top and more shells around the centre under the cake wedges. Decorate with chocolate triangles and sift a little sugar over the gâteau before serving.

Stages in making Mocha wedge gâteau

Rich 'n moist chocolate gâteau

150 g/5 oz plain flour (U.S. 1¼ cups all-purpose flour)
25 g/1 oz cornflour (U.S. ¼ cup cornstarch)
65 g/2½ oz cocoa powder (U.S. ⅔ cup unsweetened cocoa)
¼ teaspoon bicarbonate of soda (U.S. baking soda)
175 g/6 oz caster sugar (U.S. ¾ cup granulated sugar)
50 g/2 oz (U.S. ½ cup) ground almonds
2 eggs
100 ml/4 fl oz (U.S. ½ cup) corn oil
175 ml/6 fl oz golden syrup (U.S. ¾ cup light corn syrup)
175 ml/6 fl oz (U.S. ¾ cup) milk
FROSTING
225 g/8 oz plain chocolate (U.S. 1⅓ cups semi-sweet chocolate pieces)
175 g/6 oz (U.S. ¾ cup) butter
350 g/12 oz icing sugar, sifted (U.S. 2⅔ cups sifted confectioners' sugar)
2 egg yolks

Heat the oven to 160°C/325°F, Gas Mark 3, grease a 17.5-cm/7-inch square cake tin and line with greaseproof paper (U.S. waxed paper).

Sift the flour with the cornflour, cocoa and bicarbonate of soda into a bowl. Stir in the sugar and nuts. Put the eggs, oil, syrup and milk into another bowl and whisk until smooth. Add to the dry ingredients and beat to make a smooth batter. Transfer to the prepared tin.

Bake for 1½ hours, or until just firm to the touch. Leave in the tin for 5 minutes then turn out on a wire rack, remove the paper and allow to cool.

To make the frosting, melt the chocolate in a bowl over a pan of hot water then cool. Beat the butter and sugar together in a bowl until smooth. Add the egg yolks, one at a time, beating well after each addition. Finally, beat in the chocolate.

Split the cake into two layers and sandwich together with half the frosting. Spread half the remainder over the top and mark into swirls with a knife blade. Put the rest into a piping bag fitted with a medium-sized star tube and pipe a shell border all round the edge of the cake and rosettes in the centre.

Double chocolate gâteau

(Illustrated on the cover)

50 g / 2 oz cocoa powder (U.S. ½ cup unsweetened cocoa), sifted
65 ml / 2½ fl oz (U.S. scant ⅓ cup) milk
150 ml / ¼ pint (U.S. ⅔ cup) water
175 g / 6 oz plain flour (U.S. 1½ cups all-purpose flour)
½ teaspoon baking powder
1 teaspoon bicarbonate of soda (U.S. baking soda)
pinch of salt
100 g / 4 oz whipped white vegetable fat (U.S. ½ cup shortening)
250 g / 9 oz caster sugar (U.S. generous 1 cup granulated sugar)
2 eggs, beaten
FILLING AND DECORATION
175 g / 6 oz plain chocolate (U.S. 6 squares semi-sweet chocolate)
25 g / 1 oz cocoa powder (U.S. ¼ cup unsweetened cocoa), sifted
3 tablespoons (U.S. 4 tablespoons) boiling water
175 g / 6 oz (U.S. ¾ cup) butter or margarine
350 g / 12 oz icing sugar, sifted (U.S. 2⅔ cups sifted confectioners'
sugar)
½ teaspoon vanilla essence (U.S. vanilla extract)
4 glacé cherries (U.S. candied cherries)

Heat the oven to 180°C/350°F, Gas mark 4, grease 2 × 20-cm/8-inch shallow cake tins and line the bases with greaseproof paper (U.S. waxed paper).

Put the cocoa in a bowl and gradually work in the milk and water, keeping the mixture smooth. Sift the flour with the baking powder, bicarbonate of soda and salt. Cream the fat and sugar in a large bowl until really soft and fluffy. Gradually beat in the egg then add spoonfuls of the dry ingredients alternately with the cocoa mixture, stirring the mixture lightly but thoroughly. Divide between the prepared tins.

Bake for about 30 minutes, or until firm to the touch. An extra test for this cake is to insert a wooden cocktail stick (U.S. toothpick) in the centre. It should come out clean if the cake is ready. Turn out on a wire rack, peel off the lining paper and leave to cool.

To make the chocolate triangles, draw a rectangle measuring 10 cm/4 inches by 5 cm/2 inches on a sheet of non-stick baking parchment (U.S. waxed paper). Melt one third of the chocolate and spread inside the marked shape. Leave to set then trim the edges with a sharp knife. Cut the shape into 2 × 5-cm/2-inch squares and cut the squares diagonally to make 4 triangles. Make chocolate curls from the remaining chocolate (see page 10). Blend the cocoa with the water until smooth. Cool. Cream the butter and sugar and gradually beat in the cocoa mixture and vanilla essence.

Sandwich the cake layers together with one quarter of the filling. Spread the chocolate curls on a sheet of greaseproof paper (U.S. waxed paper). Cover the sides of the cake thinly with about half of the remaining filling. Holding the cake between your hands, one on the top and one on the base, roll the sides of the cake very lightly in the chocolate curls until evenly coated. Place on a serving plate. Put half the rest of the filling in a piping bag fitted with a large star tube. Use the remainder to cover the top of the cake. Mark into swirls with the tip of a knife, drawing it from the edge of the cake into the centre. Pipe eight rosettes around the edge of the cake and top these alternately with a chocolate triangle and a cherry.

Nusstorte

6 large eggs
100 g / 4 oz caster sugar (U.S. ½ cup granulated sugar)
50 g / 2 oz plain flour (U.S. ½ cup all-purpose flour), sifted
100 g / 4 oz ground hazelnuts (U.S. 1 cup ground filberts)
FILLING AND DECORATION
50 g / 2 oz (U.S. ¼ cup) butter
100 g / 4 oz icing sugar, sifted (U.S. scant 1 cup sifted
confectioners' sugar)
2 tablespoons (U.S. 3 tablespoons) brandy
4 tablespoons (U.S. 6 tablespoons) apricot jam, sieved
1 (200-g / 7-oz) pack plain chocolate flavour cake covering (U.S.
7-oz pack semi-sweet chocolate flavor cake covering)

Heat the oven to 180°C/350°F, Gas Mark 4, grease 2 × 20-cm/8-inch shallow cake tins, line with greaseproof paper (U.S. waxed paper) and grease the paper.

Place 2 eggs and 4 extra egg yolks in a large bowl and add the sugar. Whisk, using an electric mixer if possible, until thick and foamy. Fold in the flour and hazelnuts. Whisk the egg whites in a separate bowl until stiff and fold them into the nut mixture lightly but thoroughly. Divide between the prepared tins.

Bake for about 40 minutes, or until just firm to the touch. Leave in the tins for 5 minutes then turn out on a wire rack and peel off the paper. Allow to cool.

Meanwhile, make the filling. Cream the butter and icing sugar and gradually beat in the brandy. Set aside. Warm the jam slightly.

Split each cake in half and sandwich the 2 halves together with brandy filling. Then put the cake layers together with the jam and transfer to a serving plate.

Melt the cake covering as directed, pour it over the cake and spread over the top and sides with a spatula dipped in hot water and dried. Mark the cake into 8 portions before the chocolate sets.

VARIATION

Hazelnut cream layer cake Omit the brandy filling, jam and chocolate covering. Bake the cakes as above then cool and split to make 4 layers altogether. Toast 50 g/2 oz hazelnuts (U.S. ½ cup filberts) then chop finely. Blend 1 tablespoon cocoa powder (U.S. unsweetened cocoa) with 2 tablespoons (U.S. 3 tablespoons) sweet sherry. Beat 50 g/2 oz (U.S. ¼ cup) butter until soft and add 100 g/4 oz icing sugar, sifted (U.S. scant 1 cup sifted confectioners' sugar) and the cocoa mixture. Mix in the nuts. Use to sandwich the pairs of cake layers together. Whip 300 ml/½-pint double cream (U.S. 1¼ cups heavy cream) with 1 tablespoon sweet sherry and use some to sandwich the 2 filled cake layers together. Place on a serving plate. Mask the cake with the remaining cream, marking it into swirls, and decorate the top with 8 whole hazelnuts (U.S. filberts) round the edge and grated chocolate in the centre.

Strawberry sponge layer

=== SERVES 6 ===

(Illustrated below)

100 g/4 oz plain flour (U.S. 1 cup all-purpose flour)
4 large eggs
100 g/4 oz caster sugar (U.S. ½ cup granulated sugar)
FILLING AND DECORATION
225 g/8 oz (U.S. ½ lb) medium-sized strawberries
1 (100-g/3½-oz) pack melt-in-the-bag plain chocolate flavour cake covering (U.S. 3½-oz pack semi-sweet chocolate flavor cake covering)
300 ml/½ pint (U.S. 1¼ cups) whipping cream, whipped

Heat the oven to 190°C/375°F, Gas Mark 5, grease 3 × 17.5-cm/7-inch shallow cake tins, line the bases with greaseproof paper (U.S. waxed paper) and grease the paper lightly.

Sift the flour twice and set aside. Put the eggs and sugar in a large bowl and stand this over a pan of simmering water, without allowing the bowl to touch the water. Whisk steadily, using an electric beater if possible, until thick and mousse-like. When ready, the mixture should fall back on itself in a thick ribbon when the beaters are lifted. Remove from the heat and continue whisking until cool. Sift about half the flour again over the whisked mixture and fold in lightly but thoroughly. Repeat with the rest of the flour. Divide among the prepared tins and tilt these to make even layers.

Bake for about 15 minutes, or until golden and springy to the touch. Leave in the tins for 2 minutes then turn out on a wire rack, peel off the lining paper and allow to cool.

Meanwhile, halve the strawberries and divide into 2 portions. Melt the cake covering as directed.

Place one cake layer on a serving dish and cover with half the cream. Using one portion of fruit, first lay strawberry halves evenly around the edge of the cake, cut-surface downwards on the cream, then arrange any strawberries remaining from this portion over the rest of the cream. Cover with another layer of cake and top with the rest of the cream and strawberries in the same manner. Snip off the corner of the bag of cake covering and pour on top of the cake. Spread to the edges and swirl with the tip of a round-bladed knife before the covering sets.

Dark cherry gâteau

SERVES 10

(Illustrated opposite)

190 g/6½ oz plain flour (U.S. generous 1½ cups all-purpose flour)
2 teaspoons (U.S. 1 tablespoon) baking powder
40 g/1½ oz cocoa powder (U.S. ⅓ cup unsweetened cocoa)
175 g/6 oz (U.S. ¾ cup) butter or margarine
200 g/7 oz caster sugar (U.S. scant 1 cup granulated sugar)
3 eggs, beaten
3 tablespoons (U.S. 4 tablespoons) milk
FILLING AND DECORATION
1 (397-g/14-oz) can dark cherries, drained
300 ml/½ pint double cream (U.S. 1¼ cups heavy cream), whipped
1½ (200-g/7-oz) packs plain chocolate flavour cake covering (U.S.
1½ × 7-oz packs semi-sweet chocolate flavor cake covering)

Heat the oven to 160°C/325°F, Gas Mark 3, grease a 20-cm/8-inch cake tin and line with greaseproof paper (U.S. waxed paper).

Sift the flour with the baking powder and cocoa. Cream the butter and sugar in a bowl until light and fluffy. Gradually add the egg, beating well after each addition and adding a little of the dry ingredients with the last of the egg. Fold in the remaining flour mixture and the milk. Transfer to the prepared tin and level the surface.

Bake for about 1 hour, or until firm to the touch. Turn out on a wire rack, peel off the lining paper and leave to cool.

Stone the cherries (U.S. pit the cherries) and roughly chop half of them. Fold these into half the cream. Split the cake into 3 even layers and sandwich them together again with the cherry cream. Transfer to a serving dish. Make 30 large curls from the blocks of cake covering (see page 10). Set aside. Melt the remaining covering and spread it over the top and sides of the cake, using a spatula dipped in hot water and dried. Leave to set.

Put the rest of the cream in a piping bag fitted with a large star tube. Pipe rosettes around the edge of the cake and top each with a chocolate curl. Put 4 cherries in the centre of the cake then place the rest, in a ring, inside the border of cream rosettes. Set the last of the curls radiating out from the centre of the cake.

Left: Dark cherry gâteau. Right: Chocolate walnut tartlets
(recipe page 55)

Dobostorte

SERVES 8

150 g / 5 oz plain flour (U.S. *1¼ cups all-purpose flour*)
1 teaspoon baking powder
pinch of salt
4 large eggs
175 g / 6 oz caster sugar (U.S. *¾ cup granulated sugar*)
FILLING
100 g / 4 oz plain chocolate (U.S. *⅔ cup semi-sweet chocolate pieces*)
175 g / 6 oz (U.S. *¾ cup*) *unsalted butter*
175 g / 6 oz (U.S. *¾ cup*) *granulated sugar*
75 ml / 3 fl oz (U.S. *⅓ cup*) *water*
2 egg yolks
DECORATION
150 g / 5 oz (U.S. *⅔ cup*) *granulated sugar*
150 ml / ¼ pint (U.S. *⅔ cup*) *water*
75 g / 3 oz plain chocolate (U.S. *3 squares semi-sweet chocolate*),
coarsely grated

The cake is baked in 6 separate layers requiring 20-cm/8-inch shallow cake tins if possible, or it can be made in 20-cm/8-inch rounds on baking sheets (U.S. cookie sheets). If necessary, make up the mixture and bake the layers in batches. Heat the oven to 190°C/375°F, Gas Mark 5 and grease and flour the chosen tins or sheets. Mark 20-cm/8-inch circles on prepared sheets.

Sift the flour with the baking powder and salt 3 times and set aside. Put the eggs and sugar in a large bowl and stand this over a pan of simmering water, without allowing the bowl to touch the water. Whisk steadily, using an electric beater if possible, until the mixture falls back on itself in a thick ribbon when the beaters are lifted. Remove from the heat and continue whisking until cool. Fold in the dry ingredients, one third at a time.

Spoon into the prepared tins or circles. The mixture should be no more than 6 mm/¼ inch deep.

Bake for about 6 minutes, or until golden and springy to the touch. Leave for 1 minute then turn out on a wire rack to cool. If baking the layers on sheets, trim round the edges with a sharp knife before transferring to the rack.

To make the filling, melt the chocolate over a pan of hot water and leave to cool. Put the butter in another bowl and beat until soft and creamy. Place the sugar and water in a pan and stir over gentle heat until the sugar has dissolved. Then boil to a temperature of 107°C/225°F. To test the syrup without using a thermometer, place 2 teaspoons back to back and dip them in the syrup. Then lift out and pull them apart. The syrup is ready if a short thread forms between the 2 spoons. Remove the pan from the heat and leave until the bubbles subside. Put the egg yolks in a third bowl, whisk lightly then add the syrup in a thin stream, whisking vigorously all the time, until thick and mousse-like. Start adding the mousse to the butter a little at a time, beating constantly. Then beat in the chocolate and leave until cold and thick.

Lightly oil a baking sheet (U.S. cookie sheet). Choose the cake with the best surface and place on the prepared sheet. Brush away any crumbs. To make the caramel, put the sugar and water in a pan and heat gently, stirring, until the sugar has dissolved. Then boil without stirring until the caramel is golden brown. Pour at once over the cake on the sheet, allowing it to flow over the edges. As soon as the caramel starts to set, mark the cake into 8 portions with a sharp knife, cutting through the caramel. Trim around the edges.

To assemble the cake, use three-quarters of the filling to sandwich all the layers together, putting the caramel-coated layer on top. Spread the sides of the cake thinly with more filling and press on grated chocolate. Place on a serving dish. Put any remaining filling in a piping bag fitted with a medium-sized star tube and pipe one rosette on each section of the cake.

Frosted carrot cake

SERVES 6–8

(Illustrated below)

175 g/6 oz (U.S. ¾ cup) butter or margarine
175 g/6 oz soft brown sugar (U.S. ¾ cup light brown sugar)
3 eggs, beaten
finely grated rind of 1 orange
2 teaspoons (U.S. 1 tablespoon) orange juice
150 g/5 oz (U.S. 1¼ cups) finely grated carrot
25 g/1 oz cocoa powder (U.S. ¼ cup unsweetened cocoa)
2 teaspoons (U.S. 1 tablespoon) baking powder
175 g/6 oz wheatmeal flour (U.S. 1½ cups wholewheat flour)
FILLING AND DECORATION
100 g/4 oz (U.S. ½ cup) butter or margarine
225 g/8 oz icing sugar, sifted (U.S. 1¾ cups sifted confectioners'
sugar)
2 tablespoons (U.S. 3 tablespoons) orange juice
100 g/4 oz marzipan (U.S. ¼ lb almond marzipan)
few drops green food colouring
few drops orange food colouring
few drops brown food colouring

Heat the oven to 180°C/350°F, Gas Mark 4, grease a 17.5-cm/7-inch cake tin and line the base with greaseproof paper (U.S. waxed paper).

Cream the butter and sugar in a bowl until light and fluffy.

Gradually add the egg, orange rind and juice, beating well after each addition. Stir in the carrot. Sift the cocoa with the baking powder and add to the creamed mixture with the flour. Fold in thoroughly. Transfer to the prepared tin and level the surface.

Bake for about 1¼ hours, or until firm to the touch. Leave in the tin for 5 minutes then turn out on a wire rack to cool. When cold, peel off the lining paper.

To make the filling, beat the butter and sugar until smooth, then gradually beat in the orange juice. To make the carrot decorations, pinch off a tiny piece of the marzipan and tint this green with food colouring. Roll out into a very thin string about 22.5 cm/9 inches long. Snip into 18 × 1.25-cm/½-inch lengths. Tint the remaining marzipan orange with food colouring and divide into 6 equal pieces. Form each into a carrot shape, about 5 cm/2 inches long. Using a small paintbrush, dipped in brown food colouring, or even gravy browning, mark a few tiny lines across each carrot.

Split the cake into 2 layers and sandwich them together with just under half the filling. Place on a serving plate. Take about 3 tablespoons (U.S. 4 tablespoons) of the remaining icing and place in a piping bag fitted with a small star tube. Spread the rest of the icing smoothly on top of the cake and pipe a shell border around the edge. Arrange the marzipan carrots evenly on the cake and press 3 tiny pieces of green marzipan 'stalk' into the top of each, pinching the ends into points.

Russian soured cream cake

═══ SERVES 8–10 ═══

50 g/2 oz plain chocolate, roughly chopped (U.S. ⅓ cup semi-sweet chocolate pieces)
150 ml/¼ pint (U.S. ⅔ cup) very hot strong black coffee
25 g/1 oz cocoa powder (U.S. ¼ cup unsweetened cocoa)
150 ml/¼ pint (U.S. ⅔ cup) soured cream
225 g/8 oz plain flour (U.S. 2 cups all-purpose flour)
½ teaspoon salt
2 teaspoons (U.S. 1 tablespoon) baking powder
½ teaspoon bicarbonate of soda (U.S. baking soda)
100 g/4 oz (U.S. ½ cup) butter
275 g/10 oz caster sugar (U.S. 1¼ cups granulated sugar)
1 teaspoon vanilla essence
2 eggs, separated
FILLING AND DECORATION
225 g/8 oz plain chocolate (U.S. 1⅓ cups semi-sweet chocolate pieces)
300 ml/½ pint double cream (U.S. 1¼ cups heavy cream)
1 (225-g/8-oz) can unsweetened chestnut purée
2 marrons glacés, each cut into 3 pieces

Heat the oven to 180°C/350°F, Gas Mark 4, grease 2 × 20-cm/8-inch shallow cake tins and line the bases with greaseproof paper (U.S. waxed paper).

Put the chocolate in a bowl and pour over the coffee. Leave for about 5 minutes then stir well until smooth. Put the cocoa in a pan and gradually add the chocolate liquid to it, mixing well until creamy. Heat very gently, stirring, until the mixture boils. Remove from the heat and leave to cool. Stir in the cream.

Sift the flour with the salt, baking powder and bicarbonate of soda. Cream the butter with the sugar until light and fluffy. Add the vanilla essence and egg yolks, one at a time, beating well after each addition. Fold in a little of the dry ingredients, with some of the chocolate mixture. Repeat until all are incorporated. Whisk the egg whites in a clean bowl until stiff and fold in evenly. Divide between the prepared tins.

Bake for about 45 minutes, or until just firm to the touch. Leave in the tins for 5 minutes then turn out on a wire rack and allow to cool. Remove the lining paper and split each cake in half, giving 4 layers in all.

To make the chocolate cream, put the chocolate in a bowl with 2 tablespoons (U.S. 3 tablespoons) of the cream and place over hot water until the chocolate has melted. Stir lightly to blend and leave until cool but not set. Whip the remaining cream until thick and gradually blend in the chocolate, whisking until firm and holding its shape. Take just under half the chocolate cream and whisk in the chestnut purée. Use to sandwich the cake layers together on a serving plate. Mark the cake with the remaining chocolate cream and mask the surface in lines with the tip of a round-bladed knife. Decorate the top with pieces of marron glacé.

Gâteau Diane

═══ SERVES 8–10 ═══

(Illustrated opposite)

3 egg whites
2 teaspoons (U.S. 1 tablespoon) instant coffee powder
175 g/6 oz caster sugar (U.S. ¾ cup granulated sugar)
FILLING AND DECORATION
150 g/5 oz plain chocolate (U.S. generous ¾ cup semi-sweet chocolate pieces)
175 g/6 oz (U.S. ¾ cup) unsalted butter
3 egg yolks
175 g/6 oz (U.S. ¾ cup) granulated sugar
75 ml/3 fl oz (U.S. ⅓ cup) water
50 g/2 oz flaked almonds (U.S. ½ cup slivered almonds), toasted
icing sugar (U.S. confectioners' sugar) for sprinkling

Heat the oven to 110°C/225°F, Gas Mark ¼. Mark 3 × 15-cm/6-inch circles on non-stick baking parchment (U.S. waxed paper) and place on baking sheets (U.S. cookie sheets).

Put the egg whites in a large bowl and whisk until stiff. Mix the coffee with the sugar and gradually add to the egg whites, a tablespoon at a time, beating vigorously after each addition until the meringue is firm and glossy. Spread or pipe the meringue inside the marked circles.

Bake for about 4 hours, or until completely dry, turning the layers over for the last 1 hour of baking time. When cool, the layers may be stored in an airtight container for up to 1 week.

To make the chocolate filling, melt the chocolate in a bowl over a pan of hot water. Cool. Place the butter in a bowl and beat until soft. In another bowl, whisk the egg yolks until pale, if possible using an electric mixer. Put the sugar and water in a pan and heat gently, stirring, until the sugar has dissolved. Then boil to a temperature of 107°C/225°F. To test the syrup without a thermometer, take 2 teaspoons, place them back to back, then dip them into the syrup. Lift them out and pull apart. If ready, a short thread of syrup should form between the 2 spoons.

Whisking the egg yolks constantly with the mixer, add the syrup in a thin stream. Whisk until cool then gradually beat the egg mousse into the butter. Finally, beat in the chocolate. Leave until cold and thick.

To assemble the gâteau, sandwich the meringue layers together with just over half the filling. Place on a serving dish and spread the remainder over the top and sides. Cover with the almonds, pressing them in lightly. Lay 3 × 2.5-cm/1-inch wide strips of paper over the cake and sift the top lightly with icing sugar. Carefully remove the paper.

Gâteau Diane

Milk chocolate layer cake

(Illustrated opposite)

175 g/6 oz (U.S. ¾ cup) butter or margarine
175 g/6 oz caster sugar (U.S. ¾ cup granulated sugar)
3 eggs
225 g/8 oz self-raising flour, sifted (U.S. 2 cups all-purpose flour
sifted with 2 teaspoons baking powder)
1 teaspoon vanilla essence (U.S. vanilla extract)
3 tablespoons (U.S. 4 tablespoons) cold water
FILLING AND DECORATION
2 (200-g/7-oz) packs milk chocolate flavour cake covering (U.S.
2 × 7-oz packs sweet chocolate flavor cake covering)
100 g/4 oz (U.S. ½ cup) butter or margarine
175 g/6 oz icing sugar, sifted (U.S. 1⅓ cups sifted confectioners'
sugar)
4 glacé cherries (U.S. candied cherries)

Heat the oven to 160°C/325°F, Gas Mark 3, grease a 20-cm/8-inch cake tin and line with greaseproof paper (U.S. waxed paper).

Cream the butter and sugar in a bowl until light and fluffy. Beat in the eggs, one at a time, adding a little of the flour with the last of the eggs. Beat in the vanilla essence then fold in the flour and water. Mix lightly but thoroughly. Transfer to the prepared tin and level the surface.

Bake for about 1 hour, or until firm to the touch. Leave in the tin for 5 minutes then turn out on a wire rack, peel off the paper and leave to cool.

To make the filling, melt the cake covering in a bowl over a pan of hot water and leave to cool slightly. Cream the butter and sugar in another bowl until soft and fluffy. Add about 3 tablespoons (U.S. 4 tablespoons) of the cake covering and beat well. Set aside. Use a little of the remaining cake covering to make about 12 chocolate 'leaves' (see page 10). Keep chilled. Cut 3 of the cherries into small pieces and place about a quarter of the chocolate filling in a piping bag fitted with a large star tube.

Split the cake into 3–5 even layers and sandwich them together again with the remaining chocolate filling. Transfer to a serving dish and spread the top and sides with cake covering, using a spatula dipped in hot water and dried. Leave to set. Pipe a continuous twisted line of chocolate icing around the edge of the cake and spike this with chocolate leaves and pieces of cherry. Put the whole cherry in the centre of the cake surrounded by more leaves.

Right: Milk chocolate layer cake. Left: Apricot and coconut florentines (recipe page 47)

Bavarian mustorte

225 g/8 oz plain chocolate (U.S. 1⅓ cups semi-sweet chocolate pieces)
8 eggs, separated
65 g/2½ oz icing sugar, sifted (U.S. generous ½ cup sifted confectioners' sugar)
225 g/8 oz (U.S. 1 cup) unsalted butter, softened
2 tablespoons (U.S. 3 tablespoons) Kirsch or Maraschino
50 g/2 oz (U.S. ½ cup) fine dried breadcrumbs
50 g/2 oz (U.S. ½ cup) finely chopped walnuts or pecans

Heat the oven to 180°C/350°F, Gas Mark 4 and grease a 22.5-cm/9-inch spring-sided or loose-based cake tin.

Melt the chocolate in a bowl over a pan of hot water then allow to cool. Put the egg yolks in another bowl and whisk, using an electric mixer if possible, until very pale. Reserve 3 tablespoons (U.S. 4 tablespoons) of the sugar and add the remainder to the yolks with the butter, chocolate and Kirsch. Whisk on high speed until velvety.

In a clean bowl lightly whisk the egg whites. Sprinkle on the reserved sugar and whisk until the meringue is firm and glossy. Fold into the chocolate mixture. Take half to another bowl, fold in the breadcrumbs and nuts and spread in the prepared tin. Cover the rest and chill.

Bake for about 20 minutes, or until a fine skewer or wooden cocktail stick (U.S. toothpick) inserted in the centre comes out clean. Leave in the tin until cold. (The centre will sink on cooling.)

Remove the sides of the cake tin and transfer the cake, still on the metal base, to a serving plate. Use the chilled mixture to fill the hollow in the cake, lifting it into peaks with a knife blade.

Praline gâteau

500 ml/18 fl oz (U.S. generous 2 cups) Chocolate ice cream (see page 117), slightly softened
50 g/2 oz (U.S. ½ cup) unblanched whole almonds
50 g/2 oz caster sugar (U.S. ¼ cup granulated sugar)
2 (20-cm/8-inch) cake layers as in Rich chocolate button cake (see page 84)
about 75 ml/3 fl oz (U.S. ⅓ cup) apricot jam
300 ml/½ pint double cream (U.S. 1¼ cups heavy cream), whipped

Line a 20-cm/8-inch cake tin with greaseproof paper (U.S. waxed paper) and press in the ice cream to make a flat layer. Cover and freeze until firm.

Meanwhile, make the praline powder. Have ready a greased baking sheet (U.S. cookie sheet). Put the nuts and sugar in a heavy-based pan over very low heat, shaking the pan frequently, until the sugar melts to a liquid. Using a metal spoon, stir carefully until the syrup and nuts are rich golden brown. Turn immediately on to the prepared sheet and cool. Grind or pound the praline to a coarse powder.

Assemble the cake just before serving. Place one cake layer on a plate and spread with jam. Turn the ice cream round out on it and peel off the paper. Spread the ice cream with more jam and press the second cake layer on top. Fold the praline powder into the cream and use to mask the cake.

NOTE Praline powder can be stored in an airtight container for many months. It is not necessary to freeze it.

Arctic surprise

(Illustrated opposite)

175 g/6 oz (U.S. ¾ cup) butter
175 g/6 oz caster sugar (U.S. ¾ cup granulated sugar)
3 eggs, beaten
175 g/6 oz self-raising flour, sifted (U.S. 1½ cups all-purpose flour sifted with 1½ teaspoons baking powder)
1 tablespoon milk
FILLING AND DECORATION
500 ml/18 fl oz (U.S. generous 2 cups) Chocolate ice cream (see page 54)
100 g/4 oz plain chocolate (U.S. 4 squares semi-sweet chocolate)
12 medium-sized strawberries, sliced
150 ml/¼ pint double cream (U.S. ⅔ cup heavy cream), whipped

Heat the oven to 190°C/375°F, Gas Mark 5, grease 2 × 20-cm/8-inch shallow cake tins and line the bases with greaseproof paper (U.S. waxed paper).

Cream the butter and sugar in a bowl until light and fluffy. Gradually add the egg, beating well after each addition. Fold in the flour and milk. Divide between the prepared tins and level the surface.

Bake for 25 minutes, or until firm to the touch. Turn out on a wire rack, remove the lining paper and leave to cool.

Meanwhile, mark a 20-cm/8-inch circle on a sheet of greaseproof paper (U.S. waxed paper). Spoon the ice cream into the marked shape and press down to make a fairly even layer. This does not have to be accurate. Freeze until firm. Grate a quarter of the chocolate and set aside. Melt the remainder and use to make 5 chocolate cones (see page 11).

Only assemble the gâteau immediately before serving time. Set one cake on a plate and put the ice cream layer on top. Reserve 15 good strawberry slices and arrange the remainder over the ice cream. Top with the second cake. Spread two-thirds of the cream over the top and sides of the cake and press the grated chocolate over the sides. Put the remaining cream in a piping bag fitted with a medium-sized star tube. Pipe a little cream into each chocolate cone and arrange these on the cake, alternating them with overlapping lines of strawberry slices. Finish with rosettes of cream in the centre of the cake and serve at once.

Arctic surprise

Simple Puddings and Sweets

Although it may be true that the main meal no longer consists always of a savoury course followed by a sweet one, puddings are still in demand. Taste buds seem to crave for something sweet to follow the more substantial main course, and chocolate is the preferred flavour. The blander vanilla and almond blancmanges and creams are almost always passed up in favour of chocolate and mocha. The latter is an intriguing blend of cocoa with coffee. For everyday meals, you will probably opt to use cocoa powder instead of melted chocolate, as this gives a strong flavour without adding much to the cost of the ingredients.

Most frequently served to the family are milk puddings, and sponges resembling in texture light cakes or cookies. This section includes the sponge types, with that popular surprise, the upside-down pudding. Here you have plenty of scope to ring the changes. Pears, apples, peaches and apricots all taste good with chocolate, equally so with mocha. The best way to incorporate the blended flavour in this case is to moisten the cocoa powder and instant coffee together with boiling water, mix to a thin cream and add to the liquid ingredients. Another alternative is to add almond or orange essence (U.S. almond or orange extract) to the mixture. This could give a new flavour-way if you were to serve the pudding with a clear orange sauce or a thin pouring almond sauce. Arrowroot is the ideal thickener, as it has an entirely neutral flavour, does not have to be cooked to remove rawness, and thickens at a lower temperature than flour or cornflour (U.S. cornstarch). Moisten as for cornflour and stir into the sauce as it reaches boiling point. Three level teaspoons (U.S. 4 teaspoons) or even less gives a velvety consistency and shining purity of colour to 300 ml/$\frac{1}{2}$ pint (U.S. 1$\frac{1}{4}$ cups) liquid.

For fruit sauce, use fruit juice and a grating of some appropriate citrus fruit rind. For almond or vanilla, add essence to milk. Double the quantity of chocolate sponge mixture, and use the extra to fill small tartlet cases of pastry. Bake these using my Raspberry tartlet recipe and dress up with pink glacé icing and a raspberry topping. You could use other fruit from a can, well drained, or fresh fruit. The same mixture, baked in advance as a round layer, would make an interesting base for a Baked Alaska, and again is more flavourful than a plain vanilla sponge (page 125).

Above: Cherry chocolate bakewell (recipe page 108). Centre: Chocolate crumb pudding (recipe page 113). Below: Cheesy chocolate flan (recipe page 113).

Cherry chocolate bakewell

SERVES 6

(Illustrated on page 106)

PASTRY
175 g/6 oz plain flour (U.S. 1½ cups all-purpose flour)
40 g/1½ oz (U.S. 3 tablespoons) lard or other white fat
40 g/1½ oz (U.S. 3 tablespoons) block margarine
1–2 tablespoons (U.S. 2–3 tablespoons) water
FILLING
150 ml/¼ pint (U.S. ⅔ cup) cherry jam
50 g/2 oz (U.S. ¼ cup) margarine
50 g/2 oz caster sugar (U.S. ¼ cup granulated sugar)
1 egg, beaten
1 (100-g/3½-oz) packet melt-in-the-bag plain chocolate flavour cake covering (U.S. 3½-oz pack semi-sweet chocolate flavor cake covering)
50 g/2 oz self-raising flour, sifted (U.S. ½ cup all-purpose flour sifted with ½ teaspoon baking powder)
50 g/2 oz (U.S. ½ cup) ground almonds

Heat the oven to 200°C/400°F, Gas Mark 6 and have ready a 20-cm/8-inch tin or shallow cake tin.

To make the pastry, sift the flour into a bowl. Rub or cut in the fats until the mixture resembles breadcrumbs. Add sufficient water to make a firm dough. Roll out almost all the pastry on a lightly floured surface and use to line the tin. Reserve the trimmings.

Spread the jam in the pastry case. Cream the margarine and sugar in a bowl until light and fluffy. Gradually beat in the egg. Melt the cake covering as directed, add to the creamed mixture with the flour and almonds. Mix well. Spoon evenly over the jam and level the surface.

Gather the pastry trimmings and reserved pastry into a ball and roll out to a rectangle. Cut into 6-mm/¼-inch strips. Lay these in a lattice design over the chocolate filling. Trim to fit, dampen the ends of the strips and press them to the pastry case.

Bake for 20 minutes, then reduce the oven temperature to 180°C/350°F, Gas Mark 4 and continue cooking for a further 20 minutes, or until the pastry is golden brown. Serve hot or cold.

Upside-down pear pudding

SERVES 4–5

(Illustrated opposite)

1 (411-g/14½-oz) can pear halves
25 g/1 oz cocoa powder (U.S. ¼ cup unsweetened cocoa)
100 g/4 oz (U.S. ½ cup) butter or margarine
100 g/4 oz caster sugar (U.S. ½ cup granulated sugar)
2 eggs
75 g/3 oz self-raising flour, sifted (U.S. ¾ cup all-purpose flour sifted with ¾ teaspoon baking powder)
75 ml/3 fl oz double cream (U.S. ⅓ cup heavy cream), whipped
5 maraschino cherries (U.S. cocktail cherries)

Heat the oven to 190°C/375°F, Gas Mark 5, grease a 15-cm/6-inch cake tin, line the base with greaseproof paper (U.S. waxed paper) and grease the paper.

Drain the pears and reserve the syrup. Arrange the pear halves, rounded sides upwards, in the base of the prepared tin.

Blend the cocoa with 2 tablespoons (U.S. 3 tablespoons) of the pear syrup. Cream the butter and sugar in a bowl until light and fluffy. Add the eggs, one at a time, beating well after each addition. Fold in the flour and the blended cocoa. Spoon evenly over the pears and level the surface.

Bake for about 30 minutes, or until firm to the touch. Turn out on a serving dish and leave to cool.

Put the cream in a piping bag fitted with a medium-sized star tube and pipe rosettes around the base of the pudding. Top each pear half with a cherry. Serve with single cream (U.S. light cream).

NOTE If liked, whisk left-over pear syrup into the pouring cream using 2 tablespoons syrup to 150 ml/¼ pint cream (U.S. 3 tablespoons syrup to ⅔ cup cream).

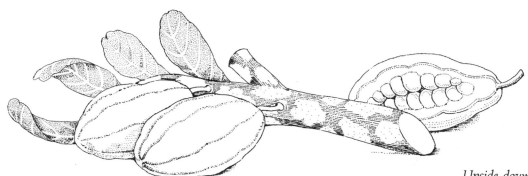

Upside-down pear pudding

Steamed mocha nut pudding

SERVES 6

(Illustrated opposite)

150 g / 5 oz plain flour (U.S. 1¼ cups all-purpose flour)
2 teaspoons (U.S. 1 tablespoon) baking powder
50 g / 2 oz (U.S. ¼ cup) margarine
50 g / 2 oz soft brown sugar (U.S. ¼ cup light brown sugar)
1 (113-g / 4-oz) packet chocolate dots (U.S. ⅔ cup chocolate chips)
25 g / 1 oz (U.S. ¼ cup) chopped walnuts or pecans
1 egg, beaten
100 ml / 4 fl oz (U.S. ½ cup) strong black coffee
1 tablespoon granulated sugar
small knob of butter

Sift the flour and baking powder into a bowl. Rub or cut in the margarine until the mixture resembles breadcrumbs. Stir in the brown sugar, one quarter of the chocolate dots and the nuts. Whisk the egg with half the coffee and add to the bowl. Mix well.

Transfer to a greased 600-ml / 1-pint (U.S. 1¼-pint) pudding bowl. Cover with a double layer of greased foil with a pleat in the centre and crimp the edges well under the rim of the bowl. Stand it in a pan and pour in boiling water to come halfway up the side of the bowl. Put on the lid and keep the water boiling steadily for 1½ hours, adding more boiling water during cooking if necessary.

Just before the pudding is ready, make the sauce. Put the rest of the chocolate dots, the remaining coffee, the white sugar and butter in a bowl. Stand this over a pan of hot water and stir until the sauce is smooth. Beat until glossy.

Turn the pudding out on a warm serving dish and spoon some of the sauce over it. Hand the rest separately. Serve at once.

VARIATIONS

Dotty pudding Omit the nuts and use all the chocolate dots in the pudding mixture. Use more to make the sauce or serve it with single cream (U.S. light cream).

Prunie pudding Stone (U.S. pit) 8 tenderized dried prunes and chop the flesh roughly. Use in the pudding mixture in place of the nuts. When the pudding is almost cooked, make up this Fluffy sauce. Prepare the Mocha sauce as in the main recipe then leave to cool slightly. Whisk 1 egg white in a clean bowl until stiff, add 25 g / 1 oz icing sugar, sifted (U.S. ¼ cup sifted confectioners' sugar) and whisk until the meringue is firm and glossy. Gradually whisk in the mocha sauce and serve separately with the hot pudding.

Above: Steamed mocha nut pudding. Below: Sweet 'n sour flan (recipe page 113)

111

Half-and-half sponge pudding

(Illustrated below)

50 g / 2 oz (U.S. scant ¼ cup) orange marmalade
50 g / 2 oz (U.S. ¼ cup) soft margarine
50 g / 2 oz caster sugar (U.S. ¼ cup granulated sugar)
50 g / 2 oz self-raising flour, sifted (U.S. ½ cup all-purpose flour
sifted with ½ teaspoon baking powder)
1 egg, beaten
1 tablespoon cocoa powder (U.S. unsweetened cocoa), sifted
1 tablespoon plain flour (U.S. all-purpose flour), sifted
finely grated rind of ½ orange

Grease a 600-ml / 1-pint (U.S. 1¼-pint) pudding bowl and spoon in the marmalade. Level the surface.

Put the margarine, sugar, self-raising flour and egg into a bowl and stir well until combined. Do not beat. Take half the mixture to a second bowl. Stir the cocoa into one portion and add the plain flour and orange rind to the other. Spread the orange mixture over the marmalade, making a well in the centre. Spoon the chocolate mixture into the centre and around the edges, to cover the orange mixture completely. Level the surface.

Cover the bowl with a double layer of greased foil with a pleat in the centre, crimping the edges under the rim of the bowl. Stand it in a pan and pour in boiling water to come half way up the side of the bowl. Put on the lid and keep the water boiling steadily for 1¼ hours, adding more boiling water to the pan during cooking if necessary.

Turn the pudding out on a warm serving plate and serve at once with custard or vanilla ice cream.

Fruit cap chocolate pudding Grease the pudding bowl and spoon in 50 g / 2 oz (U.S. ⅓ cup) seedless raisins, 6 glacé cherries (U.S. candied cherries), chopped and 1 tablespoon golden syrup (U.S. light corn syrup) instead of the marmalade. Make up the pudding mixture and add 2 tablespoons cocoa powder (U.S. 3 tablespoons unsweetened cocoa), omitting the cocoa, extra flour and orange rind in the main recipe. Cook as above and serve with scoops of chocolate ice cream.

Marbled lemon chocolate pudding Omit the marmalade in the pudding bowl and use lemon rind instead of orange rind in the pudding mixture. Spoon the chocolate and lemon mixtures alternatively into the greased bowl then swirl lightly with a knife blade. Serve the pudding with Lemon curd cream. Whip 150 ml / ¼ pint double cream (U.S. ⅔ cup heavy cream) and when thick whisk in 3 tablespoons (U.S. 4 tablespoons) lemon curd.

112

Chocolate crumb pudding

(Illustrated on page 106)

150 g / 5 oz (U.S. ⅔ cup) butter or margarine
1 tablespoon clear honey
1 (425-g / 15-oz) can apricot halves, drained
50 g / 2 oz soft brown sugar (U.S. ¼ cup light brown sugar)
1 egg, beaten
1 (100-g / 3½-oz) packet melt-in-the-bag plain chocolate flavour
cake covering (U.S. 3½-oz pack semi-sweet chocolate flavor cake
covering)
75 g / 3 oz self-raising flour, sifted (U.S. ¾ cup all-purpose flour
sifted with ¾ teaspoon baking powder)
75 g / 3 oz (U.S. 1½ cups) soft breadcrumbs
4 tablespoons (U.S. 6 tablespoons) milk

Heat the oven to 180°C / 350°F, Gas Mark 4 and grease a 900-ml / 1½-pint (U.S. 2-pint) ovenproof dish.

Beat together 25 g / 1 oz (U.S. 2 tablespoons) of the butter and the honey and spread evenly over the base of the prepared dish. Roughly chop the apricots and spoon into the dish.

Cream the remaining butter and the sugar in a bowl until light and fluffy. Gradually add the egg, beating well all the time. Melt the cake covering as directed and add to the creamed mixture with the flour, breadcrumbs and milk. Mix well and spread over the apricots.

Bake for about 1 hour, or until firm to the touch. Leave to stand for 10 minutes, then turn out on a warm serving dish.

Cheesy chocolate flan

(Illustrated on page 106)

1 (100-g / 3½-oz) packet melt-in-the-bag milk chocolate flavour cake
covering (U.S. 3½-oz pack sweet chocolate cake covering)
50 g / 2 oz (U.S. ¼ cup) soft butter or margarine
200 g / 7 oz gingernut biscuits, crushed (U.S. 2⅓ cups gingersnap
cookie crumbs)
350 g / 12 oz (U.S. 1½ cups) cream cheese
finely grated rind and juice of 1 large orange
50 g / 2 oz caster sugar (U.S. ¼ cup granulated sugar)

Have ready a 17.5-cm / 7-inch fluted flan ring standing on a flat serving plate, or a flan tin with a loose base.

Melt the cake covering in hot water as directed. Put the butter in a bowl and add the biscuit crumbs. Snip off the corner of the bag and squeeze in half the cake covering. Mix well. Return the remaining covering, still in the bag, to the hot water, so that it does not harden. Press the crumb mixture inside the flan ring, making a flat base and raising the sides. Chill until firm.

Put the cheese in a bowl with the orange rind and juice and the sugar. Beat vigorously until light and fluffy. Spoon into the crumb case. Carefully remove the flan ring. If using a tin, remove this and transfer the flan, still on the metal base, to a serving plate. Drizzle the rest of the cake covering over the top of the cheese filling and chill for about 1 hour before serving.

Sweet 'n sour flan

(Illustrated on pages 110–111)

75 g / 3 oz (U.S. ⅓ cup) margarine
100 g / 4 oz digestive biscuits, crushed (U.S. 1⅓ cups graham
cracker crumbs)
50 g / 2 oz chocolate dots (U.S. ⅓ cup chocolate chips)
3 tablespoons (U.S. 4 tablespoons) water
15 g / ½ oz powdered gelatine (U.S. 1 envelope gelatin)
200 ml / 7 fl oz double cream (U.S. scant 1 cup heavy cream),
whipped
150 ml / ¼ pint blackcurrant or bilberry yogurt (U.S. ⅔ cup
blackcurrant or blueberry yogurt)
extra chocolate dots (U.S. chocolate chips)

Lightly grease a 17.5-cm / 7-inch loose-based cake tin.

Melt the margarine in a pan and stir in the biscuit crumbs. Leave to cool slightly then mix in the chocolate dots. Press this mixture to the base of the prepared tin, raising the sides to a height of about 5 cm / 2 inches. Chill for 10 minutes.

Put the water in a small bowl and sprinkle on the gelatine. Leave to stand for 5 minutes then place the bowl over a pan of hot water until the gelatine has completely dissolved. Cool. Reserve half the cream for the decoration. Add the yogurt to the remainder and mix well. Stir in the dissolved gelatine. Pour into the prepared crumb case and chill until set.

Remove the cake tin but transfer the flan, still on the metal base, to a serving dish. Put the reserved cream in a piping bag fitted with a large star tube. Pipe rosettes around the top of the flan and decorate these with chocolate dots.

Apple chocolate pudding

(Illustrated opposite)

2 tablespoons (U.S. 3 tablespoons) white rum
50 g/2 oz sultanas (U.S. ⅓ cup seedless white raisins)
100 g/4 oz (U.S. ½ cup) margarine, softened
100 g/4 oz caster sugar (U.S. ½ cup granulated sugar)
2 eggs, beaten
100 g/4 oz self-raising flour (U.S. 1 cup all-purpose flour sifted with
1 teaspoon baking powder)
25 g/1 oz cocoa powder (U.S. ¼ cup unsweetened cocoa)
3 tablespoons (U.S. 4 tablespoons) rhubarb and ginger jam
1 medium-sized cooking apple, peeled, cored and thinly sliced
SAUCE
3 tablespoons (U.S. 4 tablespoons) rhubarb and ginger jam
3 tablespoons (U.S. 4 tablespoons) water

Pour the rum over the sultanas and leave to soak for 1 hour. Cream the margarine and sugar in a bowl until light and fluffy. Gradually beat in the egg. Sift the flour and cocoa together and fold into the creamed mixture. Add the sultanas and mix well.

Place the jam in the base of a greased 1.4-litre/2½-pint (U.S. 3-pint) pudding bowl. Cover with 2 large spoonfuls of the pudding mixture and a layer of apple slices. Repeat the layers until all the ingredients are used, ending with a layer of pudding mixture.

Cover the bowl with a double layer of greased foil with a pleat in the centre and crimp this well under the rim of the bowl. Stand it in a large pan and pour in boiling water to come halfway up the side of the bowl. Put on the lid and keep the water boiling steadily for 1½ hours, adding more boiling water during cooking if necessary.

To make the sauce, place the jam and water in a small pan and stir over gentle heat until piping hot. Turn the pudding out on a warm dish, top with a little of the sauce and hand the remainder in a sauceboat.

Speyside raspberry tartlets

(Illustrated opposite)

100 g/4 oz plain flour (U.S. 1 cup all-purpose flour)
pinch of salt
50 g/2 oz (U.S. ¼ cup) block margarine
little water
FILLING
50 g/2 oz (U.S. ¼ cup) margarine, softened
50 g/2 oz caster sugar (U.S. ¼ cup granulated sugar)
1 egg, beaten
50 g/2 oz self-raising flour (U.S. ½ cup all-purpose flour sifted
with ½ teaspoon baking powder)
2 teaspoons cocoa powder (U.S. 1 tablespoon unsweetened cocoa),
sifted
1 (425-g/15-oz) can raspberries
75 g/3 oz icing sugar, sifted (U.S. ⅔ cup sifted confectioners' sugar)

First make the pastry. Sift the flour and salt into a bowl. Rub or cut in the margarine until the mixture resembles breadcrumbs. Add enough cold water to make a stiff dough. Roll out thinly on a lightly floured surface and stamp out 12 rounds using a 7-cm/2¾-inch fluted biscuit cutter (U.S. cookie cutter). Use the pastry rounds to line buns tins (U.S. muffin pans). Chill. Meanwhile, heat the oven to 190°C/375°F, Gas Mark 5.

To make the filling, cream the margarine and sugar in a bowl until light and fluffy. Gradually beat in the egg. Sift the flour and cocoa together and fold into the creamed mixture. Drain the raspberries, reserving the syrup. Set aside 12 berries and divide the remainder among the pastry cases. Spoon the chocolate mixture over to cover the fruit.

Bake for about 20 minutes, or until firm to the touch. Turn on to a wire rack to cool. Combine the icing sugar with enough of the reserved fruit syrup to make a thick smooth mixture. Top each tartlet with a little icing and a reserved raspberry. Leave to set before serving.

Raspberry congress tartlets Make the tartlet cases as above and spoon in all the raspberries. Omit the cocoa powder from the filling mixture and substitute 25 g/1 oz (U.S. ¼ cup) ground almonds and ¼ teaspoon almond essence (U.S. almond extract). Bake as instructed. Ice the top of each tartlet and sprinkle with grated chocolate before the icing sets.
Scottish strawberry tart Use the pastry to line a 17.5-cm/7-inch flan tin or shallow cake tin. Substitute a can of strawberries for the raspberries, drain and arrange all the fruit in the pastry case. Make up the chocolate filling and fold in 50 g/2 oz (U.S. ½ cup) chopped walnuts. Spread over the strawberries and bake for about 30 minutes, or until the pastry and filling are golden and firm. Serve hot with scoops of chocolate ice cream, or allow to cool and trickle the icing over the top in a random pattern.

Above: Apple chocolate pudding. Below: Speyside raspberry tartlets

Iced mocha mousse

(Illustrated below)

1 (35-g/1¼-oz) sachet cream topping mix
150 ml/¼ pint (U.S. ⅔ cup) cold milk
1 tablespoon instant coffee powder
2 tablespoons (U.S. 3 tablespoons) hot water
50 g/2 oz plain chocolate (U.S. ⅓ cup semi-sweet chocolate pieces)
3 eggs, separated
75 g/3 oz caster sugar (U.S. ⅓ cup granulated sugar)
chocolate flavour quick-setting ice cream topping, or melted
chocolate

Make up the topping mix with the milk as directed on the pack. Dissolve the coffee in the water in a bowl, put in the chocolate and stand the bowl over hot water until the chocolate melts. Stir to blend. Remove from the heat.

Whisk the egg yolks and sugar in a separate bowl until thick and creamy. Whisk in the chocolate mixture, then fold in two-thirds of the cream topping. Whisk the egg whites in a clean bowl until stiff and fold into the mousse. Divide among 6 individual serving dishes, cover and freeze until firm.

Just before serving, remove the dishes from the freezer, take off the wrappings and cover the surface with the chocolate-flavoured topping. When set, put the remaining cream topping in a piping bag fitted with a large star tube and pipe a rosette on top of each mousse.

Mocha granita

100 g/4 oz plain chocolate (U.S. ⅔ cup semi-sweet chocolate pieces)
3 tablespoons (U.S. 4 tablespoons) freeze-dried instant coffee
granules
50 g/2 oz caster sugar (U.S. ¼ cup granulated sugar)
600 ml/1 pint (U.S. 2½ cups) boiling water
150 ml/¼ pint (U.S. ⅔ cup) whipping cream
1 tablespoon icing sugar (U.S. confectioners' sugar)

Put the chocolate in a bowl. Dissolve the coffee and sugar in the water and pour over the chocolate. Leave to stand for 5 minutes, by which time the chocolate should be soft. Stir until the mixture is smooth. If the chocolate is still firm, stand the bowl over hot water for a short time. Leave to cool.

Pour into a shallow container and freeze until the edges are firm. Transfer to a bowl and beat until smooth. Return to the container and refreeze.

Whip the cream until thick then whisk in the icing sugar. Serve small portions of granita scooped into stemmed glasses and topped with the sweetened cream. For special occasions, spoon 1 tablespoon Tia Maria or Kahlua over the ice before adding the cream.

Chocolate swirl ice cream

SERVES 6

(Illustrated below)

100 g/4 oz (U.S. ½ cup) sugar
300 ml/½ pint (U.S. 1¼ cups) water
finely grated rind and juice of 2 large or 3 small lemons
1 (35-g/1¼-oz) sachet cream topping mix
100 ml/4 fl oz (U.S. ½ cup) cold milk
DECORATION
orange chocolate flavour quick-setting ice cream topping, or
melted chocolate
lemon slices

Put the sugar and water in a pan. Heat gently, stirring, until the sugar has dissolved, then boil steadily for 10 minutes. Add lemon rind and cook for a further 2 minutes. Stir in the lemon juice, remove from the heat, cool and chill.

Make up the cream topping mix with the milk and gradually whisk in the lemon syrup. Measure 3 tablespoons (U.S. 4 tablespoons) of the chocolate topping and very lightly swirl this through the lemon mixture. Transfer to a loaf-shaped tin, cover and freeze.

Remove the ice cream from the freezer 10 minutes before serving time. Turn out on a dish and if liked top with more chocolate topping. Decorate with lemon slices.

Chocolate ice cream

MAKES ABOUT 750 ML/1¼ PINTS (U.S. 3 CUPS)

100 g/4 oz plain chocolate (U.S. ⅔ cup semi-sweet chocolate pieces)
1 (198-g/7-oz) can condensed milk (U.S. 7-oz can sweetened condensed milk)
3 tablespoons (U.S. 4 tablespoons) water
½ teaspoon vanilla essence (U.S. vanilla extract)
300 ml/½ pint double cream (U.S. 1¼ cups heavy cream)
2 egg whites
25 g/1 oz icing sugar, sifted (U.S. ¼ cup sifted confectioners' sugar)

Put the chocolate and condensed milk in a bowl and stand this over a pan of simmering water until the chocolate has melted. Stir the mixture, which will be thick. Remove the bowl from the heat and blend in the water and vanilla essence. Chill.

Whip the cream until thick and fold into the chocolate mixture. Transfer to a shallow container, slightly larger than needed to contain the mixture. Cover and freeze until firm round the edges.

Turn the mixture out into a cold bowl and beat until smooth. Whisk the egg whites in a clean bowl until stiff. Gradually whisk in the sugar, a tablespoon at a time, until the meringue is firm and glossy. Fold into the ice cream until evenly blended. Return to the container, cover and freeze again.

Serving individual portions – tilt glass, spoon in crumbs, pour in apple mixture, returning glass to upright

Build up layers in each glass

Chocolate and apple layer

SERVES 6

450 g / 1 lb cooking apples, peeled, cored and sliced
1 tablespoon water
caster sugar (U.S. granulated sugar)
75 g / 3 oz (U.S. ⅓ cup) butter
225 g / 8 oz (U.S. 4 cups) fresh white breadcrumbs
100 g / 4 oz plain chocolate (U.S. 4 squares semi-sweet chocolate), coarsely grated
icing sugar (U.S. confectioners' sugar) for sprinkling

Put the apple and water in a pan and cook gently, stirring frequently, until soft. Beat to a smooth purée and sweeten to taste. Leave to cool.

Melt the butter in a large pan, add the breadcrumbs and fry over moderately high heat, stirring, until golden brown. Remove from the heat and stir in 2 tablespoons (U.S. 3 tablespoons) sugar. Cool. When cold, stir in the chocolate.

Spread half the apple purée in a straight-sided glass dish and cover with half the chocolate crumbs. Repeat the layers once. Sift the top with icing sugar and serve with whipped cream or ice cream.

Lemon cream crunch pie

SERVES 6–8

(Illustrated on pages 2–3)

75 g / 3 oz plain chocolate (U.S. ½ cup semi-sweet chocolate pieces)
25 g / 1 oz (U.S. 2 tablespoons) butter or margarine
2 tablespoons golden syrup (U.S. 3 tablespoons light corn syrup)
75 g / 3 oz (U.S. 3¾ cups) crisp rice cereal
FILLING
150 ml / ¼ pint double cream (U.S. ⅔ cup heavy cream)
1 (198-g / 7-oz) can condensed milk (U.S. 7-oz can sweetened condensed milk)
finely grated rind and juice of 2 large or 3 small lemons
DECORATION
150 ml / ¼ pint double cream (U.S. ⅔ cup heavy cream), whipped
15 small pieces glacé pineapple (U.S. candied pineapple)

Break up the chocolate and place in a large heavy-based pan with the butter and syrup. Heat gently, stirring frequently, until the chocolate melts. Stir in the cereal and mix well. Transfer to a greased 20-cm / 8-inch pie plate and press the base down with the back of a spoon, building up the sides evenly all round. Chill until firm.

To make the filling, place the cream, milk and lemon rind in a bowl and stir to mix. Gradually whisk in the lemon juice. When the mixture begins to thicken, pour it into the prepared case and leave until completely set.

At serving time, move the pie carefully to a serving dish. Place the cream in a piping bag fitted with a large star tube and pipe shells all round the edge of the pie. Decorate with the pineapple pieces.

Chocolate pancakes with raisin sauce

25 g/1 oz plain chocolate (U.S. scant ¼ cup semi-sweet chocolate pieces)
175 ml/6 fl oz (U.S. ¾ cup) milk
75 g/3 oz plain flour (U.S. ¾ cup all-purpose flour)
25 g/1 oz cocoa powder (U.S. ¼ cup unsweetened cocoa)
1½ teaspoons (U.S. 2 teaspoons) baking powder
¼ teaspoon salt
2 eggs, beaten
1 tablespoon oil
little oil for cooking
SAUCE
100 g/4 oz (U.S. ⅔ cup) seedless raisins
50 g/2 oz (U.S. ¼ cup) granulated sugar
300 ml/½ pint (U.S. 1¼ cups) orange juice
2 teaspoons cornflour (U.S. 1 tablespoon cornstarch)
2 tablespoons (U.S. 3 tablespoons) sweet sherry

First, make the sauce. Put the raisins, sugar and orange juice in a pan and stir over gentle heat until the sugar has dissolved. Then boil gently for 10 minutes, until the fruit is soft and plump. Moisten the cornflour with the sherry, add to the pan and stir until boiling. Simmer for 5 minutes and keep hot while cooking the pancakes.

Put the chocolate in a bowl with a little of the milk. Stand the bowl over a pan of hot water until the chocolate has melted. Stir to blend then mix in the rest of the milk. Sift the flour with the cocoa, baking powder and salt into a bowl. Add the egg, oil and chocolate milk and whisk until just smooth.

Heat a griddle or heavy frying pan (U.S. skillet) and brush very lightly with oil. Make 12 pancakes, using about 2 tablespoons (U.S. 3 tablespoons) batter for each one. Cook gently until bubbles start to break on the surface then turn and cook until the second side is golden. Keep warm in a covered dish. When all the pancakes are ready, serve on warm plates with the hot raisin sauce.

Monday macaroni pudding

about 600 ml/1 pint (U.S. 2½ cups) milk
100 g/4 oz (U.S. 1⅓ cups) short cut macaroni
25 g/1 oz cocoa powder (U.S. ¼ cup unsweetened cocoa)
2 eggs, separated
25 g/1 oz soft brown sugar (U.S. 2 tablespoons light brown sugar)
½ teaspoon vanilla essence (U.S. vanilla extract)
100 g/4 oz caster sugar (U.S. ½ cup granulated sugar)
25 g/1 oz plain chocolate (U.S. 1 square semi-sweet chocolate), grated

Put the measured milk into a heavy-based pan and stir in the pasta. Bring to the boil, stirring constantly. Reduce the heat and simmer for 20 minutes, stirring now and then. Just before the pasta is cooked, heat the oven to 190°C/375°F, Gas Mark 5 and grease an ovenproof dish.

Blend the cocoa with just enough extra milk to make a smooth paste. Add to the pan and stir briskly until boiling. Remove from the heat, beat in the egg yolks, brown sugar and vanilla and transfer to the prepared dish.

Put the egg whites in a clean bowl and whisk until stiff. Gradually add the white sugar, a tablespoon at a time, whisking well after each addition until the meringue is firm and glossy. Fold in the chocolate. Put the meringue into a piping bag fitted with a large star tube and pipe rosettes all over the surface of the chocolate mixture. Alternatively, spread the meringue over the pudding and lift into peaks with a knife blade.

Bake for 15 minutes, until the meringue is just turning golden. Serve hot.

Pineapple fudge tart

100 g/4 oz digestive biscuits, crushed (U.S. 1⅓ cups graham cracker crumbs)
25 g/1 oz desiccated coconut (U.S. ⅓ cup shredded coconut)
75 g/3 oz (U.S. ⅓ cup) butter or margarine, melted
FILLING
150 g/5 oz plain flour (U.S. 1¼ cups all-purpose flour)
1½ teaspoons (U.S. 2 teaspoons) baking powder
25 g/1 oz cocoa powder (U.S. ¼ cup unsweetened cocoa)
1 (225-g/8-oz) can pineapple pieces
about 50 ml/2 fl oz (U.S. ¼ cup) milk
about 100 g/4 oz (U.S. ½ cup) butter or margarine
75 g/3 oz soft brown sugar (U.S. ⅓ cup light brown sugar)

Heat the oven to 190°C/375°F, Gas Mark 5 and grease a 20-cm/8-inch flan tin or shallow cake tin.

Put the biscuit crumbs and coconut in a bowl and stir in the butter. Press into the prepared tin and bake for 5 minutes.

To make the filling, sift the flour with the baking powder and cocoa. Drain the pineapple syrup into a jug and make up to 150 ml/¼ pint (U.S. ⅔ cup) with milk. Cream the butter and sugar in a bowl until light and fluffy. Gradually stir in the dry ingredients and milk liquid and mix well. Arrange the pineapple pieces in the crumb base and spoon over the fudge topping.

Bake for about 30 minutes, or until just firm to the touch. Serve cold with whipped cream or ice cream. The tart is delicious eaten hot, but the case tends to be rather crumbly.

Mandarin fudgy squares Substitute 25 g/1 oz (U.S. ¼ cup) very finely chopped roasted peanuts in place of the coconut and press the crumb mixture into a 17.5-cm/7-inch square shallow tin. Use a 311-g/11-oz can of mandarin orange segments instead of the can of pineapple. Cut the tart into 9 squares.

Peachy custard pie

SERVES 6

PASTRY
175 g / 6 oz plain flour (U.S. 1½ cups all-purpose flour)
pinch of salt
75 g / 3 oz block margarine or a mixture of lard and margarine
1–2 tablespoons (U.S. 2–3 tablespoons) water
FILLING
2 tablespoons cornflour (U.S. 3 tablespoons cornstarch)
about 350 ml / 12 fl oz (U.S. 1½ cups) milk
1 (225-g / 8-oz) can peach slices
50 g / 2 oz plain chocolate (U.S. 2 squares semi-sweet chocolate),
coarsely grated
pinch of salt
100 g / 4 oz caster sugar (U.S. ½ cup granulated sugar)
40 g / 1½ oz (U.S. ⅔ cup) tenderized shredded coconut

Heat the oven to 200°C / 400°F, Gas Mark 6 and have ready a 20-cm / 8-inch flan tin or shallow cake tin.

Sift the flour and salt into a bowl and rub or cut in the fat until the mixture resembles breadcrumbs. Add enough water to make a firm dough. Roll out on a lightly floured surface and use to line the tin. Put in a sheet of greaseproof paper (U.S. waxed paper) and fill with baking beans.

Bake for 15 minutes then remove the paper and beans and return to the oven for a further 5–10 minutes, or until the pastry is just turning golden. Leave to cool.

Meanwhile, mix the cornflour with a little of the milk to make a thin paste. Drain the syrup from the peaches into a jug and make up to 350 ml / 12 fl oz (U.S. 1½ cups) with milk. Pour into a pan and add just over half the chocolate, the salt and sugar. Heat gently, stirring all the time, until the chocolate has melted. Bring to the boil, add the cornflour mixture and stir constantly until thickened. Simmer for 3 minutes then stir in about three-quarters of the coconut. Cool slightly, stirring now and then.

Arrange the peach slices in the pastry case, pour the custard mixture over, then sprinkle with the remaining coconut. When cold, chill briefly. Scatter the rest of the chocolate over the pie before serving.

Apricot and chocolate rice

SERVES 4

1 (225-g / 8-oz) can apricot halves
1 (368-ml / 13-fl oz) can evaporated milk (U.S. 1⅔ cups
unsweetened evaporated milk)
50 g / 2 oz (U.S. scant ⅓ cup) short grain rice
25 g / 1 oz caster sugar (U.S. 2 tablespoons granulated sugar)
150 ml / ¼ pint single cream (U.S. ⅔ cup light cream)
50 g / 2 oz plain chocolate (U.S. 2 squares semi-sweet chocolate),
grated

Drain the syrup from the apricots into a measuring jug. Add the evaporated milk and make up to 900 ml / 1½ pints (U.S. 3¾ cups) with water. Pour into a heavy-based pan. Rinse the rice in a sieve, drain and add to the pan. Bring slowly to boiling point, stirring frequently, then reduce the heat and simmer for about 1¾ hours, stirring occasionally, or until the rice is soft and the mixture creamy. Blend in the sugar and cool, stirring now and then.

Slice the apricots and reserve 12 slices for the decoration. Fold the remainder into the rice mixture with the cream and about three-quarters of the chocolate. Spoon into 4 serving dishes and top each portion with apricot slices sprinkled with chocolate.

VARIATIONS

Mandarin and chocolate rice mould Omit the apricots and use a 311-g / 11-oz can mandarin orange segments. When the rice is almost cooked, put 2 tablespoons (U.S. 3 tablespoons) water in a small bowl and sprinkle on 15 g / ½ oz gelatine (U.S. 1 envelope gelatin). Leave to stand for 5 minutes then add to the hot cooked rice and stir for 2 minutes, until completely dissolved. Leave until cool but not set, then fold in the mandarins and chocolate. Use 150 ml / ¼ pint double cream (U.S. ⅔ cup heavy cream) instead of the thin cream and whip until thick before folding into the rice mixture. Turn into a rinsed 900-ml / 1½-pint (U.S. 3¾-cup) mould and leave to set. Turn out to serve.

Chocolate rice with peaches Use a can of peach slices instead of the apricots. As soon as the rice is cooked, stir in the chocolate until melted. Add the sugar and when cool, mix in the cream. Spoon the chocolate rice into 4 glass serving dishes and top with peach slices, arranging them radiating out from the centre of each dessert like the petals of a flower.

Semolina chocolate mould

SERVES 4–6

600 ml / 1 pint (U.S. 2½ cups) milk
50 g / 2 oz (U.S. ⅓ cup) semolina
2 eggs, separated
1 teaspoon vanilla essence (U.S. vanilla extract)
50 g / 2 oz plain chocolate, roughly chopped (U.S. ⅓ cup semi-sweet
chocolate pieces)
40 g / 1½ oz caster sugar (U.S. 3 tablespoons granulated sugar)

Have ready a 1-litre / 1¾-pint (U.S. 2¼-pint) mould.

Place the milk in a heavy-based pan and heat slowly to boiling point. Sprinkle in the semolina, stirring briskly. Boil gently, stirring all the time, for 8 minutes or until the semolina grains are soft and transparent. Remove from the heat and immediately beat in the egg yolks. Add the vanilla and chocolate and stir until the mixture is smooth.

Whisk the egg whites in a clean bowl until stiff, then gradually add the sugar, a tablespoon at a time, whisking well after each addition until the meringue is firm and glossy. Fold into the chocolate semolina.

Rinse the chosen mould with cold water and pour in the chocolate mixture. Leave to set. Loosen the mould and turn out on a flat dish for serving.

Lime mousse

(Illustrated below)

1 (135-g/4¾-oz) lime flavour jelly tablet (U.S. 4-oz package lime-
flavor gelatin)
175 g/6 oz (U.S. ¾ cup) cream cheese
4 tablespoons (U.S. 6 tablespoons) lime juice cordial
2 egg whites
50 g/2 oz caster sugar (U.S. ¼ cup granulated sugar)
2 large milk chocolate flakes, split into short narrow lengths

Dissolve the jelly in a little boiling water then make up to
600 ml/1 pint (U.S. 2½ cups) with cold water.

Place the cream cheese in a bowl and beat until soft. Gradually
whisk in the lime juice cordial and then the jelly, keeping the
mixture quite smooth. Leave to stand until beginning to set.

Whisk the egg whites in a clean bowl until stiff, then add the
sugar and whisk until the meringue is firm and glossy. Fold this
into the lime mixture. Transfer to a serving dish and leave to
set.

Decorate the edge of the mousse with pieces of chocolate
flake.

Chilly banana pie

175 g/6 oz plain chocolate (U.S. 1 cup semi-sweet chocolate
pieces)
2 tablespoons golden syrup (U.S. 3 tablespoons light corn syrup)
25 g/1 oz (U.S. 2 tablespoons) butter or margarine
100 g/4 oz (U.S. 4 cups) cornflakes
3 bananas, peeled and sliced
600 ml/1 pint (U.S. 2½ cups) chocolate or vanilla ice cream
2 tablespoons (U.S. 3 tablespoons) chopped walnuts or pecans

Have ready a 20-cm/8-inch deep flan tin or shallow cake tin.

Put the chocolate, syrup and butter in a bowl and stand this
over a pan of hot water until the chocolate has melted. Stir to
blend then mix in the flakes. Press to the base and sides of the
tin, smoothing well with the back of a spoon. Chill for 10
minutes.

Arrange the banana slices evenly in the chocolate case and
cover with scoops of ice cream. Allow to soften slightly then
press to flatten the ice cream. Scatter nuts over the top. Cover
and freeze until required. Allow to soften at room temperature
for 10 minutes before serving.

Chocolate velvet

(Illustrated opposite)

2 tablespoons custard powder (U.S. 3 tablespoons Bird's English dessert mix)
25 g / 1 oz (U.S. 2 tablespoons) sugar
900 ml / 1½ pints (U.S. 3¾ cups) cold milk
75 g / 3 oz plain chocolate, roughly chopped (U.S. ½ cup semi-sweet chocolate pieces)
4 tablespoons (U.S. 6 tablespoons) brandy
15 g / ½ oz powdered gelatine (U.S. 1 envelope gelatin)
2 (35-g / 1¼-oz) sachets cream topping mix

Put the custard powder and sugar in a bowl. Take 600 ml / 1 pint (U.S. 2½ cups) of the milk, add a little to the custard powder and mix to a thin cream. Heat the remainder in a pan. When nearly boiling, pour into the bowl and stir briskly. Return the custard to the pan, add the chocolate and stir constantly until the mixture boils and the chocolate has melted. Cover the surface with cling film and leave until cold.

Reserve 1 tablespoon of the brandy and place the rest in a small bowl. Sprinkle on the gelatine and leave for 5 minutes. Stand the bowl over a pan of hot water until the gelatine has completely dissolved. Cool. Make up the topping mixes with the remaining milk. Stir the dissolved gelatine into the cold custard, then fold in half the topping. Rinse a 900-ml / 1½-pint (U.S. 2-pint) mould with water and pour in the chocolate mixture. Leave to set.

Invert the mould on to a serving dish. Stir the reserved brandy into the remaining topping and place in a piping bag fitted with a large star tube. Pipe large shells around the base of the mould before serving.

=== VARIATION ===

Italian meringue dessert Use only 1 sachet of cream topping mix and reduce the brandy by 1 tablespoon. Make up the recipe as above until the cream topping has been folded in. Roughly crush about 4 meringue shells or almond macaroons and fold into the chocolate mixture. Rinse a 1-litre / 1¾-pint (U.S. 2¼-pint) plain ring mould and transfer the mixture to it. Level the surface and leave to set. Turn the ring out on a serving dish and fill the centre with very well drained canned dark cherries.

Orange filled sponge flan

SERVES 6–8

(Illustrated below)

40 g / 1½ oz plain flour (U.S. ⅓ cup all-purpose flour)
15 g / ½ oz cocoa powder (U.S. 2 tablespoons unsweetened cocoa)
pinch of salt
2 eggs
75 g / 3 oz caster sugar (U.S. ⅓ cup granulated sugar)
FILLING AND DECORATION
1 (311-g / 11-oz) can mandarin segments in syrup
2 teaspoons powdered gelatine (U.S. ⅔ envelope gelatin)
75 g / 3 oz (U.S. ⅓ cup) cream cheese
2 tablespoons icing sugar (U.S. 3 tablespoons confectioners'
sugar), sifted
150 ml / ¼ pint double cream (U.S. ⅔ cup heavy cream), whipped

Heat the oven to 190°C/375°F, Gas Mark 5, grease a 17.5-cm/7-inch sponge flan tin, line the base with a circle of greaseproof paper (U.S. waxed paper) and then grease the paper. Finally, dust the tin with a light coating of flour and tip out as much as possible.

Sift the flour with the cocoa and salt twice. Set aside. Put the eggs and sugar in a large bowl and stand this over a pan of simmering water. Make sure the base of the bowl is above the surface of the water. Whisk the mixture steadily by hand or with an electric mixer until it is thick and mousse-like. When ready, the mixture should fall back into the bowl in the form of a thick ribbon when the beaters are lifted. Remove the bowl from the heat and continue whisking until the mixture is cold. Fold in the dry ingredients lightly but thoroughly. Transfer to the prepared tin and tilt this until the mixture is level.

Bake for about 20 minutes, or until firm to the touch. Turn out on a wire rack to cool. Peel off the lining paper.

To make the filling, drain the mandarins and reserve the syrup. Place 2 tablespoons (U.S. 3 tablespoons) of the syrup in a bowl, sprinkle on the gelatine and leave to stand for 5 minutes. Stand the bowl over a pan of hot water until the gelatine has completely dissolved. Cool. Reserve 12 mandarin segments and liquidize the remainder with the rest of the syrup. Put the cheese in a bowl and beat until smooth. Gradually beat in the sugar, dissolved gelatine and the mandarin purée. Fold in about one third of the cream.

Place the flan case on a serving dish and pour in the filling. Smooth the top and chill until set. Put the remaining cream in a piping bag fitted with a small star tube. Decorate the edge of the sponge flan with alternating mandarin segments and pairs of cream rosettes.

Baked Alaska

(Illustrated below)

*1 chocolate bar cake (about 20 cm/8 inches by 7.5 cm/3 inches
and 5 cm/2 inches deep)*
1 (311-g/11-oz) can mandarin segments
*500 ml/18 fl oz (U.S. 1-pint pack) vanilla ice cream (not the soft-
scoop variety)*
TOPPING
3 egg whites
150 g/5 oz caster sugar (U.S. ⅔ cup granulated sugar)

Split the cake into 2 layers and place these side by side on an
ovenproof plate. Drain the mandarins, reserving the syrup.
Spoon 3 tablespoons (U.S. 4 tablespoons) of the syrup over the
cake. Shape the ice cream into a round and place on the cake.
Freeze until the ice cream is firm again. Meanwhile, heat the
oven to 230°C/450°F, Gas Mark 8.

Put the egg whites in a clean bowl and whisk until stiff.
Gradually add the sugar, a tablespoon at a time, whisking
vigorously after each addition until the meringue is firm and
glossy. Arrange the mandarins on the ice cream, then spread
the meringue over to completely cover the fruit, ice cream and
cake, sealing it to the plate all round. Swirl the surface with a
knife.

Bake for about 5 minutes, or until the meringue is golden
brown. Serve immediately.

Raisin chocolate wonder

100 g/4 oz (U.S. ⅔ cup) seedless raisins
200 ml/7 fl oz (U.S. scant 1 cup) water
50 g/2 oz (U.S. ¼ cup) butter or margarine
50 g/2 oz soft brown sugar (U.S. ¼ cup light brown sugar)
100 g/4 oz caster sugar (U.S. ½ cup granulated sugar)
50 g/2 oz plain flour (U.S. ½ cup all-purpose flour)
25 g/1 oz cocoa powder (U.S. ¼ cup unsweetened cocoa)
1 teaspoon baking powder
pinch of salt
75 ml/3 fl oz (U.S. ⅓ cup) milk
1 teaspoon vanilla essence (U.S. vanilla extract)

Heat the oven to 190°C/375°F, Gas Mark 5 and grease a deep
ovenproof dish.

Put the raisins in a pan with the water, half the butter, the
brown sugar and half the white sugar. Heat gently, stirring,
until the sugar has dissolved, then bring to the boil and cook
steadily, uncovered, for 10 minutes.

Meanwhile, sift the flour with the cocoa, baking powder and
salt. Cream the rest of the butter and sugar in a bowl until light
and fluffy. Fold in the flour mixture and milk. Transfer to the
prepared dish and level the surface. Remove the syrup from the
heat, stir in the vanilla essence and spoon evenly over the
pudding mixture in the dish.

Bake for about 30 minutes, or until the pudding has risen
through the syrup and is firm to the touch.

Rita's baked custard

SERVES 4

25 g / 1 oz plain chocolate (U.S. scant ¼ cup semi-sweet chocolate pieces)
225 ml / 8 fl oz (U.S. 1 cup) strong hot black coffee
225 ml / 8 fl oz (U.S. 1 cup) milk
50 g / 2 oz caster sugar (U.S. ¼ cup granulated sugar)
pinch of salt
3 large eggs
little ground cinnamon

Heat the oven to 150°C/300°F, Gas Mark 2 and have ready 1 medium-sized or 4 individual ovenproof dishes standing in a roasting tin.

Put the chocolate in a bowl. Immediately pour over the hot coffee and leave to stand for 5 minutes, or until the chocolate has melted. If it is not completely soft, heat the milk, pour it into the bowl and stir occasionally until the mixture is smooth. If the chocolate melts in the coffee, just add cold milk and stir well.

Transfer to a blender or food processor, add the sugar, salt and eggs and switch on high until the mixture is frothy. Transfer to the prepared dish or dishes. Pour hot water into the roasting tin to come half way up the side of the dishes and sprinkle each custard lightly with cinnamon.

Bake, allowing about 45 minutes for individual custards or 1 hour for the large one, until set. Cool, then chill before serving.

VARIATION

Dressed-up custards Top chilled custards with piped rosettes of whipped cream and sprinkle with roughly crushed peanut brittle.

NOTE To crush the sticky brittle, place in a plastic bag and beat with a rolling pin, but do not pulverize.

Chocolate queen of puddings

SERVES 4–5

500 ml / 18 fl oz (U.S. 2¼ cups) milk
50 g / 2 oz drinking chocolate powder (U.S. ½ cup sweetened cocoa)
40 g / 1½ oz (U.S. 3 tablespoons) butter
3 eggs, separated
75 g / 3 oz (U.S. 1½ cups) fresh white breadcrumbs
150 g / 5 oz caster sugar (U.S. ⅔ cup granulated sugar)
2 tablespoons (U.S. 3 tablespoons) chocolate spread or raspberry jam

Put the milk, chocolate powder and butter into a pan and heat gently, stirring, until the butter has melted. Remove from the heat and whisk in the egg yolks. Stir in the breadcrumbs then transfer to a greased ovenproof pie dish and leave to stand for 20 minutes. Meanwhile, heat the oven to 180°C/350°F, Gas Mark 4.

Bake the pudding for 30 minutes. At the same time, whisk the egg whites in a clean bowl until stiff then gradually add the sugar, a tablespoon at a time, whisking well after each addition until the meringue is firm and glossy.

Thinly cover the pudding with chocolate spread or jam and pile the meringue evenly on top. Return to the oven for a further 15 minutes, or until the meringue is turning golden.

Tipsy chocolate trifle

SERVES 4–6

(Illustrated opposite)

1 chocolate flavour Swiss roll (U.S. 1 chocolate flavor jelly roll)
3 tablespoons (U.S. 4 tablespoons) rum
750 ml / 1¼ pints (U.S. generous 3 cups) milk
1 (600-ml / 1-pint) packet chocolate blancmange powder (U.S. 1¼-pint pack chocolate flavor cornstarch pudding mix)
2 tablespoons (U.S. 3 tablespoons) sugar
1 teaspoon instant coffee powder
1 (35-g / 1¼-oz) sachet cream topping mix
1 small milk chocolate flake, crumbled

Cut the Swiss roll into 6 slices and arrange these in a glass serving dish. Sprinkle over the rum.

Set aside 150 ml / ¼ pint (U.S. ⅔ cup) of the milk for the decoration. Put the blancmange powder and the sugar in a bowl and mix in enough of the remaining milk to make a smooth cream. Put the rest of the milk in a pan and bring almost to boiling point. Pour on to the blended mixture and stir briskly. Return to the pan and stir constantly until boiling. Simmer for 1 minute and pour over the soaked cake in the dish. Leave until cold.

Add the coffee to the reserved milk and use to make up the topping mix. Swirl about one third of the mix over the top of the trifle and put the rest in a piping bag fitted with a large star tube. Pipe large shells all round the edge of the dish and sprinkle the flake in the centre.

VARIATIONS

Banana and chocolate trifle Slice 2 ripe but firm bananas and mix with 4 tablespoons (U.S. 6 tablespoons) strawberry jam. Spread over the cake in the dish, omitting the rum. Make up the chocolate blancmange as above, pour into the dish and leave to set. Omit the coffee from the cream topping and substitute 3 tablespoons (U.S. 4 tablespoons) strawberry jam, sieved. Mix it into the topping before spreading over the trifle. Mark the surface into swirls with the tip of a knife and sprinkle with chocolate flake.

Kiwi trifle Use a raspberry or strawberry jam Swiss roll (U.S. jelly roll) instead of a chocolate roll. Moisten with Cointreau or Grand Marnier and omit the rum. To decorate, make up the cream topping without adding the coffee and spread half over the trifle. Pipe the remainder in rosettes around the edge of the dish. Peel and slice 1 kiwi fruit. Halve the slices and use to spike the rosettes. Sprinkle coarsely grated chocolate in the centre of the dessert instead of the chocolate flake.

Tipsy chocolate trifle

Special Desserts

Cheesecakes, mousses and creams all come into this category. Richer than everyday recipes, but not necessarily more difficult to make. Perhaps the most tricky are cheesecakes, because the crust must hold together and not disintegrate when the cake is cut. If the ingredients are to be blended and pressed into the base of the pan, be sure you use sufficient pressure with your fingertips or the back of a spoon. Pre-baking firms up the crust and I have included a base which is partly cooked. This could be oven-baked at a moderate temperature for 10 minutes to give a more chewy, easy-to-cut crust. Cool before adding the filling.

Mousses are the most delicate and airy of sweets. For parties, they can include various liqueurs which enhance chocolate flavour; of which Tia Maria or Kahlua, Orange Curaçao or Grand Marnier are particularly successful. Other fruit brandies, such as cherry or apricot, are also good choices, along with Crème-de-menthe. Among the spirits, rum, brandy and whisky blend well with slightly heavier chocolate confections, in which the inclusion of cream is more important than the egg whites. These creams are usually served in small pots or custard cups, as they are so rich. Try switching the recommended liqueurs and spirits, for they all underline and complement chocolate deliciously. Another good partner in these more exotic sweets is a purée of chestnuts. This again is very rich and a little goes a long way. As it usually comes sweetened in cans, don't be tempted to add more sugar.

Soufflés, hot and cold, fall in this special dessert category. Hot ones, like my Chocolate soufflé, need careful timing to succeed. You can prepare them up to the stage of folding in the egg whites, but this final step should only be carried out when the oven is preheated and the guests around the table, eating the main course. Then you have a captive audience ready to appreciate a perfect, puffed-up beauty of a soufflé which will be eaten before it can collapse. To have complete success with cold ones, your most important requirement is a smaller soufflé dish than you imagined necessary! A band of greaseproof paper, non-stick baking parchment (U.S. waxed paper), or foil fixed round the edge in a cuff allows you to fill it above the edge of the dish. The mixture should be well set before you ease away the cuff. Decorate the edge that is revealed by pressing finely chopped nuts, chocolate vermicelli (U.S. chocolate sprinkles) or grated chocolate against it before you pipe the top with whipped cream.

Chestnut creams (recipe page 130)

Festive cheesecake

(Illustrated opposite)

75 g/3 oz (U.S. $\frac{1}{3}$ cup) butter
2 tablespoons cocoa powder (U.S. 3 tablespoons unsweetened
cocoa), sifted
25 g/1 oz caster sugar (U.S. 2 tablespoons granulated sugar)
100 g/4 oz digestive biscuits, crushed (U.S. 1$\frac{1}{3}$ cups graham
cracker crumbs)

FILLING
4 tablespoons (U.S. 6 tablespoons) water
15 g/$\frac{1}{2}$ oz powdered gelatine (U.S. 1 envelope unflavored gelatin)
225 g/8 oz (U.S. 1 cup) cream cheese
150 ml/$\frac{1}{4}$ pint (U.S. $\frac{2}{3}$ cup) natural yogurt
2 eggs, separated
finely grated rind of 1 small orange
2 teaspoons (U.S. 1 tablespoon) clear honey
50 g/2 oz caster sugar (U.S. $\frac{1}{4}$ cup granulated sugar)
1 large milk chocolate flake, crushed

DECORATION
75 g/3 oz plain chocolate (U.S. $\frac{1}{2}$ cup semi-sweet chocolate pieces)
small quantity of marzipan (U.S. almond marzipan)
few drops red food colouring
2 large milk chocolate flakes, split into short narrow lengths

Grease a 20-cm/8-inch loose-based cake tin. Melt the butter in a pan, stir in the cocoa and sugar and cook, stirring, for 1 minute. Mix in the biscuit crumbs and press evenly to the base of the prepared tin. Chill.

To make the filling, place the water in a small bowl, sprinkle on the gelatine and leave for 5 minutes. Stand the bowl over a pan of hot water until the gelatine has completely dissolved. Cool. Place the cream cheese in a bowl and beat until soft. Gradually add the yogurt, egg yolks, orange rind, honey and gelatine, beating constantly to keep the mixture quite smooth. Whisk the egg whites in a clean bowl until stiff, add the sugar and whisk again until the meringue is firm and glossy. Fold into the cheese mixture with the flake. Spoon into the tin and chill until set.

Meanwhile, make the decorations. Melt the chocolate in a bowl over a pan of hot water. Transfer to a paper icing bag (see page 11). Draw holly leaves on a sheet of non-stick baking parchment (U.S. waxed paper). Snip off the end of the bag and pipe the outlines of the leaves then flood the centres (see page 11). Leave to set. Colour the marzipan with food colouring, divide into 6 pieces and roll each into a ball to make the red berries.

Carefully remove the tin from the cheesecake but transfer it, still on the metal base, to a serving plate. Place a border of pieces of flake on the cheesecake, then group the chocolate holly leaves and berries attractively inside this. Festive cheesecake is best eaten within 24 hours of making.

Chestnut creams

(Illustrated on page 128)

2 trifle sponges
4 tablespoons (U.S. 6 tablespoons) rum
100 g/4 oz plain chocolate (U.S. $\frac{2}{3}$ cup semi-sweet chocolate pieces)
1 (225-g/8-oz) can sweetened chestnut purée·
300 ml/$\frac{1}{2}$ pint double cream (U.S. 1$\frac{1}{4}$ cups heavy cream), whipped
6 'langues de chat' biscuits (U.S. 6 thin sweet cookies)

Cut the sponges into neat cubes and divide among 6 stemmed wine glasses. Spoon rum over each portion.

Melt the chocolate in a bowl over a pan of hot water, then leave to cool slightly. Place the chestnut purée in a bowl and beat in the chocolate. Fold in the cream until no traces of white remain.

Place the mixture in a piping bag fitted with a large star tube and pipe a large swirl into each glass. Chill for 10 minutes.

Decorate each chestnut cream with a biscuit and serve at once.

Baked marble cheesecake

(Illustrated opposite)

BASE
100 g/4 oz plain flour (U.S. 1 cup all-purpose flour)
pinch of salt
50 g/2 oz caster sugar (U.S. $\frac{1}{4}$ cup granulated sugar)
50 g/2 oz (U.S. $\frac{1}{4}$ cup) margarine

FILLING
100 g/4 oz plain chocolate (U.S. $\frac{2}{3}$ cup semi-sweet chocolate pieces)
350 g/12 oz (U.S. 1$\frac{1}{2}$ cups) cream cheese
175 g/6 oz caster sugar (U.S. $\frac{3}{4}$ cup granulated sugar)
50 g/2 oz plain flour (U.S. $\frac{1}{2}$ cup all-purpose flour), sifted
1 teaspoon vanilla essence (U.S. vanilla extract)
4 eggs
150 ml/$\frac{1}{4}$ pint (U.S. $\frac{2}{3}$ cup) natural yogurt

Heat the oven to 200°C/400°F, Gas Mark 6 and grease a 20-cm/8-inch loose-based cake tin.

Sift the flour twice with the salt. Stir in the sugar and rub or cut in the margarine. Gather the mixture together and press it to the base of the prepared tin. Bake for 10 minutes.

Melt the chocolate in a small bowl over a pan of hot water. Place the cheese and sugar in a large bowl and beat until smooth. Mix in the flour and vanilla essence then beat in the eggs, one at a time, and finally add the yogurt. Pour half the filling over the base. Mix the melted chocolate into the remainder and drop it in spoonfuls over the vanilla filling. Lightly swirl the 2 colours together to give a marbled effect.

Lower the oven temperature to 160°C/325°F, Gas Mark 3 and bake the cheesecake for 1 hour. Turn off the heat but leave the cake in the oven for a further 1 hour. Leave until cold before removing from the tin.

Above: Baked marble cheesecake. Centre: Chocolate and orange cheesecake (recipe page 134). Below: Festive cheesecake.

Tropical lime cups

(Illustrated opposite)

100 g / 4 oz plain chocolate (U.S. ⅔ cup semi-sweet chocolate pieces)
100 ml / 4 fl oz double cream (U.S. ½ cup heavy cream)
150 ml / ¼ pint (U.S. ⅔ cup) lime or lemon curd
2 tablespoons (U.S. 3 tablespoons) natural yogurt

Melt the chocolate and use it to coat the inside of 6 paper cake cases (see page 11). Use all the chocolate, coating the cases a second time if possible. Chill until set then carefully peel away the paper cases. Stand the chocolate cups on a serving plate.

Whip the cream until thick then stir in three-quarters of the curd and the yogurt. Spoon this into the chocolate cups and place in the freezer for 30 minutes, until half frozen but not solid. Spoon a little of the remaining curd on top of the filling in each cup and swirl it with a wooden cocktail stick (U.S. toothpick) to give an attractive finish. Serve still chilled.

Chocolate crunchy cake

SERVES 8

(Illustrated on page 9)

175 g / 6 oz glacé cherries (U.S. ⅔ cup candied cherries)
175 g / 6 oz plain chocolate, broken up (U.S. 1 cup semi-sweet chocolate pieces)
100 g / 4 oz (U.S. ½ cup) butter
225 ml / 8 fl oz double cream (U.S. 1 cup heavy cream)
100 g / 4 oz digestive biscuits, crushed (U.S. 1⅓ cups graham cracker crumbs)
50 g / 2 oz (U.S. 2 cups) cornflakes
50 g / 2 oz (U.S. ⅓ cup) seedless raisins
50 g / 2 oz hazelnuts, roughly chopped (U.S. ½ cup roughly chopped filberts)

Lightly grease a 20-cm / 8-inch fluted flan ring and place it on a serving plate.

Reserve 11 cherries and chop the remainder. Put the chocolate in a large bowl with the butter and 4 tablespoons (U.S. 6 tablespoons) of the cream. Stand the bowl over hot water until the chocolate and butter have melted. Stir to blend and remove from the heat. Add the biscuit crumbs, cornflakes, raisins, chopped cherries and nuts. Mix well. Turn into the flan ring, press down lightly and level the surface. Chill for 1 hour.

Remove from the flan ring. Whip the rest of the cream and place in a piping bag fitted with a large star tube. Pipe rosettes around the edge of the cake and top each with a cherry.

Tropical lime cups

Chocolate and orange cheesecake

SERVES 8

(Illustrated on page 128)

50 g/2 oz (U.S. $\frac{1}{4}$ cup) butter or margarine
100 g/4 oz digestive biscuits, crushed (U.S. 1$\frac{1}{3}$ cups graham cracker crumbs)
1 tablespoon cornflour (U.S. cornstarch)
1 tablespoon cocoa powder (U.S. unsweetened cocoa), sifted
1 tablespoon caster sugar (U.S. granulated sugar)
300 ml/$\frac{1}{2}$ pint (U.S. 1$\frac{1}{4}$ cups) milk
small piece of butter
2 eggs, separated
1 (135-g/4$\frac{3}{4}$-oz) orange jelly tablet (U.S. 4-oz package orange-flavored gelatin)
4 tablespoons (U.S. 6 tablespoons) water
175 g/6 oz (U.S. $\frac{3}{4}$ cup) cream cheese
150 ml/$\frac{1}{4}$ pint (U.S. $\frac{2}{3}$ cup) natural yogurt
DECORATION
20 milk chocolate buttons
5 glacé cherries (U.S. candied cherries)

Grease a 20-cm/8-inch loose-based cake tin. Melt the butter, mix in the biscuit crumbs and press this to the base of the tin. Chill.

Blend the cornflour, cocoa and sugar with a little of the cold milk in a bowl. Place the remaining milk in a pan and bring to boiling point. Pour it on to the cocoa mixture, whisking well. Return to the pan and bring to the boil, stirring constantly. Remove from the heat and beat in the butter, then the egg yolks. Cover and cool.

Meanwhile, dissolve the jelly in the water. Place the cream cheese in a bowl and beat until soft. Gradually add the chocolate custard, the jelly and yogurt, beating vigorously to keep the mixture smooth. Leave in a cool place until the filling is on the point of setting. Whisk the egg whites in a clean bowl and fold them in evenly. Pour over the cheesecake base and chill until set.

Carefully remove the tin and transfer the cheesecake, still on the metal base, to a serving plate. Decorate the top with a border of chocolate buttons and cherries.

Pineapple and walnut tart

SERVES 4–6

225 g/8 oz plain flour (U.S. 2 cups all-purpose flour)
$\frac{1}{2}$ teaspoon salt
50 g/2 oz (U.S. $\frac{1}{4}$ cup) block margarine
50 g/2 oz (U.S. $\frac{1}{4}$ cup) lard
3 tablespoons (U.S. 4 tablespoons) water
FILLING
1 (225-g/8-oz) can pineapple pieces
3 tablespoons (U.S. 4 tablespoons) apricot jam
25 g/1 oz (U.S. $\frac{1}{4}$ cup) chopped walnuts
75 g/3 oz plain chocolate (U.S. 3 squares semi-sweet chocolate), grated
2 tablespoons cocoa powder (U.S. 3 tablespoons unsweetened cocoa), sifted
50 g/2 oz (U.S. $\frac{1}{4}$ cup) margarine
50 g/2 oz caster sugar (U.S. $\frac{1}{4}$ cup granulated sugar)
1 egg, beaten
50 g/2 oz self-raising flour, sifted (U.S. $\frac{1}{2}$ cup all-purpose flour sifted with $\frac{1}{2}$ teaspoon baking powder)
9 walnut halves

Heat the oven to 190°C/375°F, Gas Mark 5 and have ready a 20-cm/8-inch flan tin or shallow cake tin, or a flan ring standing on a baking sheet (U.S. cookie sheet).

Sift the flour with the salt into a bowl. Rub or cut in the fats until the mixture resembles breadcrumbs. Add the water and mix to a firm dough. Knead briefly until smooth. Roll out on a lightly floured surface and use to line the flan tin. Gather the trimmings together and roll out again. Cut into 4 narrow strips about 25 cm/10 inches long.

Drain the pineapple, reserving the syrup. Roughly chop the fruit and drain again. Spread the jam in the pastry case and sprinkle with the chopped nuts and pineapple, then the chocolate.

Blend the cocoa with enough pineapple syrup to make a smooth paste and set aside. Cream the margarine and sugar in a bowl until light and fluffy. Gradually beat in the egg and blended cocoa. Fold in the flour. When evenly combined, spoon carefully over the filling and level the surface. Twist the pastry strips and arrange on top of the tart in a lattice design. Trim to fit, dampen the ends and press to the edge of the pastry case. Place a walnut half on each exposed section of filling.

Bake for about 40 minutes, or until the pastry is golden and the filling firm to the touch. Serve hot or cold with cream or ice cream.

Dreamy chocolate pye

(Illustrated below)

100 g / 4 oz (U.S. ½ cup) butter
1 teaspoon ground ginger
2 (150-g / 5-oz) packets milk chocolate digestive biscuits, roughly crushed (U.S. 3⅓ cups mixed chocolate wafer and graham cracker crumbs)

FILLING AND DECORATION
150 ml / ¼ pint (U.S. ⅔ cup) milk
75 g / 3 oz plain chocolate (U.S. ½ cup semi-sweet chocolate pieces)
2 teaspoons powdered gelatine (U.S. ⅔ envelope gelatin)
finely grated rind and juice of 1 small orange
2 eggs, separated
2 tablespoons caster sugar (U.S. 3 tablespoons granulated sugar)
150 ml / ¼ pint (U.S. ⅔ cup) whipping cream
8 milk chocolate buttons

Melt the butter and stir in the ginger and biscuit crumbs. Press this mixture to the base and sides of a 22.5-cm/9-inch loose-based flan tin or shallow cake tin. Chill.

Place the milk in a pan and add the chocolate. Heat gently, stirring frequently, until the chocolate has melted. Sprinkle on the gelatine and add the orange rind and juice. Stir until the gelatine has completely dissolved.

Meanwhile, place the egg yolks and sugar in a bowl and whisk until thick. Gradually whisk in the chocolate mixture. Leave to stand until beginning to set. Whisk the egg whites until stiff. Fold into the chocolate mixture with about one quarter of the cream. Pour into the crumb base and smooth the top. Chill until set.

Remove the tin and transfer the pye, still on the metal base, to a serving plate. Put the remaining cream in a piping bag fitted with a large star tube and pipe it in scrolls around the edge. Decorate the cream with the buttons.

VARIATIONS

Chocolate flan with grapes Make the pye as in the above recipe then cover the surface with halved and pipped (U.S. pitted) green grapes, cut surface down. Melt 50 g / 2 oz plain chocolate (U.S. ⅓ cup semi-sweet chocolate pieces), place in a paper icing bag (see page 11), snip off the end and pipe a long swirl of chocolate from the centre point of the flan to the outside, in ever-increasing circles. Finish by piping rosettes of cream around the outside edge.

Cream-topped chocolate orange pie Add the juice of 1 more orange to the chocolate filling and don't fold in any of the cream. When set firmly, whip the cream until stiff then whisk in 1 tablespoon icing sugar (U.S. confectioners' sugar), sifted and 2 tablespoons Grand Marnier or Cointreau. Spread the flavoured cream over the pie to cover it completely then sprinkle with grated chocolate.

Strawberry chocolate mousse

SERVES 8

225 g/8 oz (U.S. ½ lb) strawberries, sliced
175 g/6 oz plain chocolate (U.S. 1 cup semi-sweet chocolate pieces)
25 g/1 oz (U.S. 2 tablespoons) butter
3 eggs, separated
225 ml/8 fl oz double cream (U.S. 1 cup heavy cream), whipped
25 g/1 oz icing sugar, sifted (U.S. ¼ cup sifted confectioners' sugar)
8 chocolate leaves (see page 10)

Reserve 8 neat strawberry slices for the decoration. Put the chocolate and butter in a bowl and stand this over a pan of hot water until the chocolate has melted. Stir lightly, remove from the heat and beat in the egg yolks, one at a time, until the mixture is smooth. Fold in about two-thirds of the cream.

Whisk the egg whites in a clean bowl until stiff then add the icing sugar, a tablespoon at a time, whisking vigorously after each addition until the meringue is firm and glossy. Fold into the chocolate mixture with the remaining strawberries. Transfer to a glass serving dish and chill for 2 hours.

Put the reserved cream in a piping bag fitted with a large star tube and pipe 8 rosettes around the edge of the mousse. Top each with a strawberry slice and a chocolate leaf.

VARIATIONS

Cherry chocolate cream pots Substitute 350 g/12 oz (U.S. ¾ lb) dark sweet cherries for the strawberries. Reserve 8 whole cherries with stalks. Stone (U.S. pit) the rest then roughly chop before folding into the mousse. Divide among 8 individual serving pots or stemmed glasses and top each with a rosette of cream and a whole cherry.

Pineapple ratafia mousse Drain a 350-g/12-oz can of pineapple pieces in syrup. Put 16 small ratafia biscuits (U.S. tiny almonds macaroons) in a bowl and spoon over about 75 ml/3 fl oz (U.S. ⅓ cup) of the syrup. Leave to stand for 30 minutes. Make up the chocolate mousse and fold in the soaked ratafias. Spoon half the mixture into a glass serving dish. Reserve 8 pieces of pineapple and spoon the rest evenly over the mousse. Top with the remainder. Decorate with 8 rosettes of cream as in the main recipe and spike each rosette with a piece of pineapple.

Pear cream pots Drain 8 canned pear halves and sandwich them together in pairs with a little of the cream, pressing them so that they stick together. Stand each 'pear' in a deep individual serving dish, trimming a little off the base of each to make them stand firm. Make up the chocolate mousse, folding in all the remaining cream, and spoon round the pears in the dishes.

Maraschino cherry mousse Drain a 100-g/4-oz jar of maraschino cherries (U.S. cocktail cherries), reserving the syrup. Quarter the cherries and fold into the chocolate mousse together with 3 tablespoons (U.S. 4 tablespoons) of the syrup. Decorate the top of the mousse with piped cream rosettes and chocolate curls (see page 10).

Apricot pocket mousse

SERVES 6

(Illustrated opposite)

3 tablespoons cocoa powder (U.S. 4 tablespoons unsweetened cocoa), sifted
175 ml/6 fl oz (U.S. ¾ cup) boiling water
1 (135-g/4¾-oz) orange flavour jelly tablet (U.S. 4-oz package orange-flavored gelatin)
300 ml/½ pint double cream (U.S. 1¼ cups heavy cream)
3 eggs, separated
2 tablespoons caster sugar (U.S. 3 tablespoons granulated sugar)
2 tablespoons (U.S. 3 tablespoons) apricot jam
about 20 milk chocolate buttons

Put the cocoa in a pan and add a little of the water to make a smooth paste. Gradually add the remaining water and bring to the boil. Remove from the heat and add the jelly. Stir until completely dissolved. Leave to cool until the mixture begins to set.

Whip half the cream until it will hold its shape. In a separate bowl, whisk the egg yolks and sugar together until pale. Stir in the whipped cream, then add the setting jelly and mix lightly but thoroughly. Whisk the egg whites in a clean bowl until stiff and fold into the mousse.

Rinse a 900-ml/1½-pint (U.S. 2-pint) mould with water. Put 3 small spoonfuls of jam into the base, keeping them separate. Pour in half the mousse. Carefully add 3 more small spoonfuls of jam, pour in the remaining mousse, and push the last spoonfuls of jam into it. Chill for at least 6 hours.

Dip the mould quickly into hot water and invert the mousse on to a serving plate. Whip the rest of the cream and place in a piping bag fitted with a large star tube. Pipe shells around the base of the mousse and a rosette in the centre. Spike the cream with chocolate buttons at regular intervals.

Apricot pocket mousse

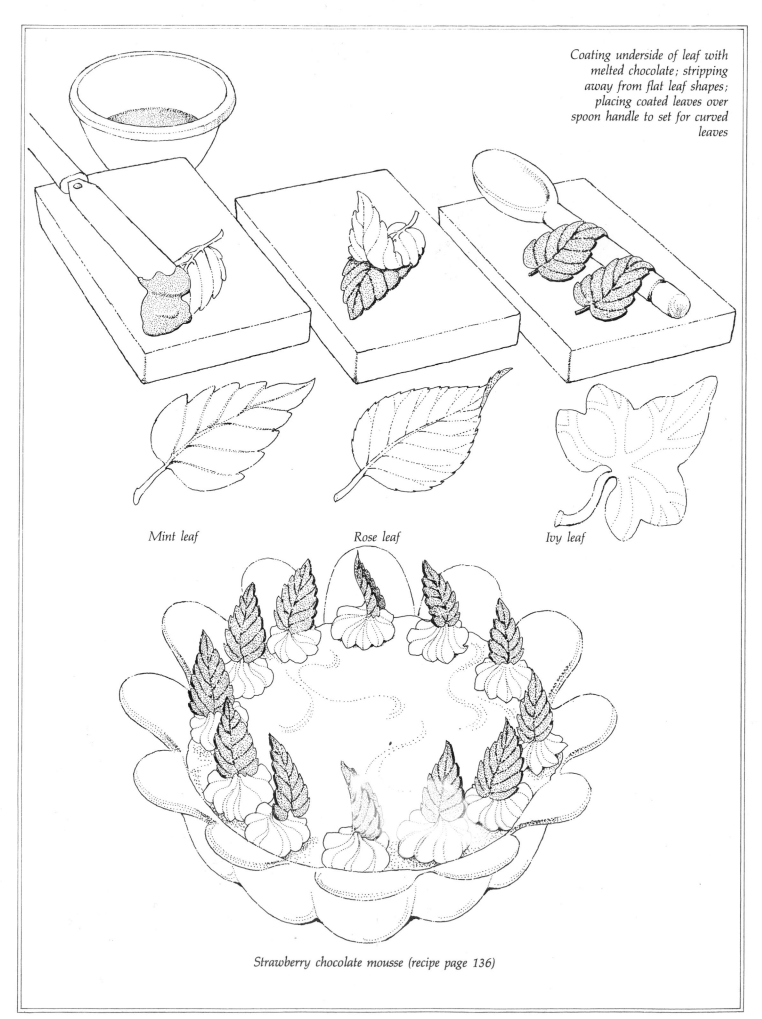

Coating underside of leaf with melted chocolate; stripping away from flat leaf shapes; placing coated leaves over spoon handle to set for curved leaves

Mint leaf   Rose leaf   Ivy leaf

Strawberry chocolate mousse (recipe page 136)

Moist chocolate pudding

SERVES 8

(Illustrated on the cover)

150 g/5 oz plain flour (U.S. 1¼ cups all-purpose flour)
25 g/1 oz cocoa powder (U.S. ¼ cup unsweetened cocoa)
½ teaspoon salt
2 teaspoons (U.S. 1 tablespoon) baking powder
150 g/5 oz soft brown sugar (U.S. ⅔ cup light brown sugar)
2 eggs, separated
6 tablespoons (U.S. 9 tablespoons) oil
6 tablespoons (U.S. 9 tablespoons) milk
½ teaspoon vanilla essence (U.S. vanilla extract)
SYRUP
100 g/4 oz (U.S. ½ cup) sugar
150 ml/¼ pint (U.S. ⅔ cup) water
3 tablespoons (U.S. 4 tablespoons) brandy
DECORATION
300 ml/½ pint double cream (U.S. 1¼ cups heavy cream), whipped
chocolate leaves (see page 10)

Heat the oven to 180°C/350°F, Gas Mark 4 and generously grease a 1.4-litre/2½-pint (U.S. 3-pint) decorative fluted tin.

Sift the flour with the cocoa, salt and baking powder. Stir in the brown sugar. Make a well in the centre and drop in the egg yolks, oil, milk and vanilla essence. Beat with a wooden spoon until smooth. Place the egg whites in a clean bowl, whisk until stiff then fold in. Transfer to the prepared tin.

Bake for about 50 minutes, or until firm to the touch. Turn out on a wire rack to cool.

To make the syrup, place the sugar and water in a pan and heat gently, stirring, until the sugar has dissolved. Boil steadily for 5 minutes. Remove from the heat and stir in the brandy.

Place the cold cake on a plate and slowly pour the hot syrup over it. Leave to stand for about 8 hours.

Transfer the cake to a serving plate. Place the cream in a piping bag fitted with a medium-sized star tube. Decorate the pudding with piped shells of cream and chocolate leaves.

VARIATIONS

Sherry chocolate pudding Grate 100 g/4 oz plain chocolate (U.S. 4 squares semi-sweet chocolate) and stir half of it into the pudding mixture just before baking. Make the soaking syrup with sweet sherry instead of brandy. Decorate the pudding by sprinkling it with the remaining chocolate and sifting over icing sugar (U.S. confectioners' sugar). Hand single cream (U.S. light cream) separately.

Almond chocolate pudding Lightly toast 50 g/2 oz flaked almonds (U.S. ½ cup slivered almonds) and fold most of them into the pudding mixture before baking, together with 1 teaspoon almond essence (U.S. almond extract). Use apple juice in place of the brandy in the syrup. Whip the cream until thick then add ½ teaspoon almond essence (U.S. almond extract) and 1 tablespoon caster sugar (U.S. granulated sugar) and whip until it holds its shape well. Sprinkle the reserved nuts over the pudding and serve the Almond cream in a bowl alongside.

Dark secret

SERVES 10

(Illustrated on page 9)

350 g/12 oz (U.S. 1½ cups) cream cheese
2 tablespoons caster sugar (U.S. 3 tablespoons granulated sugar)
75 g/3 oz (U.S. ¾ cup) chopped almonds, toasted
100 g/4 oz plain chocolate (U.S. ⅔ cup semi-sweet chocolate pieces)
300 ml/½ pint (U.S. 1¼ cups) milk
100 g/4 oz soft brown sugar (U.S. ½ cup light brown sugar)
3 tablespoons plain flour (U.S. 4 tablespoons all-purpose flour), sifted
2 egg yolks, beaten
40 g/1½ oz (U.S. 3 tablespoons) butter
BASE
65 g/2½ oz (U.S. 5 tablespoons) butter
150 g/5 oz plain chocolate-coated digestive biscuits, crushed (U.S. 1⅔ cups mixed chocolate wafer and graham cracker crumbs)
25 g/1 oz (U.S. ¼ cup) chopped almonds, toasted
DECORATION
10 canned drained apricot halves
chocolate curls (see page 10)

Line a deep 17.5 cm/7-inch loose-bottomed cake tin with foil.

Beat together the cream cheese, sugar and almonds. Press this mixture to the base and 5 cm/2 inches up the sides of the prepared tin, making it about 6 mm/¼ inch thick all over. Chill well.

Break up the chocolate and place with the milk in a heavy-based pan. Heat gently, stirring frequently, until the chocolate has melted. In a bowl, whisk together the sugar, flour and egg yolks. Gradually whisk in the chocolate mixture. Pour back into the pan and heat almost to boiling point, stirring constantly. Beat in the butter and simmer until the mixture is thick. Do not let it boil. Remove from the heat, cover and cool. When cold, pour into the cream cheese case and chill thoroughly.

To make the base, melt the butter, then stir in the biscuit crumbs and almonds. Mix well. Spoon into the tin and press down lightly with the back of a metal spoon to give a level surface. Chill for about 1 hour. Invert on to a serving plate and peel off the foil. Decorate the top edge with apricot halves and fill the centre with chocolate curls.

Special chocolate pots

SERVES 4–6

(Illustrated opposite)

200 g / 7 oz plain chocolate (U.S. 1 square semi-sweet chocolate
and 1 cup semi-sweet chocolate pieces)
300 ml / ½ pint single cream (U.S. 1¼ cups light cream)
1 tablespoon dark rum
1 egg, beaten

Use 25 g / 1 oz of the chocolate (U.S. use the square of chocolate) to make chocolate curls (see page 10). Reserve these for decoration.

Break up the remaining chocolate and place in a heavy-based pan with the cream. Heat gently, stirring frequently, until the chocolate melts. Stir well and bring to the boil. Remove the pan from the heat and whisk in the rum and egg. When well blended, divide among 4–6 individual dishes and chill for 24 hours. Serve decorated with the chocolate curls.

Macaroon ice cream dessert

SERVES 8

(Illustrated on page 9)

1 litre / 1¾ pints (U.S. 4¼ cups) chocolate ice cream, slightly
softened
50 g / 2 oz plain chocolate (U.S. ⅓ cup semi-sweet chocolate pieces)
150 ml / ¼ pint double cream (U.S. ⅔ cup heavy cream), whipped
75 g / 3 oz almond macaroons, crushed (U.S. ¾ cup almond
macaroon crumbs)

Press the ice cream into a 1-kg / 2-lb loaf-shaped tin and freeze until solid again. Melt the chocolate and use to make 4 chocolate cones (see page 11). Leave to set. Place the cream in a piping bag fitted with a large star tube.

At serving time, remove the paper from the chocolate cones. Dip the tin of ice cream into hot water for a couple of seconds then turn the ice cream out on to a serving dish. Press macaroon crumbs all over the surface. Top with the chocolate cones and pipe a rosette of cream inside each one. Pipe shells of the remaining cream around the base.

NOTE Home-made chocolate ice cream (see page 117) or commercial ice cream is suitable for this dessert but do not use the 'soft scoop' variety.

Chocolate chiffon flan

SERVES 8

150 g / 5 oz plain flour (U.S. 1¼ cups all-purpose flour)
50 g / 2 oz caster sugar (U.S. ¼ cup granulated sugar)
75 g / 3 oz (U.S. ⅓ cup) butter or block margarine, chilled and diced
1 egg yolk
FILLING
1 tablespoon water
1 teaspoon powdered gelatine (U.S. gelatin)
225 g / 8 oz plain chocolate (U.S. 1⅓ cups semi-sweet chocolate
pieces)
3 tablespoons (U.S. 4 tablespoons) black coffee
pinch of ground cloves
3 eggs, separated
150 ml / ¼ pint (U.S. ⅔ cup) whipping cream, whipped
few chocolate curls (see page 10)

Sift the flour into a bowl, add the sugar, butter and egg yolk and mix to a dough. Knead lightly until smooth, then cover and chill for 15 minutes.

Heat the oven to 190°C / 375°F, Gas Mark 5 and have ready a deep 20-cm / 8-inch flan tin. Roll out the pastry on a lightly floured surface and fit into the tin. Line with a sheet of greaseproof paper (U.S. waxed paper) and baking beans. Bake 'blind' for 10 minutes. Remove the lining paper and beans, and return the pastry case to the oven for a further 5 minutes, or until just turning golden. Turn on to a wire rack to cool, then transfer to a serving plate.

To make the filling, place the water in a small bowl, sprinkle on the gelatine and leave to stand for 5 minutes. Put the chocolate, coffee and cloves in a large bowl and stand this over a pan of hot water, until the chocolate has melted. Stir lightly and remove from the heat. Stand the gelatine over the hot water until completely dissolved. Beat the egg yolks into the chocolate mixture then add the dissolved gelatine and leave to cool. Fold about two-thirds of the cream into the chocolate mixture. Whisk the egg whites in a clean bowl until stiff and fold in lightly but thoroughly. Transfer to the pastry case and leave to set.

Put the remaining cream in a piping bag fitted with a medium-sized star tube and pipe rosettes around the edge of the pie. Top the rosettes with chocolate curls.

Special chocolate pots

Chocolate orange bombe

=== SERVES 6–8 ===

(Illustrated opposite)

1 (35-g/1¼-oz) sachet cream topping mix
300 ml/½ pint (U.S. 1¼ cups) cold milk
finely grated rind of 1 orange
juice of ½ orange
150 ml/¼ pint single cream (U.S. ⅔ cup light cream)
1 (64-g/2¼-oz) sachet chocolate orange flavour whipped dessert mix
chocolate orange flavour quick-setting ice cream topping, or melted chocolate
1 orange, sliced

Make up the cream topping mix with half the milk. Reserve a little for the decoration and stir the orange rind and juice into the remainder. Use this mixture to line the base and sides of a 600-ml/1-pint (U.S. 1¼-pint) bowl. Try to keep an even thickness. Freeze until firm.

Use the remaining milk and the cream to make up the dessert mix. Spoon into the centre of the lined bowl. Measure 2 tablespoons (U.S. 3 tablespoons) of the chocolate topping and swirl this through the soft centre of the bombe. Cover and freeze again until firm.

Invert the bombe on to a serving plate. Pour over chocolate topping to make a cap. When set, put the reserved cream topping in a piping bag fitted with a star tube and pipe a rosette on top of the dessert. Decorate with orange slices and serve at once.

=== VARIATIONS ===

Fruit cocktail bombe Make up the cream topping mix and stir in 50 g/2 oz plain chocolate (U.S. 2 squares semi-sweet chocolate), grated. Use to line the bowl and freeze. Make up a vanilla-flavoured dessert mix. Drain a 225-g/8-oz can of fruit cocktail, fold into the dessert mix and spoon into the bombe. Cover and freeze then turn out and spoon over chocolate topping to make a cap. Leave for 15 minutes before serving.

Strawberry cream bombe Make up the cream topping mix, use to line the bowl and freeze. Make up a strawberry dessert mix using cream and milk, as in main recipe, and fold in 100 g/4 oz (U.S. ¼ lb) sliced strawberries. Swirl chocolate topping through lightly, spoon into the bombe and freeze. Turn out and press grated chocolate all over the surface before serving.

Banana bombe surprise Make up a banana dessert mix using half milk and half cream. Slice 2 bananas and stir in with 2 tablespoons (U.S. 3 tablespoons) Crème de cacao or Irish cream liqueur. Turn into the bowl and press a smaller bowl in the centre. Cover and freeze. Pour warm water into the small bowl and remove. Make up the cream topping mix, marble lightly with chocolate topping, turn into the hollow and freeze. Serve decorated with a random trickle of chocolate topping and allow this to harden before cutting.

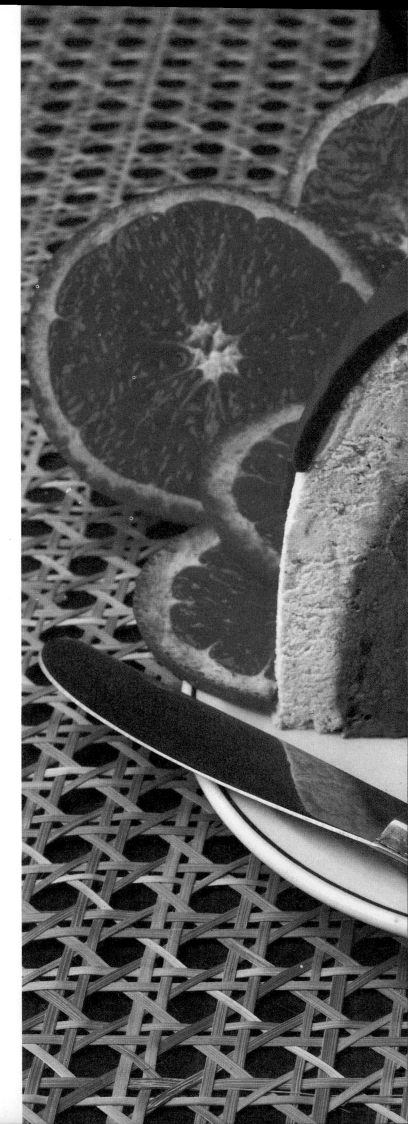

Amaretto cheesecake

BASE
225 g/8 oz digestive biscuits, crushed (U.S. 2⅔ cups graham
cracker crumbs)
100 g/4 oz (U.S. ½ cup) butter or margarine, melted
FILLING
50 g/2 oz plain chocolate (U.S. ⅓ cup semi-sweet chocolate pieces)
225 ml/8 fl oz double cream (U.S. 1 cup heavy cream)
225 g/8 oz (U.S. 1 cup) cream cheese
50 g/2 oz (U.S. ½ cup) ground almonds
½ teaspoon almond essence (U.S. almond extract)
2 tablespoons Amaretto or maraschino liqueur
2 eggs, separated
50 g/2 oz caster sugar (U.S. ¼ cup granulated sugar)
TOPPING
25 g/1 oz flaked almonds (U.S. ¼ cup slivered almonds) toasted
1 tablespoon coarsely grated chocolate

Heat the oven to 160°C/325°F, Gas Mark 3, and grease a 20-cm/8-inch loose-based cake tin.

Mix together the biscuit crumbs and butter, transfer to the base of the tin and press with the back of a spoon to make a smooth case, raising the sides evenly all round to about half the depth of the tin. Chill while making the filling.

Put the chocolate and 2 tablespoons (U.S. 3 tablespoons) of the cream in a bowl. Stand this over a pan of hot water until the chocolate has melted. Stir lightly.

In a large bowl, beat the cheese until smooth then gradually add the ground almonds, almond flavouring, liqueur and chocolate mixture. In a separate bowl put the egg yolks and sugar and whisk until thick. Reserve 3 tablespoons (U.S. 4 tablespoons) of the remaining cream for the topping and whip the rest. Gradually add the egg mousse to the cheese mixture and then fold in the whipped cream. Finally, whisk the egg whites until stiff and fold them in lightly but evenly. Transfer to the crumb case.

Bake for about 35 minutes, or until the centre is just firm. Turn off the oven, open the door slightly and leave the cheesecake until cold. Remove the tin and transfer the cheesecake, still on the metal base, to a serving dish.

To decorate, whip the reserved cream lightly and spread over the surface of the cheesecake to make a flat surface. (The centre of the cheesecake sinks slightly after baking.) Scatter with the almonds and grated chocolate just before serving.

Chocolate raisin mousse

50 g/2 oz (U.S. ⅓ cup) seedless raisins
2 tablespoons (U.S. 3 tablespoons) Cointreau or Grand Marnier
juice of 1 orange
1½ teaspoons powdered gelatine (U.S. ½ envelope gelatin)
100 g/4 oz plain chocolate (U.S. ⅔ cup semi-sweet chocolate pieces)
4 eggs
50 g/2 oz caster sugar (U.S. ¼ cup granulated sugar)
finely grated rind of ½ orange
75 ml/3 fl oz double cream (U.S. ⅓ cup heavy cream), whipped
DECORATION
little whipped cream
grated rind of ½ orange

Put the raisins in a small bowl and sprinkle over the liqueur. Leave to stand, stirring occasionally, until the raisins are plump and the liqueur has been absorbed. Meanwhile, put the orange juice in another small bowl and sprinkle on the gelatine. Leave for 5 minutes then place over hot water until the gelatine has completely dissolved. Melt the chocolate over the hot water then cool.

Put 2 whole eggs and 2 egg yolks in a bowl with the sugar and stand this over the pan of simmering water. Whisk until thick then remove from the heat and continue whisking until cool. Whisk in the chocolate, gelatine and orange rind. Fold in the raisins and cream. Whisk the remaining egg whites until stiff and fold in evenly.

Transfer to a serving dish and leave to set but do not chill. Serve topped with rosettes of cream and the orange rind.

Sultana cream mousse Use sultanas (U.S. seedless white raisins) instead of the seedless raisins and soak them in cherry brandy instead of orange liqueur. Make up the mousse, using 150 ml/¼ pint double cream (U.S. ⅔ cup heavy cream) and omitting the orange rind. When completely set, decorate the top with a circle of small ratafia biscuits (U.S. tiny almond macaroons) that have been half-dipped in melted chocolate and allowed to set on non-stick baking parchment (U.S. waxed paper).

Buttered crumb mousse Melt 40 g/1½ oz (U.S. 3 tablespoons) butter in a pan and use to fry 75 g/3 oz fresh wholemeal breadcrumbs (U.S. 1½ cups fresh wholewheat bread crumbs), stirring, until golden brown. Mix in 2 tablespoons demerara sugar (U.S. 3 tablespoons light brown sugar) and ½ teaspoon ground cinnamon. Put about half the crumbs into a glass serving dish, spoon over the raisin mousse and top evenly with the remaining crumbs. Leave for 1 hour. Omit the cream decoration but place 2 narrow strips of paper across the mousse and sift with icing sugar (U.S. confectioners' sugar). Carefully lift off the paper strips and serve at once.

Speedy dress-ups for ice cream

(Illustrated below)

To serve an impressive dessert with very little effort, make some chocolate cups in advance (see page 11). These store well in a rigid airtight container in the freezer for 1 month or in the refrigerator for 1 week. At serving time, simply spoon in a mixture of half and half crumbled cake and ground almonds moistened with a fruit liqueur. Top this with a generous scoop of rich dairy ice cream. Pretty rolled wafers make a good accompaniment.

Here are the liqueurs I recommend to serve with these special rich ice cream flavours. Mocha Coffee ice cream is delicious with Tia Maria or Kahlua in the crumb base. Dark Chocolate contrasts well with Grand Marnier or Cointreau, and Cherry Marnier or Kirsch bring out the fresh fruit flavour of Strawberry Royale.

Mallow chocolate chip ice cream

═══ SERVES 8 ═══

450 g / 1 lb marshmallows
600 ml / 1 pint (U.S. 2½ cups) freshly-made very strong black coffee
300 ml / ½ pint double cream (U.S. 1¼ cups heavy cream)
100 g / 4 oz plain chocolate dots (U.S. ⅔ cup semi-sweet chocolate chips)

Put the marshmallows in a large bowl and stand this over a pan of hot water. Pour the fresh coffee over the marshmallows and stir them together until the marshmallows have melted to the size of hazelnuts (U.S. filberts). Remove the bowl from the heat and leave to cool. Whip the cream until thick and fold into the mallow mixture. Transfer to a shallow container and freeze until the edges are just firm.

Stir the ice cream lightly in the container, scattering in the chocolate dots as you do so. Level the surface again and freeze until solid. Allow to stand at room temperature for 15 minutes before serving.

This ice cream is very rich and sweet, so serve small portions scooped into stemmed glasses with sponge fingers (U.S. ladyfingers).

Boules de neige

275 g/10 oz plain chocolate, roughly chopped (U.S. 1⅔ cups semi-sweet chocolate pieces)
175 ml/6 fl oz (U.S. ¾ cup) freshly brewed strong black coffee
275 g/10 oz caster sugar (U.S. 1¼ cups granulated sugar)
175 g/6 oz (U.S. ¾ cup) unsalted butter, softened
5 eggs
1 tablespoon rum
DECORATION
450 ml/¾ pint double cream (U.S. 2 cups heavy cream)
100 g/4 oz (U.S. 4 squares) white chocolate, grated

It takes time and patience to coat the shaped balls evenly with cream but the effect is very French indeed!

Heat the oven to 180°C/350°F, Gas Mark 4, grease a 1-kg/2-lb loaf-shaped tin and line with non-stick baking parchment (U.S. waxed paper).

Put the chocolate, coffee and sugar in a large bowl and stand this over a pan of hot water, stirring occasionally, until the chocolate has melted and the sugar dissolved. Leave to cool. Add the butter to the bowl and beat, using an electric mixer if possible, until smooth. Beating constantly, add the eggs, one at a time, and then the rum. Spread in the prepared tin and level the surface.

Bake for 1 hour and ignore the fact that the top looks split. Leave in the tin to cool and then chill for 8 hours.

Line a baking sheet (U.S. cookie sheet) with non-stick baking parchment (U.S. waxed paper). Mark the chocolate mixture into 8 equal sections. Scoop out 1 section and shape into a ball on the parchment using a spoon and palette knife (U.S. spatula). Repeat with the other sections, to make 8 balls altogether. Chill thoroughly or freeze.

Whip the cream. Place a chocolate ball on a serving plate and carefully cover with a thin layer of cream. When all the balls are coated, sprinkle the tops with white chocolate 'snow' and serve before the snowballs melt.

NOTE If preferred, pipe the cream to cover the chocolate balls using a small star tube. The effect is very pretty but you will probably need another 150 ml/¼ pint (U.S. ⅔ cup cream) for this.

=== VARIATION ===

Ice cream snowballs Use block chocolate ice cream (not soft scoop) instead of the butter mixture to shape the balls, then refreeze. Transfer to the serving dish, coat with cream and freeze again. Serve as a frozen dessert, sprinkling with the white chocolate at the last moment.

Cassata

(Illustrated opposite)

2 (35-g/1¼-oz) sachets cream topping mix
300 ml/½ pint (U.S. 1¼ cups) cold milk
2 tablespoons (U.S. 3 tablespoons) brandy or sweet sherry
50 g/2 oz (U.S. ½ cup) chopped mixed nuts
100 g/4 oz red, green and yellow glacé cherries (U.S. ½ cup red, green and yellow candied cherries), chopped
chocolate flavour quick-setting ice cream topping or melted chocolate
DECORATION
2 each red, green and yellow glacé cherries (U.S. candied cherries), cut into neat pieces

Make up the cream topping mix with the milk. Reserve about one fifth for the decoration. Whisk the brandy or sherry into the remainder, then fold in the nuts and chopped cherries. Transfer to a 15-cm/6-inch loose-based cake tin and level the surface. Cover with a generous layer of the chocolate topping. Freeze until solid.

Take the cassata from the freezer 15 minutes before serving time. Remove it from the tin to a serving dish, or serve the cassata on the metal base and place this on a serving plate. Put the reserved cream topping in a piping bag fitted with a star tube and pipe rosettes all round the top edge and 3 small rosettes in the centre. Spike the rosettes with pieces of cherry.

Double delights
Melt 100 g/4 oz plain chocolate (U.S. ⅔ cup semi-sweet chocolate pieces) in one large bowl over hot water and the same quantity of milk chocolate (U.S. sweet chocolate) in another. Put the grated rind and juice of 2 oranges in a small bowl, sprinkle on 15 g/½ oz powdered gelatine (U.S. 1 envelope gelatin) and leave for 5 minutes. Place over hot water until the gelatine has completely dissolved. Add 2 egg yolks, 1 tablespoon of Tia Maria or Kahlua and half the gelatine to the bowl of plain chocolate and stir briskly until blended. Add 2 egg yolks, 1 tablespoon Grand Marnier or Cointreau and the rest of the gelatine to the milk chocolate and mix as before. Whisk 150 ml/¼ pint (U.S. ⅔ cup) whipping cream until holding its shape. In a clean bowl, whisk 2 egg whites until stiff, add 3 tablespoons caster sugar (U.S. 4 tablespoons granulated sugar), one at a time, whisking well after each addition until the meringue is firm and glossy. Fold half the cream and half the meringue into each bowl of chocolate. In 6 stemmed glasses, layer up the two mixtures carefully, making 4 layers in each glass. Chill. To serve, spoon unwhipped whipping cream over the surface of each delight.

Cassata

Speckled pecan soufflé

SERVES 4–6

(Illustrated opposite)

5 tablespoons (U.S. 7 tablespoons) water
4 teaspoons powdered gelatine (U.S. 1⅓ envelopes gelatin)
4 large eggs, separated
100 g / 4 oz caster sugar (U.S. ½ cup granulated sugar)
few drops vanilla essence (U.S. vanilla extract)
75 g / 3 oz plain chocolate (U.S. 3 squares semi-sweet chocolate),
coarsely grated
40 g / 1½ oz (U.S. ⅓ cup) finely chopped pecans
300 ml / ½ pint double cream (U.S. 1¼ cups heavy cream)
2 tablespoons (U.S. 3 tablespoons) milk
7 glacé cherries (U.S. candied cherries), halved
7 pecan halves

Prepare a soufflé dish, with a capacity of about 900 ml / 1½ pints (U.S. 2 pints) or very slightly smaller, by tying a double thickness of foil or greaseproof paper around the dish which extends at least 5 cm / 2 inches above the rim. Secure with adhesive tape or string.

Put 2 tablespoons (U.S. 3 tablespoons) of the water in a small bowl and sprinkle on the gelatine. Set aside. Put the egg yolks, the remaining water, the sugar and vanilla essence in a large bowl. Stand this over a pan of simmering water, having the base of the bowl above the level of the water. Keeping this at simmering point, whisk the ingredients steadily, using an electric mixer if possible, until thick and mousse-like. When ready, the mixture should fall back on itself in a firm ribbon when the beaters are lifted. Remove the bowl from the heat and continue whisking until cold.

Meanwhile, stand the container of soaked gelatine over hot water until the gelatine has dissolved. Whisk into the mousse, then fold in the chocolate and nuts. Leave until the mixture is on the point of setting.

Whip half the cream with the milk until thick. Fold into the setting mixture. Put the egg whites in a clean bowl and whisk until stiff. Fold these in lightly but thoroughly. Transfer to the prepared dish, level the surface and chill until set.

Whip the remaining cream and place in a piping bag fitted with a large star tube. Remove the collar from the soufflé dish, peeling it carefully away from the exposed mixture. Pipe the cream in a looped crown on top of the soufflé and decorate with cherries. Arrange the nuts round the outside of the cream.

Hot chocolate soufflé

SERVES 4–6

300 ml / ½ pint (U.S. 1¼ cups) milk
1 teaspoon instant coffee powder
75 g / 3 oz plain chocolate (U.S. ½ cup semi-sweet chocolate pieces)
50 g / 2 oz (U.S. ¼ cup) butter or margarine
40 g / 1½ oz plain flour (U.S. ⅓ cup all-purpose flour), sifted
50 g / 2 oz caster sugar (U.S. ¼ cup granulated sugar)
3 egg yolks
1 tablespoon brandy
4 egg whites
little icing sugar (U.S. confectioners' sugar) for sprinkling

Heat the oven to 190°C / 375°F, Gas Mark 5 and grease a 1-litre / 2-pint (U.S. 2½-pint) soufflé dish.

Put the milk, coffee and chocolate in a pan and heat gently, stirring, until the chocolate has melted. Stir until smooth. In a clean pan, melt the butter and stir in the flour. Cook and stir for 1 minute, without allowing the roux to colour. Gradually blend in the chocolate milk and half the sugar and bring to the boil, stirring constantly, until the sauce is smooth and very thick. Remove from the heat and beat in the egg yolks, one at a time, and the brandy. Leave to cool to lukewarm. The mixture can be prepared ahead up to this point.

Put the egg whites in a clean bowl and whisk until stiff. Gradually add the remaining sugar, a tablespoon at a time, whisking vigorously after each addition until the meringue is thick and glossy. Fold one third into the chocolate mixture. When well blended, fold in the remainder and transfer to the prepared dish. Mark a 12.5-cm / 5-inch circle lightly in the top with the back of a teaspoon.

Bake for about 40 minutes, or until well risen and firm to the touch. Sift the top with sugar and serve immediately, straight from the oven.

Speckled pecan soufflé

Chilled chocolate dessert cake

1 teaspoon powdered gelatine (U.S. $\frac{1}{3}$ envelope gelatin)
1 tablespoon water
2 tablespoons cornflour (U.S. 3 tablespoons cornstarch)
450 ml/$\frac{3}{4}$ pint (U.S. 2 cups) milk
175 g/6 oz plain chocolate (U.S. 1 cup semi-sweet chocolate pieces)
2 egg yolks
25 g/1 oz (U.S. 2 tablespoons) butter
300 ml/$\frac{1}{2}$ pint double cream (U.S. 1$\frac{1}{4}$ cups heavy cream), whipped
25 g/1 oz (U.S. $\frac{1}{4}$ cup) finely chopped almonds, toasted
about 30 sponge fingers (U.S. ladyfingers)
25 g/1 oz flaked almonds (U.S. $\frac{1}{4}$ cup slivered almonds), toasted

Line a 1-kg/2-lb loaf-shaped tin with non-stick parchment (U.S. waxed paper).

Dissolve the gelatine in the water in a small bowl over a pan of hot water. Set aside. Moisten the cornflour with a little of the milk. Break up the chocolate and heat gently in the remaining milk until melted. Mix in the blended cornflour and stir constantly until boiling. Cook gently for 3 minutes. Remove from the heat and beat in the egg yolks, butter and dissolved gelatine. Leave to cool, stirring occasionally. Fold in half the cream and the chopped nuts.

Arrange sponge fingers neatly over the base of the prepared tin, then stand more of them all round the sides, with the sugared surface facing the parchment. Carefully pour in half the chocolate mixture, put in another layer of fingers, then add the rest of the chocolate mixture. Trim the tops of the fingers level with the filling and use these to make the last layer. Press down lightly and chill for at least 8 hours.

Turn the cake out on a serving dish and peel off the parchment. Put the remaining cream into a piping bag fitted with a star tube. Pipe rosettes round the base of the cake and on the top 4 corners. Spike the rosettes with the flaked almonds.

Tia Maria soufflé

(Illustrated opposite)

6 tablespoons (U.S. 9 tablespoons) water
3 tablespoons (U.S. 4 tablespoons) Tia Maria
2 tablespoons powdered gelatine (U.S. 2 envelopes gelatin)
175 g/6 oz milk chocolate (U.S. 6 squares sweet chocolate)
6 large eggs, separated
175 g/6 oz caster sugar (U.S. $\frac{3}{4}$ cup granulated sugar)
300 ml/$\frac{1}{2}$ pint (U.S. 1$\frac{1}{4}$ cups) whipping cream, whipped
DECORATION
75 ml/3 fl oz (U.S. $\frac{1}{3}$ cup) whipping cream, whipped
2 tablespoons chocolate vermicelli (U.S. 3 tablespoons chocolate sprinkles or finely grated chocolate)
4 walnut halves, roughly broken up

Prepare a soufflé dish, with a capacity of about 1.1 litres/2 pints (U.S. 2$\frac{1}{2}$ pints) or very slightly smaller, by tying a double thickness of foil or greaseproof paper (U.S. waxed paper) around the dish which extends at least 5 cm/2 inches above the rim. Secure with adhesive tape or string.

Spoon 2 tablespoons (U.S. 3 tablespoons) of the water and the liqueur into a small bowl and sprinkle on the gelatine. Put the chocolate in another bowl. Set aside. Place the egg yolks, remaining water and the sugar in a large bowl and stand this over a pan of simmering water, keeping the base of the bowl above the level of the water. Whisk together, using an electric mixer if possible, until thick and creamy, keeping the water simmering all the time. When ready, the mixture should fall back on itself in a firm ribbon when the beaters are lifted. Remove the bowl from the heat and continue whisking until cold.

Meanwhile, put the bowl with the gelatine in it over the hot water until the gelatine has dissolved. Remove from the heat and replace with the bowl of chocolate. When this has melted, stir in the gelatine mixture, then gradually whisk into the mousse. Leave until on the point of setting.

Fold the cream into the setting mixture. Put the egg whites in a clean bowl and whisk until stiff. Fold these in lightly but thoroughly. Transfer to the prepared dish and chill until set.

Put the cream for the decoration in a piping bag fitted with a large star tube. Remove the collar from the soufflé dish, easing it carefully away from the exposed mixture. Press vermicelli against the sides all round. Pipe 8 rosettes of cream on the soufflé and top each with a piece of nut.

Tia Maria soufflé

Norah's favourite dessert

225 g/8 oz plain chocolate (U.S. 1⅓ cups semi-sweet chocolate pieces)
2 tablespoons (U.S. 3 tablespoons) milk
4 eggs, separated
50 g/2 oz caster sugar (U.S. ¼ cup granulated sugar)
175 ml/6 fl oz (small can) evaporated milk (U.S. ¾ cup unsweetened evaporated milk), chilled
2 egg whites

Put the chocolate in a bowl with the fresh milk and stand this over a pan of hot water until the chocolate has melted. Stir lightly and leave to cool.

Put the egg yolks and sugar in another bowl and stand this over the simmering water. Whisk constantly for 5 minutes, or until thickened. Remove from the heat and whisk until cool. Blend in the chocolate.

Whisk the evaporated milk using an electric mixer if possible, until thick. Combine with the chocolate mixture. Whisk all the egg whites together in a clean bowl until stiff and fold in lightly until no traces of white remain. Transfer to a glass serving dish and chill for 12 hours.

Dinner party pots Omit the evaporated milk and substitute 300 ml/½ pint double cream (U.S. 1¼ cups heavy cream), whipped until thick. Reserve about a quarter of the cream and fold the rest into the dessert mixture with 2 tablespoons (U.S. 3 tablespoons) rum. Divide among 8 stemmed glasses and chill for 12 hours. Serve each topped with a rosette of the reserved cream and a sprinkling of grated chocolate.

Orange liqueur pots

100 g/4 oz plain chocolate (U.S. ⅔ cup semi-sweet chocolate pieces)
finely grated rind and juice of 1 large orange
25 g/1 oz (U.S. 2 tablespoons) butter
1 tablespoon Grand Marnier
2 eggs, separated
TOPPING
2 thin slices of orange, quartered
4 teaspoons Grand Marnier

Put the chocolate in a bowl with the orange rind and juice and butter. Stand the bowl over hot water, stirring occasionally until the chocolate has melted. Remove from the heat, add the Grand Marnier and beat until smooth. Put the egg yolks in another bowl and whisk until pale. Strain in the hot chocolate mixture, whisk until well blended then leave to cool. Whisk the egg whites in a clean bowl until stiff and fold in lightly but evenly. Divide among 4 individual dishes and leave to set.

To decorate, place 2 orange slice quarters, point to point on each pot. Spoon a teaspoon of liqueur over each one and swirl round to moisten the surface. Serve at once.

Cherry liqueur pots Substitute Cherry Marnier for the Grand Marnier, and use halved maraschino cherries (U.S. cocktail cherries) in place of the orange slices.

Sylvabella

100 g/4 oz plain chocolate (U.S. ⅔ cup semi-sweet chocolate pieces)
175 g/6 oz (U.S. ¾ cup) unsalted butter
150 g/5 oz caster sugar (U.S. ⅔ cup granulated sugar)
4 eggs, separated
about 22 boudoir biscuits or sponge fingers (U.S. ladyfingers)
SYRUP
1 tablespoon caster sugar (U.S. granulated sugar)
50 ml/2 fl oz (U.S. ¼ cup) warm water
50 ml/2 fl oz (U.S. ¼ cup) rum
DECORATION
150 ml/¼ pint double cream (U.S. ⅔ cup heavy cream), whipped
crystallized violets

Have ready a 15-cm/6-inch soufflé dish. Melt the chocolate in a bowl over a pan of hot water. Put the butter and sugar into a bowl and beat until really soft and fluffy. Add the egg yolks, one at a time, beating well after each addition. Gradually add the chocolate. Whisk the egg whites in a clean bowl until stiff and fold in lightly.

To make the syrup, dissolve the sugar in the water and add the rum. Working as quickly as possible, dip the biscuits into the rum liquid to about half their depth, and stand them side by side around the edge of the dish. Spoon the chocolate mixture into the centre and use any of the remaining biscuits, dipped in rum liquid, to cover the top of the chocolate mixture. Press them in lightly.

Chill for 2 hours. At serving time spread or pipe the cream over the surface of the dessert and scatter with pieces of crystallized violet.

Icebergs

3 egg yolks
25 g/1 oz self-raising flour, sifted (U.S. ¼ cup all-purpose flour
sifted with ¼ teaspoon baking powder)
100 g/4 oz icing sugar, sifted (U.S. scant 1 cup sifted
confectioners' sugar)
300 ml/½ pint (U.S. 1¼ cups) milk
50 g/2 oz plain chocolate (U.S. 2 squares semi-sweet chocolate),
grated
2 tablespoons (U.S. 3 tablespoons) Tia Maria
TOPPING
about 300 ml/½ pint double cream (U.S. 1¼ cups heavy cream)
1 tablespoon Tia Maria

Put the egg yolks, flour and sugar in a bowl and whisk until blended. Heat the milk in a heavy pan. When almost boiling pour on to the egg mixture and whisk vigorously. Pour the mixture into the pan and stir constantly over very gentle heat until it begins to thicken. Add the chocolate and continue stirring until the custard is thick enough to coat the back of the spoon. Blend in the liqueur then divide among 4–5 individual deep dishes or custard cups. When cool, chill.

Whip the cream until thick then add the liqueur and whip until holding its shape. Place in a piping bag fitted with a medium-sized star tube. Press the tip of the tube slightly into the centre of one custard and pipe in cream generously, pulling it up into a point at the end, so that it becomes an 'iceberg' with only the tip rising above the surface. Serve with brandy snaps (see page 171).

Festive Novelties

Family birthdays keep coming around and so do the festivities of Christmas and Easter, and other special occasions. For even a formally decorated cake, the basic mixture need no longer be one made dark with fruit. A chocolate spongy mixture goes well with any kind of icing or frosting, especially a classic frosting that is ideal to pull up into peaks for a snow-scene cake. There's a pretty one shown on page 157; and remember to save the bought decorations from the top for next year. Other Christmas delights include a new version of the Yule log, with a crisp, crackly chocolate bark, and a tiny robins' nest on top (see page 166). The birds can be purchased, or moulded from coloured marzipan, as the eggs are from sugar paste. You may think of other novel ideas for the log; a moulded owl with three baby owlets would be fun.

For those who want to celebrate Christmas with biscuits or cookies instead of a cake, the mixture can be rolled and then stamped out in all sorts of shapes appropriate to the season. 'Bottles' are iced to bring cheery greetings. Other ideas would be Father Christmas shapes, stars or angels. The gold leaf used to decorate hand-made chocolates could be most effective here, and if you have an artistic bent, plain ice the shapes in white, then draw in the design with food colourings and a fine paint brush copying a suitable greetings card. It helps to mark the outer dimensions of the colour work with a pin-prick here and there in the icing first, so you keep the design central.

Easter novelties are exciting to make too. Children accustomed to weird creatures from outer space will love Golden straw balls. Cereals make all sorts of crispy nests to hold marzipan eggs, or bought ones of chocolate encased in a candy coat or foil paper. Melted chocolate combines with practically any cereal to form an edible container for small sweets. The more chocolate you use the firmer the case will be. Clean non-stick bun tins (U.S. muffin pans) mould an easy, all-purpose shape. Any leftover chocolate should be mixed in the melting bowl with nuts and raisins, or other dried fruits (chopped if necessary) and formed into mounds to make tasty small chews.

Birthday cakes wear a traditional air when the chocolate centre is covered with pastel-tinted icing; pink or peach for girls, pale blue or green for boys. Flavour with triple-distilled rose water, orange essence; or with peppermint oil as appropriate.

Above left: Snowman cake (recipe page 156). Above right: Fir cone cakes (recipe page 158). Below: Tropical Christmas cake (recipe page 159)

Snowman cake

(Illustrated on page 154)

150 g/5 oz plain flour (U.S. 1¼ cups all-purpose flour)
25 g/1 oz cocoa powder (U.S. ¼ cup unsweetened cocoa)
1 tablespoon baking powder
175 g/6 oz (U.S. ¾ cup) soft margarine
175 g/6 oz caster sugar (U.S. ¾ cup granulated sugar)
3 eggs
50 g/2 oz plain chocolate (U.S. 2 squares semi-sweet chocolate),
grated
DECORATION
75 g/3 oz (U.S. ⅓ cup) butter or margarine
175 g/6 oz icing sugar, sifted (U.S. 1⅓ cups sifted confectioners'
sugar)
75 g/3 oz desiccated coconut (U.S. 1 cup shredded coconut,
chopped)
1 chocolate-covered wagon wheel biscuit (U.S. 1 chocolate-covered
sandwich cookie, about 9 cm/3½ inches in diameter)
1 chocolate-covered marshmallow teacake (U.S. 1 chocolate-
covered marshmallow topped cookie, about 5 cm/2 inches in
diameter)
100 g/4 oz marzipan (U.S. ¼ lb almond marzipan)
red food colouring
7.5-cm/3-inch length liquorice for mouth and eyes
2 candy-covered liquorice sweets for buttons

Heat the oven to 160°C/325°F, Gas Mark 3 and grease 2 ovenproof pudding bowls, one with a capacity of about 900 ml/1½ pints (U.S. 2 pints) and the other of about 300 ml/½ pint (U.S. 1¼ cups). Stand them on a baking sheet (U.S. cookie sheet).

Sift the flour, cocoa and baking powder into a bowl. Add the margarine, sugar and eggs and beat until well blended. Fold in the chocolate. Spoon just over two-thirds of the mixture into the larger pudding bowl and the remainder into the smaller bowl. Level the surfaces.

Bake, allowing about 50 minutes for the smaller cake and 1 hour for the larger, or until the cakes are firm to the touch. Turn out on a wire rack to cool.

To make the icing, cream the butter and icing sugar until soft and fluffy. Spread icing thinly over the larger cake, avoiding the flat side. Roll the coated cake in coconut and set it on a cake board, flat side downwards. Place the smaller cake flat side downwards on a board and cut a slice from each side. Cover this smaller cake completely in butter icing and roll in coconut in the same way. Set it on the large cake, pressing one of the cut surfaces to the top of the cake on the board. Keep the flat surface at the back of the snowman's head. Use a little icing to stick the large chocolate biscuit on the top cut surface for the brim of the hat, then stick the chocolate teacake on top of this.

Tint the marzipan red with food colouring. Pinch off a small piece and shape into a cone for the nose. Roll out the rest to a narrow strip about 45 cm/18 inches long, trim neatly and cut a fringe at each end, to make the scarf. Place around the snowman's neck to cover the join in the cakes. Snip off a little piece of liquorice for each eye and keep a piece about 5 cm/2 inches in length for the smiling mouth. Use a little buttercream to stick the eyes, nose, mouth and buttons on the snowman cake, then sprinkle a little coconut over his hat. Chill any remaining buttercream then roll it into balls and coat these in coconut. Pile these snowballs on the board.

Snowscene Christmas cake

(Illustrated opposite)

225 g/8 oz self-raising flour (U.S. 2 cups all-purpose flour sifted
with 2 teaspoons baking powder)
½ teaspoon salt
½ teaspoon cream of tartar
25 g/1 oz cocoa powder (U.S. ¼ cup unsweetened cocoa), sifted
150 ml/¼ pint double cream (U.S. ⅔ cup heavy cream)
100 g/4 oz (U.S. ½ cup) soft margarine
100 g/4 oz caster sugar (U.S. ½ cup granulated sugar)
2 eggs, beaten
50 g/2 oz (U.S. ½ cup) ground almonds
½ teaspoon almond essence (U.S. almond extract)
2 tablespoons (U.S. 3 tablespoons) milk
75 g/3 oz plain chocolate (U.S. 3 squares semi-sweet chocolate),
grated
ROYAL ICING AND DECORATION
2 large egg whites
450 g/1 lb icing sugar (U.S. confectioners' sugar), sifted
1 teaspoon lemon juice
1 teaspoon glycerine (optional)
small tree and snowman cake decorations
about 1 metre/39 inches gold lacy ribbon

Heat the oven to 180°C/350°F, Gas Mark 4, grease a 20-cm/8-inch cake tin and line with greaseproof paper (U.S. waxed paper).

Sift the flour with the salt and cream of tartar. Mix the cocoa with the cream to give a thick smooth consistency. Cream the margarine and sugar in a bowl until light and fluffy. Beating all the time, gradually add the egg, almonds, almond essence and cocoa mixture. Fold in the dry ingredients and the milk. Spoon about a third of the mixture into the prepared tin and roughly level the surface. Sprinkle about half the chocolate over this. Repeat the layers once, using all the chocolate. Spread the last of the cake mixture on top. Make the layers very approximately. It does not matter if they get rather mixed up.

Bake for 1 hour, or until firm to the touch. Leave in the tin for 5 minutes, then turn out on a wire rack and allow to cool before peeling off the lining paper. If time permits, store the cake, sealed in a plastic bag, for 2 days before decorating.

To make the royal icing, put the egg whites in a bowl and beat lightly until broken up but not frothy. Gradually add the sugar, a tablespoon at a time, beating with a wooden spoon. Beat in the lemon juice and glycerine, if using.

Put a teaspoon of icing on a cake stand and set the cake on this, placing it accurately in the centre. Brush away any cake crumbs then cover the sides of the cake first with icing and then the top, spreading it with a spatula. When the cake is evenly covered, lift the icing into peaks with the tip of a knife. Allow the surface to harden then press in the decorations and finish by looping the ribbon about three-quarters of the way round the cake. Secure each side with a pin and leave the ribbon ends curling over the side of the dish. Remember to remove the pins before cutting the cake. Alternatively, tie the ribbon in a bow.

Snowscene Christmas cake

Fir cone cakes

MAKES 6 LARGE INDIVIDUAL CAKES

(Illustrated on page 154)

2 tablespoons cocoa powder (U.S. 3 tablespoons unsweetened
cocoa)
50 g/2 oz plain flour (U.S. ½ cup all-purpose flour)
¾ teaspoon baking powder
50 g/2 oz (U.S. ¼ cup) soft margarine
50 g/2 oz caster sugar (U.S. ¼ cup granulated sugar)
1 egg, beaten
1 tablespoon milk
DECORATION
1 teaspoon hot water
25 g/1 oz (U.S. 2 tablespoons) butter or margarine
50 g/2 oz icing sugar, sifted (U.S. scant ½ cup sifted
confectioners' sugar)
3 (51-g/2-oz) packs milk chocolate buttons
little extra icing sugar (U.S. confectioners' sugar)

Heat the oven to 160°C/325°F, Gas Mark 3 and grease 6
dariole moulds (U.S. individual pudding moulds). Stand the tins
on a baking sheet (U.S. cookie sheet).

Reserve 2 teaspoons (U.S. 1 tablespoon) of the cocoa and sift
the remainder with the flour and baking powder. Cream the
margarine and sugar in a bowl until light and fluffy. Gradually
add the egg then fold in the dry ingredients and the milk.
Divide among the prepared tins.

Bake for about 20 minutes, or until firm to the touch. Turn out
on a wire rack to cool.

To decorate the cakes, put the reserved cocoa in a bowl and
mix in the hot water until smooth. Add the butter and sugar
and beat until fluffy. Cover the top and sides of the cakes with
butter icing then press in the buttons, overlapping them to
resemble fir cones. Sift a little sugar over the tops to look like
snow.

To make chocolate marzipan holly leaves Tint marzipan
(U.S. almond marzipan) chocolate colour by working in a little
cocoa powder. Roll out and cut holly leaf shapes. Mark a centre
vein down each leaf with a knifeblade and arrange the leaves
over the handle of a wooden spoon to give a naturally curved
effect when dry.

To make fir tree centrepiece Invert a crisp ice cream cone on a
wire rack, spread thinly with royal icing (see page 156) and
attach an overlapping ring of milk chocolate buttons round the
base. Build up more rings, using fewer buttons every time, until
the cone is completely covered. Group a few silver balls on the
top. Mould foil over a clean jam jar top, and attach the 'tree' to
it with more icing. Sift a little icing sugar (U.S. confectioners'
sugar) over it to represent snow. Place in the centre of a plain
iced cake.

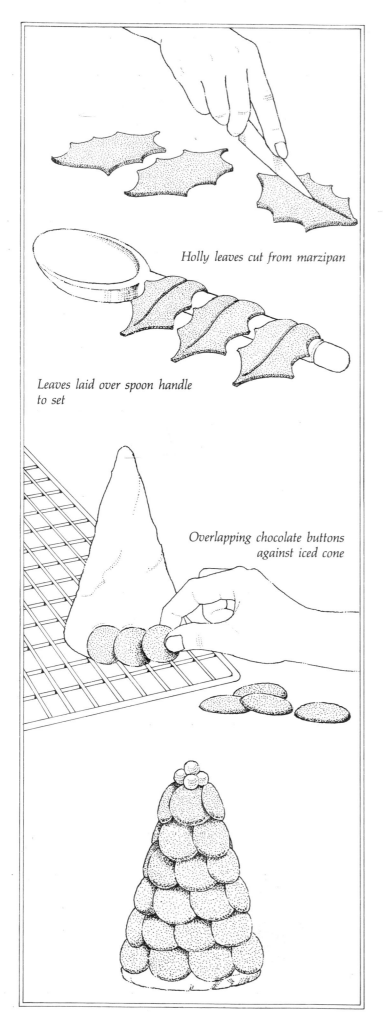

Holly leaves cut from marzipan

Leaves laid over spoon handle
to set

Overlapping chocolate buttons
against iced cone

Tropical Christmas cake

(Illustrated on page 154)

225 g/8 oz plain flour (U.S. 2 cups all-purpose flour)
1 teaspoon baking powder
225 g/8 oz (U.S. 1 cup) butter or margarine
225 g/8 oz caster sugar (U.S. 1 cup granulated sugar)
4 eggs, lightly beaten
50 g/2 oz (U.S. ½ cup) ground almonds
½ teaspoon almond essence (U.S. almond extract)
75 g/3 oz plain chocolate dots (U.S. ½ cup semi-sweet chocolate chips)
10 glacé cherries (U.S. candied cherries), chopped
25 g/1 oz (U.S. ¼ cup) chopped walnuts
25 g/1 oz crystallized ginger, chopped (U.S. scant ¼ cup chopped candied ginger)
DECORATION
3 tablespoons (U.S. 4 tablespoons) apricot jam, sieved
1 tablespoon water
3 rings glacé pineapple (U.S. candied pineapple)
17 glacé cherries (U.S. candied cherries)
14 walnut halves
10 whole almonds
about 25 cm/10 inches wide ribbon

Heat the oven to 140°C/275°F, Gas Mark 1, grease a 20-cm/8-inch cake tin and line it with a double thickness of greaseproof paper (U.S. waxed paper). Tie a double thickness of brown paper round the outside of the tin.

Sift the flour with the baking powder. Cream the butter and sugar in a bowl until light and fluffy. Gradually beat in the egg, then the almonds and almond essence. Fold in the dry ingredients with the chocolate dots, cherries, nuts and ginger. Transfer to the prepared tin and level the surface.

Bake for about 3½ hours, or until a fine skewer inserted in the cake comes out clean, with no uncooked mixture clinging to it. Leave in the tin until cold. If time permits, the texture of the cake is improved if wrapped in foil and stored for up to 1 month before cutting.

Place the cake on a board or plate. Heat the jam with the water in a small pan. Stir until boiling. Remove from the heat. Brush the top of the cake with apricot glaze and lay the pineapple rings across the centre. Put a cherry in each ring and arrange the rest of the cherries and nuts decoratively in rows on either side. Brush generously with the glaze. Finish the cake with a band of ribbon round the middle.

Hazelnut chocolate roulade

175 g/6 oz plain chocolate (U.S. 1 cup semi-sweet chocolate pieces)
2 teaspoons (U.S. 1 tablespoon) instant coffee powder
2 tablespoons (U.S. 3 tablespoons) water
5 eggs, separated
175 g/6 oz caster sugar (U.S. ¾ cup granulated sugar)
icing sugar (U.S. confectioners' sugar) for sprinkling
FILLING
75 g/3 oz plain chocolate (U.S. 3 squares semi-sweet chocolate), grated
50 g/2 oz ground toasted hazelnuts (U.S. ½ cup ground toasted filberts)
1 tablespoon rum or milk
300 ml/½ pint double cream (U.S. 1¼ cups heavy cream), whipped

Make the cake one day, for serving the next. Heat the oven to 180°C/350°F, Gas Mark 4 and line a shallow tin measuring 32.5 cm/13 inches by 22.5 cm/9 inches with non-stick baking parchment (U.S. waxed paper).

Put the chocolate, coffee and water in a bowl and stand this over simmering water until the chocolate has melted. Stir then cool. Put the egg yolks and sugar in a bowl and whisk, if possible using an electric mixer, until pale and thick. Whisk in the chocolate mixture. Put the egg whites in a clean bowl and whisk until stiff. Fold in lightly. Transfer to the prepared tin and level the surface.

Bake for about 15 minutes, or until the crust is firm, although the underneath will still be soft. Remove from the oven, lay a sheet of non-stick baking parchment (U.S. waxed paper) over the cake and cover this with a damp tea towel. Leave at least 8 hours for the crust to soften.

Remove the towel. Transfer the top sheet of parchment to a board and sprinkle thickly with icing sugar. Turn the roulade out on the sugared surface and remove the lining paper. Trim off any hard edges with a sharp knife.

To make the filling, put the chocolate and nuts in a bowl, add the rum and just enough of the cream to make a spreading consistency. Use to lightly cover the roulade. Spread the remaining cream on top. Using the parchment to help lift the roulade, and starting from one short side, roll up carefully and transfer to a serving dish. The surface will probably crack and this is to be expected. Sift more sugar over the roulade before serving.

Siena cake

(Illustrated opposite)

75 g / 3 oz plain chocolate (U.S. ½ cup semi-sweet chocolate pieces)
75 g / 3 oz hazelnuts, chopped (U.S. ¾ cup chopped filberts)
75 g / 3 oz (U.S. ¾ cup) chopped almonds
175 g / 6 oz (U.S. 1 cup) chopped candied peel
50 g / 2 oz plain flour (U.S. ½ cup all-purpose flour), sifted
½ teaspoon ground cinnamon
¼ teaspoon ground mixed spices
100 g / 4 oz (U.S. ⅓ cup) clear honey
100 g / 4 oz caster sugar (U.S. ½ cup granulated sugar)
icing sugar (U.S. confectioners' sugar) for sprinkling
Christmas cake decorations (optional)

Heat the oven to 150°C/300°F, Gas Mark 2 and line a 17.5-cm/7-inch shallow cake tin with non-stick baking parchment (U.S. waxed paper).

Melt the chocolate in a bowl over a pan of hot water. Put the nuts, peel, flour and spices in a bowl and mix well together. Place the honey and sugar in a pan and stir over gentle heat until the sugar has dissolved. Boil steadily for 3 minutes. Remove from the heat and stir in the nut mixture and chocolate. Press into the prepared tin and level the surface.

Bake for 30 minutes. Leave to cool in the tin. Transfer the cake to a serving plate and sift the top with icing sugar. If desired, add Christmas decorations.

Yule log

(Illustrated opposite)

75 g / 3 oz plain chocolate (U.S. ½ cup semi-sweet chocolate pieces)
75 g / 3 oz (U.S. ⅓ cup) butter
1 teaspoon hot water
1 (440-g / 15½-oz) can unsweetened chestnut purée
1 teaspoon ground cinnamon
75 g / 3 oz icing sugar, sifted (U.S. ¾ cup sifted confectioners' sugar)
4 small milk chocolate flakes, chopped
Christmas holly cake decoration
little icing sugar (U.S. confectioners' sugar) for sprinkling

Make the cake the day before you plan to serve it.

Place the chocolate, butter and water in a bowl and stand this over a pan of hot water until the chocolate has melted. Stir to mix. Put the chestnut purée in a bowl and beat until smooth. Blend in the chocolate mixture, cinnamon and sugar.

Chill the mixture for 30 minutes then form it into a log shape and place on a serving dish. Cover the cake with crumbled flake and press in lightly.

Chill for at least 8 hours. Decorate the cake with the holly sprigs and sift these with sugar before serving.

Lebkuchen

(Illustrated opposite)

100 g / 4 oz (U.S. ½ cup) butter
150 g / 5 oz caster sugar (U.S. ⅔ cup granulated sugar)
1 egg, beaten
1 tablespoon set honey
200 g / 7 oz plain flour (U.S. 1¾ cups all-purpose flour)
50 g / 2 oz cornflour (U.S. scant ½ cup cornstarch)
pinch of salt
1½ teaspoons (U.S. 2 teaspoons) ground ginger
½ teaspoon ground cinnamon
¼ teaspoon ground allspice
ICING AND DECORATION
100 g / 4 oz plain chocolate (U.S. ⅔ cup semi-sweet chocolate pieces)
1 tablespoon sweet sherry
50 g / 2 oz (U.S. ¼ cup) butter
50 g / 2 oz icing sugar, sifted (U.S. scant ½ cup sifted confectioners' sugar)
small pieces of glacé cherry (U.S. candied cherry)

Make the dough the day before you intend to bake and decorate the biscuits.

Cream the butter and sugar in a bowl until soft and creamy. Gradually add the egg and honey, beating well after each addition. Sift the flour, cornflour, salt and spices together, add to the creamed mixture and mix to a dough with floured hands. Shape into a ball, place in a plastic bag and chill for at least 8 hours.

Heat the oven to 200°C/400°F, Gas Mark 6 and grease 2 baking sheets (U.S. cookie sheets).

Roll out the dough on a lightly floured surface to a thickness of about 8 mm / ⅓ inch and stamp out 5-cm/2-inch rounds with a plain cutter. Arrange these on the prepared sheets and bake for about 7 minutes, or until pale golden. Turn on to a wire rack to cool.

Place the chocolate, sherry and butter in a bowl and stand this over a pan of hot water until the chocolate has melted. Stir to blend then gradually add the sugar and beat until the mixture is glossy. Coat the biscuits with icing and top each with a piece of cherry. Leave to set before serving.

Above left and centre left: Lebkuchen. Above right: Siena cake. Below: Yule log

Vanilla and chocolate marble ring

(Illustrated opposite)

5 teaspoons cocoa powder (U.S. 2 tablespoons unsweetened cocoa),
sifted
$\frac{1}{2}$ teaspoon instant coffee powder
1 tablespoon hot water
175 g/6 oz (U.S. $\frac{3}{4}$ cup) soft block margarine
175 g/6 oz caster sugar (U.S. $\frac{3}{4}$ cup granulated sugar)
3 eggs, beaten
175 g/6 oz self-raising flour, sifted (U.S. $1\frac{1}{2}$ cups all-purpose flour
sifted with $1\frac{1}{2}$ teaspoons baking powder)
1 teaspoon vanilla essence (U.S. vanilla extract)

Heat the oven to 160°C/325°F, Gas Mark 3 and grease and
flour a 1.4-litre/$2\frac{1}{2}$-pint (U.S. 3-pint) fluted ring tin.
  Mix the cocoa and coffee with the water until smooth. Set
aside. Cream the margarine and sugar in a bowl until light and
fluffy. Gradually beat in the egg and then fold in the flour. Take
half the mixture to a separate bowl and add the blended cocoa.
Flavour the remaining cake mixture with the vanilla essence.
Place alternate tablespoons of the 2 mixtures in the prepared
tin, tap it sharply on a working surface to settle the contents but
do not actually swirl the colours together.
  Bake for about 55 minutes, or until just firm to the touch. Turn
out on a wire rack to cool.

Tutti-frutti morsels

(Illustrated opposite)

100 g/4 oz (U.S. $\frac{2}{3}$ cup) seedless raisins
2 tablespoons (U.S. 3 tablespoons) rum
225 g/8 oz milk chocolate (U.S. $\frac{1}{2}$ lb sweet chocolate)
150 g/5 oz flaked almonds (U.S. $1\frac{1}{4}$ cups slivered almonds),
toasted
6 glacé cherries (U.S. candied cherries), chopped
finely grated rind of $\frac{1}{2}$ orange

Put the raisins in a bowl and pour over the rum. Leave to soak
for at least 4 hours. Set 18 paper petits fours cases on a baking
sheet (U.S. cookie sheet).
  Melt the chocolate in a large bowl over a pan of hot water.
Add the raisins, almonds, cherries and orange rind and mix
quickly until coated with chocolate. Divide among the paper
cases and leave to set.

*Above left: Vanilla and chocolate marble ring. Centre left:
Stripey biscuits (recipe page 164). Centre right: Dougall cake
(recipe page 164). Below right: Chocolate cherry bars (recipe
page 166). Right front: Tutti-frutti morsels*

Dougall cake

(Illustrated on pages 162–163)

50 g/2 oz (¼ cup) soft block margarine
100 g/4 oz caster sugar (U.S. ½ cup granulated sugar)
2 large eggs
100 g/4 oz self-raising flour, sifted (U.S. 1 cup all-purpose flour
sifted with 1 teaspoon baking powder)
extra caster sugar (U.S. granulated sugar) for sprinkling
3 tablespoons (U.S. 4 tablespoons) apricot jam
DECORATION
1 tablespoon cocoa powder (U.S. unsweetened cocoa), sifted
1 tablespoon hot water
250 g/9 oz icing sugar, sifted (U.S. 2 cups sifted confectioners'
sugar)
1 digestive biscuit (U.S. 1 graham cracker)
1 milk chocolate button
1 red and 2 orange-covered chocolate drops
75 g/3 oz (U.S. ⅓ cup) soft block margarine

Heat the oven to 200°C/400°F, Gas Mark 6, grease a shallow tin measuring 27.5 cm/11 inches by 17.5 cm/7 inches, line with greaseproof paper (U.S. waxed paper) and grease the paper.

Put the margarine, sugar, eggs and flour in a bowl and beat with a wooden spoon until well blended. Transfer to the prepared tin and level the surface.

Bake for about 10 minutes, or until firm to the touch. While the cake is baking, place a damp tea-towel on a working surface and cover with a sheet of greaseproof paper (U.S. waxed paper). Sprinkle caster sugar evenly on the paper. Turn the cake out on the sugared paper and remove the lining paper. Trim off the crusty cake edges with a sharp knife and cut a groove across one short side, about 2 cm/¾ inch from the edge. Roll up tightly from this point, rolling the cake and paper together. Place on a wire rack with the end underneath and leave to cool for 20 minutes. Carefully unroll the cake, spread with the jam and roll up again.

Blend the cocoa with the water and leave to cool. Take 25 g/1 oz (U.S. ¼ cup) of the icing sugar and add just enough water to make a thick smooth consistency. Spread this over the biscuit to make a flat surface. When nearly set, press in the chocolate button for the nose and the coloured chocolate drops for the eyes and mouth.

Cream the margarine with the remaining icing sugar until smooth then beat in the blended cocoa. Transfer to a piping bag fitted with a medium-sized star tube. Stick the biscuit 'face' to one end of the cake with a little icing. Place the cake on a serving dish and mark a line lightly down the centre of the top. Using this as a guide, pipe icing in lines from the top down over the cake to the dish along both sides and then over the uncovered end.

Chocolate fondue

(Illustrated opposite)

1 (425-g/15-oz) jar peaches in brandy syrup
225 g/8 oz (U.S. ½ lb) fresh dates
2 bananas, peeled and sliced
2 pears or apples, cored and cut into chunks
juice of 1 lemon
100 g/4 oz icing sugar, sifted (U.S. scant 1 cup sifted
confectioners' sugar)
450 g/1 lb plain chocolate (U.S. 1 lb semi-sweet chocolate), grated
pinch of ground cinnamon
150 ml/¼ pint double cream (U.S. ⅔ cup heavy cream)

Drain the peaches, reserving the syrup, and cut the fruit into chunks. Place the 4 fruits in separate dishes and brush the banana slices and pear or apple pieces with lemon juice. Put the icing sugar in a bowl.

Just before serving time, place the chocolate and cinnamon in the fondue dish. Light the burner and leave the chocolate to melt, stirring occasionally. Gradually blend in the cream then add 3 tablespoons (U.S. 4 tablespoons) of the reserved syrup from the peaches.

Guests should spear a piece of fruit on a fondue fork, dip it in icing sugar and then into the chocolate fondue.

Stripey biscuits

(Illustrated on pages 162–163)

200 g/7 oz (U.S. scant 1 cup) soft block margarine
100 g/4 oz caster sugar (U.S. ½ cup granulated sugar)
275 g/10 oz plain flour (U.S. 2½ cups all-purpose flour), sifted
2 tablespoons cocoa powder (U.S. 3 tablespoons unsweetened
cocoa), sifted

Heat the oven to 190°C/375°F, Gas Mark 5 and have ready 2 baking sheets (U.S. cookie sheets).

Put the margarine and sugar in a bowl. Reserve 2 tablespoons (U.S. 3 tablespoons) of the flour, add the remainder to the bowl and mix to a dough. Divide the dough into 2 portions, knead the cocoa into one and the reserved flour into the other.

Roll out each piece of dough between 2 sheets of non-stick baking parchment (U.S. waxed paper) to a rectangle measuring about 30 cm/12 inches by 20 cm/8 inches. Divide each rectangle in half across then pile them up, alternating light and dark layers. Press firmly and roll out again evenly to a rectangle measuring about 25 cm/10 inches by 20 cm/8 inches.

The most economical way to use the layered dough is to cut it into squares or fingers, but animal shapes are fun and the trimmings, when gathered together and re-rolled, give unusual streaky biscuits. Arrange on the sheets.

Bake for about 10 minutes, or until the pale dough it just turning golden on the edges. Leave on the sheets until firm, then turn on to a wire rack to cool.

Chocolate fondue

Chocolate cherry bars

(Illustrated on pages 162–163)

225 g/8 oz fruit and nut milk chocolate (U.S. ½ lb sweet chocolate
with raisins and nuts)
50 g/2 oz (U.S. ¼ cup) soft block margarine
100 g/4 oz caster sugar (U.S. ½ cup granulated sugar)
1 large egg
100 g/4 oz desiccated coconut (U.S. 1⅓ cups shredded coconut)
8 glacé cherries (U.S. candied cherries), halved
50 g/2 oz (U.S. ⅓ cup) seedless raisins
½ teaspoon vanilla essence (U.S. vanilla extract)
DECORATION
25 g/1 oz plain or milk chocolate (U.S. 1 square semi-sweet or
sweet chocolate)

Heat the oven to 190°C/375°F, Gas Mark 5 and line a 20-
cm/8-inch square tin with non-stick baking parchment (U.S.
waxed paper).

Melt the chocolate in a bowl over a pan of hot water then
spread it over the base of the prepared tin. Chill until set.

Cream the margarine and sugar in a bowl until soft. Add the
egg and beat until pale and creamy. Put in the coconut, cherries,
raisins and vanilla essence and mix well. Spread over the
chocolate base.

Bake for 25 minutes, or until pale golden. Leave to cool in the
tin.

Melt the chocolate for the decoration as above and place in a
paper icing bag (see page 11). Snip off the end and pipe zig-zag
lines over the surface of the cake. When the chocolate has set,
cut into bars.

Robins' nest log

(Illustrated opposite)

75 g/3 oz plain flour (U.S. ¾ cup all-purpose flour)
pinch of salt
3 large eggs
75 g/3 oz caster sugar (U.S. ⅓ cup granulated sugar)
1 teaspoon vanilla essence (U.S. vanilla extract)
extra caster sugar (U.S. granulated sugar)
FILLING AND DECORATION
25 g/1 oz cocoa powder (U.S. ¼ cup unsweetened cocoa), sifted
2 tablespoons (U.S. 3 tablespoons) boiling water
150 g/5 oz (U.S. ⅔ cup) butter or margarine
275 g/10 oz icing sugar, sifted (U.S. 2¼ cups sifted confectioners'
sugar)
1 (200-g/7-oz) pack plain chocolate flavour cake covering (U.S.
7-oz pack semi-sweet chocolate flavor cake covering)
1 tablespoon crumbled shredded wheat cereal or shredded coconut
extra sifted icing sugar (U.S. confectioners' sugar)
two tiny plastic robins

Heat the oven to 200°C/400°F, Gas Mark 6, line a shallow tin
measuring 32.5 cm/13 inches by 22.5 cm/9 inches with
greaseproof paper (U.S. waxed paper), then grease the paper.

Sift the flour with the salt and set aside. Put the eggs and sugar
in a large bowl and set this over a pan of simmering water,
without allowing the base of the bowl to touch the water.
Whisk steadily, preferably with an electric mixer, until thick
and mousse-like. When ready, the mixture falls back on itself in
a firm ribbon when the beaters are lifted. Remove from the heat,
add the vanilla essence and whisk again until cool. Fold in the
dry ingredients. Transfer to the prepared tin and tilt this until
the mixture forms an even layer.

Bake for about 10 minutes, or until firm to the touch in the
centre. While the cake is baking, lay a damp tea-towel on a
working surface and cover with a sheet of greaseproof paper
(U.S. waxed paper). Sprinkle caster sugar evenly over the paper.

Turn the cake out on the sugared surface and peel off the
lining paper. Using a sharp knife, trim the crusty cake edges.
Cut a groove in one short side of the cake, about 2 cm/¾ inch
from the edge. Starting from this end, roll the cake and paper up
tightly together. Place on a wire rack, with the end underneath,
and leave to cool for just 30 minutes.

Meanwhile, make the filling. Blend the cocoa powder with the
water to a smooth cream. Cool. Beat the butter until smooth.
Reserve 25 g/1 oz (U.S. ¼ cup) of the sugar and add the rest to
the butter with the cocoa mixture. Beat until smooth. Add just a
drop or two of water to the remaining sugar to make a firm
mixture. Shape into 4 tiny eggs. Leave to dry.

Unroll the cake carefully and spread it with about three-
quarters of the chocolate butter icing. Roll up again.

Melt the cake covering in a bowl. Take 1 tablespoon and mix
with the cereal or coconut. Mould quickly into a nest shape and
leave to set. Spread the remaining chocolate over the top and
sides of the cake. When it is almost set, score lines in the surface
with a fork. Spread the rest of the butter icing over the ends of
the cake and mark into circles with the fork. Transfer the cake to
a serving dish and sift very lightly with sugar. Set the nest on
the top, put the eggs inside and sit the robins on the nest.

Robins' nest log

Cheery greetings

MAKES 11

(Illustrated below)

100 g / 4 oz (U.S. ½ cup) butter
50 g / 2 oz caster sugar (U.S. ¼ cup granulated sugar)
2 tablespoons mincemeat (U.S. 3 tablespoons fruit mincemeat)
100 g / 4 oz plain flour (U.S. 1 cup all-purpose flour)
50 g / 2 oz cornflour (U.S. scant ½ cup cornstarch)
DECORATION
100 g / 4 oz plain chocolate (U.S. ⅔ cup semi-sweet chocolate pieces)
40 g / 1½ oz (U.S. 3 tablespoons) butter or margarine
1 tablespoon brandy
50 g / 2 oz icing sugar, sifted (U.S. scant ½ cup sifted confectioners' sugar)
little hot water
about 1 metre / 39 inches narrow coloured ribbon

Using a piece of thin card, cut a bottle shape about 12.5 cm / 5 inches high and not more than 6.5 cm / 2½ inches wide to make a template. Grease 2 baking sheets (U.S. cookie sheets).

Cream the butter and sugar in a bowl until light and fluffy. Add the mincemeat. Sift the flour with the cornflour, add to the bowl and mix to a dough. Turn out on a lightly floured surface and roll out to a rectangle measuring about 25 cm / 10 inches by 24 cm / 9½ inches. Place the bottle shape on the bottom left-hand corner of the shortbread and cut out 5 'bottles' in a line. Turn the shape upside down and make 5 more, having the 'necks' of these 'bottles' in between those of the first set. Transfer the shapes carefully to the prepared sheets. Gather up the shortbread trimmings and use to make one more bottle shape, giving 11 in all. Chill for 30 minutes. Meanwhile, heat the oven to 160°C / 325°F, Gas Mark 3.

Bake the bottle biscuits for 20 minutes, or until very pale golden. Leave on the tins until firm then cool on a wire rack. At this stage the biscuits may be stored in an airtight container for a few days.

To decorate, melt the chocolate and butter together in a bowl over a pan of hot water. Stir until blended then add the brandy. Remove from the heat and leave to cool and thicken slightly.

Dip the base of each 'bottle' in chocolate mixture and, using a brush to help, evenly cover the biscuits almost up to the base of the necks on both sides. Then dip the tops in chocolate to make the bottle caps. Place on non-stick baking parchment (U.S. waxed paper) until set.

Mix the icing sugar with just enough water to give a stiff smooth consistency. Place in a paper icing bag (see page 11). Snip off the end and pipe a greeting on each bottle at an angle. Cut the ribbon into 11 equal lengths and finish the biscuits by wrapping a piece of ribbon round the neck of each bottle, securing the ends with dabs of icing. Once decorated, the biscuits should be eaten within 24 hours because they do soften.

Crispie nests

(Illustrated below)

50 g / 2 oz (U.S. ¼ cup) butter
100 g / 4 oz (U.S. ¼ lb) marshmallows
100 g / 4 oz (U.S. 4 cups) cornflakes or crisp rice cereal
225 g / 8 oz (U.S. ½ lb) miniature sugar-coated chocolate eggs

Stand 18 paper cake cases in bun tins (U.S. muffin pans) if possible, or on a flat tray.

Place the butter and marshmallows in a large pan and heat gently, stirring occasionally, until melted. Stir in the cereal until coated.

Divide evenly among the paper cases, then press the mixture in each case with the back of a spoon so that it will hold together, and form a hollow in the centre. Leave to get quite cold then fill each nest with eggs.

Speckled meringue nests

3 large egg whites
175 g / 6 oz caster sugar (U.S. ¾ cup granulated sugar)
100 g / 4 oz plain chocolate (U.S. 4 squares semi-sweet chocolate), grated
300 ml / ½ pint (U.S. 1¼ cups) whipping cream, whipped
24 miniature chocolate eggs or 225 g / 8 oz marzipan (U.S. ½ lb almond marzipan), formed into 24 'eggs'

Heat the oven to 130°C / 250°F, Gas Mark ¼ and line a baking sheet (U.S. cookie sheet) with non-stick baking parchment (U.S. waxed paper).

Put the egg whites in a large bowl and whisk until stiff. Gradually add the sugar, a tablespoon at a time, whisking vigorously after each addition until the meringue is firm and glossy. Fold in the chocolate. Spoon out into 8 even-sized heaps on the lined sheet, leaving space between, then hollow out the centre of each, to make a nest shape.

Bake for about 2½ hours, or until the nests lift easily from the parchment. Cool on a wire rack. The unfilled nests can be stored in an airtight container for up to 1 week.

Fill each nest with cream then rest 3 eggs lightly on top. Best eaten within 2 hours of making.

Woodland cottage cake

===== SERVES 8–10 =====

175 g / 6 oz (U.S. ¾ cup) butter or margarine
175 g / 6 oz caster sugar (U.S. ¾ cup granulated sugar)
3 eggs
1 teaspoon vanilla essence (U.S. vanilla extract)
175 g / 6 oz self-raising flour, sifted (U.S. 1½ cups all-purpose flour
sifted with 1½ teaspoons baking powder)
BUTTER ICING
275 g / 10 oz (U.S. 1¼ cups) butter or margarine
450 g / 1 lb icing sugar (U.S. confectioners' sugar), sifted
25 g / 1 oz cocoa powder (U.S. ¼ cup unsweetened cocoa)
little boiling water
DECORATION
36 chocolate finger biscuits
few sugar flower cake decorations
few angelica 'diamonds'
50 g / 2 oz desiccated coconut (U.S. ⅔ cup shredded coconut,
chopped)
green food colouring

Heat the oven to 180°C/350°F, Gas Mark 4, grease a 17.5-cm/7-inch square cake tin and line with greaseproof paper (U.S. waxed paper).

Cream the butter with the sugar until light and fluffy then add the eggs, one at a time, with the vanilla, beating well after each addition. Fold in the flour and transfer to the prepared tin. Hollow out the centre slightly so that the baked cake will be flat.

Bake for about 55 minutes, or until firm to the touch. Leave in the tin for 5 minutes then turn out on a wire rack, remove the lining paper and leave to cool.

To make up the icing, cream the butter and sugar together until soft and smooth. Reserve 3 rounded tablespoons (U.S. 4 rounded tablespoons) of the white icing for the decoration. Blend the cocoa with enough hot water to make a smooth paste and beat into the remaining icing.

Next, cut the cake into sections as shown here. Remove a 7.5-cm/3-inch strip off one side of the cake and cut this strip diagonally in half. Position the two pieces, 'back-to-back' to make a roof shape and trim away 1.25 cm/½ inch from the thin pointed 'sides' with a sharp knife. Split the large piece of cake into two layers and sandwich together again with some of the chocolate butter icing. Spread more icing over the top. Stick the two pieces of the roof together with icing and press lightly in place on the large cake. Mask the cake completely with icing, smoothing it with a palette knife (U.S. spatula) dipped in hot water and shaken. Position the cake carefully on a rectangular cake board or tray large enough to leave a 7.5-cm/3-inch border all round.

In the centre of the pitched roof, cut out a flat niche 1.25-cm/½-inch deep to make a level surface to support the finger biscuits for the chimney. Fill in with a dab of icing. Cut 2 biscuits in half and place, cut sides downwards, in the centre position for the chimney. Lay one biscuit on either side of this group to make a ridgepole. Arrange 16 biscuits, close together, on either side of these, to fill in the pitched roof.

Put the white icing in a piping bag fitted with a plain writing tube. On one side pipe in 2 windows and a front door, 2 windows on the opposite side and one window on each end.

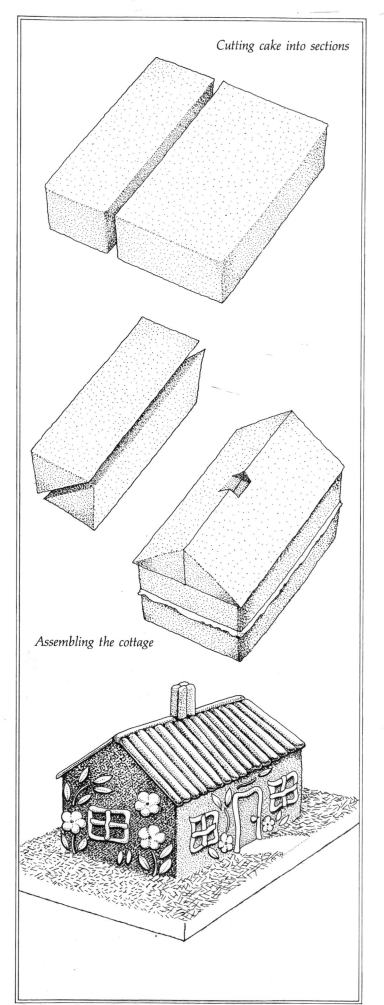

Cutting cake into sections

Assembling the cottage

Before the icing is set, press in sugar flowers and leaves made with pieces of angelica to decorate the cottage.

Put the coconut in a bowl, add 2–3 drops of food colouring and mix with a wooden spoon until the coconut is pale green. Arrange it in a border round the cottage to make a lawn.

Chestnut chocolate cake

=== SERVES 6–8 ===

100 g/4 oz plain chocolate (U.S. ⅔ cup semi-sweet chocolate pieces) pieces)
3 tablespoons (U.S. 4 tablespoons) water
4 large eggs, separated
225 g/8 oz caster sugar (U.S. 1 cup granulated sugar)
1 (225-g/8-oz) can unsweetened chestnut purée
FILLING
3 tablespoons (U.S. 4 tablespoons) water
100 g/4 oz plain chocolate (U.S. ⅔ cup semi-sweet chocolate pieces)
2 egg yolks
225 ml/8 fl oz double cream (U.S. 1 cup heavy cream)
¼ teaspoon vanilla essence (U.S. vanilla extract)
1 teaspoon caster sugar (U.S. granulated sugar)

Heat the oven to 180°C/350°F, Gas Mark 4, grease 2 × 22.5-cm/9-inch shallow cake tins and line with non-stick baking parchment (U.S. waxed paper).

Put the chocolate and water in a bowl and stand this over a pan of hot water until the chocolate has melted. Stir to mix then cool. Put the egg yolks and sugar in a large bowl and stand this over simmering water, without allowing the base to touch the water. Whisk, if possible with an electric mixer, until thick and mousse-like. When ready, the mixture falls back on itself in a thick ribbon when the beaters are lifted. Remove from the heat and whisk until cool. Whisk in the chocolate mixture then the chestnut purée. Whisk the egg whites in a clean bowl until stiff. Fold into the chocolate mixture. Divide between the prepared tins.

Bake for about 35 minutes, or until just firm to the touch. Leave to stand for 5 minutes then turn out on a wire rack, peel off the lining paper and cool.

To make the filling, put the water in a small pan with the chocolate. Place over very gentle heat, stirring frequently, until the chocolate has melted. Bring to boiling point and whisk in the egg yolks. Cool. Whip the cream until thick, add the vanilla essence and sugar and whisk again. Then fold in the chocolate mixture lightly to give a streaky appearance.

Sandwich the cake layers together with half the filling and top with the remainder.

Chocolate cream brandy snaps

=== MAKES ABOUT 20 ===

75 g/3 oz (U.S. ⅓ cup) butter
75 g/3 oz caster sugar (U.S. ⅓ cup granulated sugar)
3 tablespoons golden syrup (U.S. 4 tablespoons light corn syrup)
75 g/3 oz plain flour (U.S. ¾ cup all-purpose flour), sifted
¾ teaspoon ground ginger
1 teaspoon brandy
FILLING
225 ml/8 fl oz double cream (U.S. 1 cup heavy cream)
1 teaspoon brandy or ¼ teaspoon vanilla essence (U.S. vanilla extract)
75 g/3 oz plain chocolate (U.S. 3 squares semi-sweet chocolate), very finely grated

Heat the oven to 180°C/350°F, Gas Mark 4, grease several baking sheets (U.S. cookie sheets) and the handle of a wooden spoon.

Put the butter, sugar and syrup in a pan and place over gentle heat until the butter melts. Remove from the heat and mix in the flour, ginger and brandy. Put teaspoons of the mixture on one prepared sheet, allowing plenty of room for spreading (at least 10 cm/4 inches). Keep the rest of the mixture warm and bake only one sheet of snaps at a time.

Bake for about 7 minutes, but check after 5 minutes. The biscuits (U.S. cookies) are ready when uniformly golden brown. Meanwhile, prepare another sheet. Remove the first sheet of cookies and put the second in the oven. Leave the baked snaps to stand for 1–2 minutes, or until it is possible to slip a spatula underneath one and lift it. Wrap around the prepared spoon handle, with the smooth side inwards. Hold with your hand for a second or two then remove to a wire rack and leave to cool. Curl the remaining snaps in the same way. If they should harden on the sheet before rolling, return to the oven for about 1 minute and they will soften again. Unfilled snaps store well in an airtight container.

Just before serving time, make the filling. Whip the cream until it starts to thicken. Add the brandy or vanilla essence and whip until it holds its shape well. Fold in the chocolate and transfer to a piping bag fitted with a medium-sized star tube. Pipe chocolate cream into both ends of each brandy snap. Best eaten within 2 hours of filling.

Mushroom meringues

MAKES ABOUT 25, DEPENDING ON SIZE

4 egg whites
¼ teaspoon cream of tartar
225 g/8 oz caster sugar (U.S. 1 cup granulated sugar)
cocoa powder (U.S. unsweetened cocoa) for sifting

Heat the oven to 130°C/250°F, Gas Mark ½ and line 2 baking sheets (U.S. cookie sheets) with non-stick baking parchment (U.S. waxed paper).

Put the egg whites and cream of tartar in a bowl and whisk until stiff. Gradually add the sugar, a tablespoon at a time, whisking vigorously after each addition until the meringue is firm and glossy. Reserve about 100 ml/4 fl oz (U.S. ½ cup) of the meringue. Place the rest in a piping bag fitted with a 1.25-cm/½-inch plain tube.

Pipe out rounds about 4 cm/1½ inches in diameter on one lined sheet, leaving a little room between them. These are the mushroom 'caps'. Using a dampened finger, smooth over the piped mounds so that they are completely round. Sift cocoa very lightly over the tops.

Next pipe the 'stalks'. These are smaller rounds, drawn up into a short stem and ending in a point. The stalks should be about 5 cm/2 inches long, including the point.

Bake the mushroom caps and stalks for about 40 minutes, or until they feel hard on the outside. Remove from the oven.

To assemble the mushrooms, take a cap in one hand and a sharp pointed knife in the other. Using the point, bore a small hole in the flat base of each mushroom 'cap'. Dip the pointed end of a 'stalk' into the uncooked meringue and insert into the hole. The soft meringue will hold it in place. Put the assembled mushrooms back on the trays and return to the oven for a further 15 minutes, or until the soft meringue is dry.

Golden straw balls

MAKES 10

(Illustrated opposite)

225 g/8 oz moist chocolate cake, crumbled (U.S. 4 cups coarsely
crumbled moist chocolate cake)
50 g/2 oz (U.S. ½ cup) ground almonds
½ teaspoon almond essence (U.S. almond extract)
25 g/1 oz (U.S. 2 tablespoons) butter or margarine, melted
100 g/4 oz (U.S. 1⅓ cups) shredded coconut
yellow food colouring
about 1 tablespoon golden syrup (U.S. light corn syrup)

Combine the cake crumbs, almonds and almond essence in a bowl. Add the butter and mix well until the ingredients will hold together. Divide into 10 equal portions and shape each into a ball. Place on a dish and chill for 10 minutes.

Put the coconut in a bowl, sprinkle in a few drops of food colouring and mix with a wooden spoon until the coconut is evenly coloured. Spread the coconut on a plate. Put the syrup in a small bowl and warm slightly.

Brush each ball with syrup then roll in coconut until completely covered.

Golden straw balls

Bunny-hop cake

SERVES 8–10

200 ml/7 fl oz (U.S. scant 1 cup) water
50 g/2 oz cocoa powder (U.S. $\frac{1}{2}$ cup unsweetened cocoa)
100 g/4 oz (U.S. $\frac{1}{2}$ cup) soft margarine
275 g/10 oz caster sugar (U.S. $1\frac{1}{4}$ cups granulated sugar)
2 eggs
pinch of salt
175 g/6 oz plain flour (U.S. $1\frac{1}{2}$ cups all-purpose flour)
1 teaspoon bicarbonate of soda (U.S. baking soda)
$\frac{1}{4}$ teaspoon baking powder
DECORATION
75 g/3 oz plain chocolate (U.S. $\frac{1}{2}$ cup semi-sweet chocolate pieces)
FILLING AND COATING
175 g/6 oz (U.S. $\frac{3}{4}$ cup) butter or margarine
350 g/12 oz icing sugar, sifted (U.S. $2\frac{2}{3}$ cups sifted confectioners'
sugar)
1 teaspoon almond essence (U.S. almond extract)
few drops of green food colouring
50 g/2 oz flaked almonds (U.S. $\frac{1}{2}$ cup slivered almonds), toasted
and roughly chopped
350 g/12 oz (U.S. $\frac{3}{4}$ lb) white marzipan

Heat the oven to 180°C/350°F, Gas Mark 4, grease a 20-cm/8-inch cake tin and line with greaseproof paper (U.S. waxed paper).

Gradually mix the water into the cocoa until smooth. Place in a bowl and add all the remaining ingredients for the cake. Beat with a wooden spoon until well blended. Transfer to the prepared tin and level the surface.

Bake for about 1 hour, or until firm to the touch. Leave to cool in the tin.

Meanwhile, make the bunny decorations. Melt the chocolate in a bowl over a pan of hot water. Using the drawing here as a guide, make 8 'piped and flooded' bunny shapes (see page 11). Chill until firm.

To make the icing, cream the butter until soft then add the sugar and almond flavouring and beat until fluffy. Tint pale green with food colouring. Take a generous one third of the icing and fold in the nuts. Split the cake into 2 layers and sandwich together with nut icing. Spread more icing thinly over the top and sides of the cake.

Roll out the marzipan and cut a 20-cm/8-inch circle for the top of the cake, and a strip long enough to fit round the side of the cake and exactly the same depth. Press on the side covering first, joining the edges neatly. Then position the top piece and smooth the marzipan lightly with your fingertips to make the cake a good shape.

Put the remaining green icing in a piping bag fitted with a medium-sized star tube and pipe rosettes all round the top edge of the cake to cover the join in the marzipan, pulling each rosette up into a point as you pipe. Use up the rest of the icing in the bag by piping small rosettes around the base of the cake. Position the bunnies so that they are 'leaping' over the green 'grass' border on top of the cake.

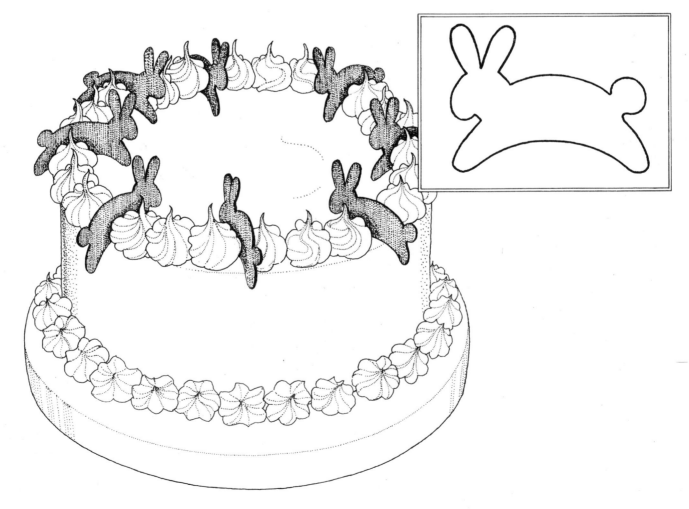

Birthday rose cake

(Illustrated below)

75 g/3 oz plain chocolate (U.S. ½ cup semi-sweet chocolate pieces)
350 g/12 oz plain flour (U.S. 3 cups all-purpose flour)
½ teaspoon salt
½ teaspoon baking powder
¾ teaspoon bicarbonate of soda (U.S. baking soda)
1 large egg
1 tablespoon oil
75 g/3 oz (U.S. ⅓ cup soft margarine)
250 g/9 oz caster sugar (U.S. generous 1 cup granulated sugar)
100 ml/4 fl oz (U.S. ½ cup) natural yogurt
75 ml/3 fl oz (U.S. ⅓ cup) water
FILLING AND DECORATION
75 g/3 oz (U.S. generous ⅓ cup) butter or margarine
250 g/9 oz icing sugar, sifted (U.S. 2 cups sifted confectioners'
sugar)
2–3 tablespoons (U.S. 3–4 tablespoons) triple distilled rose water
few drops red food colouring
1 teaspoon warm water
birthday candles and candle-holders
bought moulded pink sugar roses

Heat the oven to 180°C/350°F, Gas Mark 4, grease 2 × 20-cm/8-inch shallow cake tins and line the bases with greaseproof paper (U.S. waxed paper).

Melt the chocolate in a bowl over a pan of hot water. Sift the flour with the salt, baking powder and bicarbonate of soda into a large bowl. Put in the egg, oil, margarine, sugar, yogurt and water and beat, using an electric mixer if possible, until smooth. Add the chocolate and continue beating at high speed for 3 minutes. Divide between the prepared tins and level the surface. Bake for about 25 minutes, or until firm to the touch. Turn out on a wire rack, peel off the lining paper and leave to cool.

To make the filling, put the butter and half the icing sugar in a bowl and beat until smooth. Flavour with 4 teaspoons (U.S. 2 tablespoons) rose water and tint pale pink with food colouring. Use to sandwich the cakes together and transfer to a serving plate.

Place the remaining icing sugar in a bowl and mix in the water and then enough rose water to make a stiff smooth consistency. Tint pale pink with food colouring. Take half the icing to another bowl and tint a darker shade of pink with an extra drop or two of food colouring. Place the darker icing in a paper icing bag (see page 11).

Spread the paler icing over the top of the cake, being careful not to lift the surface. Leave to set for 15 minutes. Snip off the end of the icing bag and pipe a row of plain dots around the edge of the cake. Pipe the required name in the centre of the cake. Press the candles into the holders and push these into the cake above the piped name, alternating them with sugar roses. Arrange the remaining roses decoratively in groups.

NOTE To make emergency candle holders, hollow out the centre of sugar roses with the tip of a knife and stick the candles in with dabs of icing.

Celebration centrepiece

(Illustrated opposite)

30 sponge fingers (U.S. *ladyfingers*)
12 small milk chocolate flakes
2 tablespoons (U.S. 3 tablespoons) lime juice cordial
FILLING
2 tablespoons (U.S. 3 tablespoons) water
15 g/½ oz powdered gelatine (U.S. 1 envelope gelatin)
175 g/6 oz plain chocolate (U.S. 1 cup semi-sweet chocolate pieces)
4 eggs, separated
2 teaspoons instant coffee powder
150 ml/¼ pint double cream (U.S. ⅔ cup heavy cream)
4 tablespoons (U.S. 6 tablespoons) milk
1-metre/39-inch length wide ribbon

Trim 20 of the sponge fingers so that they are the same length as the flakes. Line a 20-cm/8-inch loose-based cake tin with these fingers and 10 of the flakes, standing the biscuits in pairs, sugared sides towards the tin, with a flake between each pair.

Crumble up the remaining sponge fingers and the trimmings, place in a bowl and sprinkle over the cordial. Stir lightly then press this mixture into the base of the tin.

To make the filling, put the water in a small bowl and sprinkle on the gelatine. Leave to stand for 5 minutes then place over hot water until the gelatine has completely dissolved. Cool. Melt the chocolate in a large bowl over the pan of hot water. Stir in the egg yolks, coffee and dissolved gelatine. Whisk the egg whites in a clean bowl and fold into the chocolate mixture. Pour into the cake tin and leave for several hours to set.

Whip the cream with the milk until just holding its shape. Spread over the chocolate mousse in the tin. Crumble the remaining flakes and scatter on top.

Carefully push up the base of the tin and transfer the dessert, still on the metal base, to a serving dish. Tie the ribbon around the centre to support the sponge fingers and flakes and tie into a bow.

VARIATION

Syllabub centrepiece Make a syllabub instead of the chocolate filling. Finely grate the rind and squeeze the juice of 2 lemons. Mix with 175 g/6 oz caster sugar (U.S. ¾ cup granulated sugar) and leave to stand for 30 minutes, stirring occasionally. Meanwhile, dissolve 15 g/½ oz powdered gelatine (U.S. 1 envelope gelatin) in 2 tablespoons (U.S. 3 tablespoons) water. Whisk 450 ml/¾ pint double cream (U.S. 2 cups heavy cream) until thick then whisk in the lemon juice mixture, 3 tablespoons (U.S. 4 tablespoons) each brandy and sweet sherry and the dissolved gelatine. Pour the syllabub into the loose-based tin and chill until set. Remove the sides of the tin, stand chocolate finger biscuits round the dessert instead of the flakes and sponge fingers and finish with the ribbon.

Chestnut ambrosia

(Illustrated opposite)

175 g/6 oz (U.S. ¾ cup) butter
175 g/6 oz caster sugar (U.S. ¾ cup granulated sugar)
275 g/10 oz plain chocolate (U.S. 1⅔ cup semi-sweet chocolate pieces)
2 teaspoons (U.S. 1 tablespoon) instant coffee powder
2 tablespoons (U.S. 3 tablespoons) water
1 tablespoon rum, brandy or defrosted frozen orange concentrate
1 (440-g/15½-oz) can unsweetened chestnut purée

Brush a 1-kg/2-lb loaf-shaped tin very lightly with oil.

Cream the butter and sugar in a bowl until pale and smooth. Reserve 25 g/1 oz (U.S. scant ¼ cup) of the chocolate. Break up the remainder and place in a bowl with the coffee, water and rum. Stand the bowl over hot water until the chocolate melts. Stir lightly to blend. Gradually beat the chestnut purée and chocolate mixture into the butter and sugar until quite smooth. Transfer to the prepared tin and level the top. Chill overnight.

Gently ease the mixture away from the tin and turn out on a serving plate.

Melt the remaining chocolate and trickle it over the top of the dessert. Serve with 'langue de chat' biscuits (U.S. thin sweet cookies).

Walnut dacquoise

75 g/3 oz (U.S. ¾ cup) chopped walnuts or pecans
4 egg whites
pinch of cream of tartar
225 g/8 oz caster sugar (U.S. 1 cup granulated sugar)
100 g/4 oz plain chocolate (U.S. ¼-lb bar semi-sweet chocolate)
150 ml/¼ pint double cream (U.S. ⅔ cup heavy cream)
icing sugar (U.S. confectioners' sugar) for sprinkling

Heat the oven to 140°C/275°F, Gas Mark 1. Have ready 2 sheets of non-stick baking parchment (U.S. waxed paper), draw a 20-cm/8-inch circle on each and place the parchment on baking sheets (U.S. cookie sheets).

Toast the nuts lightly, then grind them in a food processor or blender until fine but not oily. Put the egg whites in a large bowl and whisk until stiff. Add the cream of tartar and then the sugar, a tablespoon at a time, whisking vigorously after each addition until the meringue is firm and glossy. Fold in the nuts then spread the mixture inside the marked circles.

Bake for about 1 hour, or until the meringue layers lift off clearly when the parchment is peeled away. Move carefully to a wire rack and leave until cool.

Make some large chocolate curls, using up about half the chocolate (see page 10). Finely grate the remainder. Whip the cream and fold in the grated chocolate. Use to sandwich the meringue layers together and transfer to a serving dish. Arrange the chocolate curls on top and sift lightly with sugar.

Above: Celebration centrepiece. Below: Chestnut ambrosia

Sunny secret cake

SERVES 8

(Illustrated opposite)

50 g/2 oz plain flour (U.S. ½ cup all-purpose flour)
25 g/1 oz cocoa powder (U.S. ¼ cup unsweetened cocoa)
pinch of salt
3 large eggs
75 g/3 oz caster sugar (U.S. ⅓ cup granulated sugar)
extra caster sugar (U.S. granulated sugar)
FILLING AND DECORATION
150 g/5 oz (U.S. ⅓ cup) butter or margarine
225 g/8 oz icing sugar, sifted (U.S. 1⅔ cups sifted confectioners'
sugar)
4 teaspoons (U.S. 2 tablespoons) lemon juice
few drops yellow food colouring
4 tablespoons (U.S. 6 tablespoons) lemon jelly marmalade
birthday candles and holders (optional)

Heat the oven to 200°C/400°F, Gas Mark 6, line a shallow tin measuring 32.5 cm/13 inches by 22.5 cm/9 inches with greaseproof paper (U.S. waxed paper), then grease the paper.

Sift the flour with the cocoa powder and salt and set aside. Put the eggs and sugar in a large bowl and stand this over a pan of simmering water, without allowing the base of the bowl to touch the water. Whisk steadily, with an electric mixer if possible, until thick. When ready, the mixture will fall back on itself in a firm ribbon when the beaters are lifted. Remove from the heat and continue whisking until cool. Fold in the dry ingredients thoroughly. Transfer to the prepared tin and tilt this until the surface is level.

Bake for about 10 minutes, or until the centre of the cake springs back when lightly pressed with a fingertip. While the cake is baking, lay a damp tea-towel on a working surface and cover this with a sheet of greaseproof paper (U.S. waxed paper). Sprinkle caster sugar evenly over the paper.

Turn the cake out on the sugared surface and peel off the lining paper. Trim off the crusty cake edges with a sharp knife. Cut a groove in one short side of the cake, about 2 cm/¾ inch from the edge. Starting from this end, roll the cake and paper together. Place on a wire rack, with the end underneath, and leave to cool for just 30 minutes.

Meanwhile, make the filling. Beat the butter with the sugar and lemon juice until smooth. Tint pale yellow with food colouring. Carefully unroll the cake and spread it first with marmalade and then thinly with butter icing. Roll the cake up again and place on a serving dish. Spread the butter icing over the cake and mark the surface decoratively with the tip of a round-bladed knife. Press birthday candles and holders along the top of the cake if wished.

Sunny secret cake

Miniature Christmas 'puddings'

MAKES ABOUT 10

100 g/4 oz plain chocolate (U.S. ⅔ cup semi-sweet chocolate pieces)
25 g/1 oz (U.S. 1¼ cups) crisp rice cereal
1 tablespoon chopped preserved ginger
1 tablespoon chopped glacé cherries (U.S. candied cherries)
1 tablespoon chopped dried apricots
1 tablespoon chopped dried prunes
1 tablespoon chopped dried dates
DECORATION
50 g/2 oz icing sugar, sifted (U.S. scant ½ cup sifted confectioners'
sugar)
tiny pieces of glacé cherry (U.S. candied cherry) and angelica

Have ready about 10 pieces of cling film, each very roughly 12.5-cm/5-inches square.

Melt the chocolate in a large bowl over a pan of hot water then mix in the cereal, ginger and fruit until coated. Divide the mixture into even-sized heaps on the pieces of film. Gather each 'pudding' up to make a ball and twist the ends of the film to secure. Arrange on a baking sheet (U.S. cookie sheet), pressing each one slightly to give it a flat base. Chill until firm.

Mix the sugar with just enough water to give a smooth thick icing. Unwrap the puddings and spoon a little icing over the top of each one so that it just starts to trickle down the sides. Decorate with a tiny piece of cherry and 2 pieces of angelica on each small pudding before the icing has fully set.

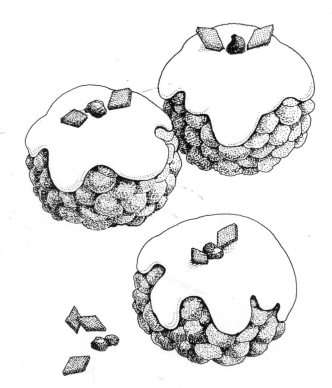

Drinks and Sauces

The trio of hot drinks preferred around the world can easily be named; tea, coffee and chocolate. Of these, tea is usually drunk with lemon or with milk. Coffee combines with milk or cream and most deliciously with chocolate, in the proportions you prefer. As little as a sprinkling of cocoa powder over a cloud of whipped cream topping the coffee; or as much as a spoonful of strong brewed coffee in a cup of frothy chocolate. Chocolate is not only a partner in many coffee drinks, it is delectable on its own, made with milk and cocoa powder, and sweetened to taste. Try any of the intriguing recipes that follow in this section. Or keep a blend of spiced cocoa ready for making up an exotic drink. You'll need a pinch of salt and 3 tablespoons (U.S. 4 tablespoons) sugar to 50 g/2 oz cocoa powder (U.S. $\frac{1}{2}$ cup unsweetened cocoa) plus $\frac{1}{2}$ teaspoon ground cinnamon and a pinch of ground nutmeg. Put all together in a screw-topped jar, shake well to blend and keep tightly closed. This amount would produce 6 good-sized cups of spiced cocoa for a bedtime drink. Fluff it up to a foam with a whisk, which prevents a skin from forming.

A chocolate syrup you can keep in the refrigerator for at least a week is handy to have in store. Make it in a bowl over hot water, first melting 100 g/4 oz plain chocolate (U.S. $\frac{2}{3}$ cup semi-sweet chocolate pieces) then stirring in a small can (198 g/7 oz) sweetened condensed milk and 100 g/4 oz (U.S. $\frac{1}{2}$ cup) sugar. Keep stirring until the sugar is dissolved, then remove from the bowl and allow to cool. Pour into an airtight container and use as required, blended with ice-cold milk or vanilla ice cream.

A drift of cocoa powder over a coffee drink intensifies the flavour; and a sprinkle of cinnamon or nutmeg does wonders for most chocolate drinks, hot or cold. Invalids who would not tolerate a raw egg whisked into a vanilla flavoured egg nog, find it quite acceptable when added to a chocolate flavoured one.

Sweet sauces can be made with cocoa powder or melted chocolate, the latter being generally richer and more expensive. To give chocolate cornflour custard a shine – stir in a few small dice of butter while it is still hot. One last word on chocolate sauces: be adventurous and serve Molé sauce with turkey. Make a fiery, spicy tomato sauce using the turkey stock; add toasted sesame seeds, pine nuts and blanched almonds. Pour it over cooked turkey portions and heat up. Just before serving, fold grated bitter chocolate into the sauce, allowing 1 tablespoon chocolate to sufficient turkey and Molé to serve 4 people generously.

Above: Chocolate ice cream soda (recipe page 182).
Below: Choc-o-mint flip (recipe page 182)

Chocolate ice cream soda

(Illustrated on page 180)

2 tablespoons (U.S. 3 tablespoons) chocolate syrup (see page 181)
½ teaspoon vanilla essence (U.S. vanilla extract)
150 ml/¼ pint (U.S. ⅔ cup) chilled milk
300 ml/½ pint fizzy lemonade (U.S. 1¼ cups 7-up)
2 scoops vanilla ice cream
2 glacé cherries (U.S. candied cherries)

Stir the chocolate syrup and vanilla essence into the milk and when blended mix in the lemonade. Divide between 2 tall glasses and top with the ice cream. Balance a cherry on each soda and serve immediately with long sundae spoons.

Choc-o-mint flip

(Illustrated on page 180)

300 ml/½ pint (U.S. 1¼ cups) milk
2 tablespoons drinking chocolate powder (U.S. 3 tablespoons sweetened cocoa)
2 tablespoons (U.S. 3 tablespoons) crème de menthe
50 ml/2 fl oz double cream (U.S. ¼ cup heavy cream), whipped
little extra drinking chocolate powder (U.S. sweetened cocoa) for sprinkling
few chocolate dots (U.S. chocolate chips)

Heat the milk in a pan to boiling point. Remove from the heat and whisk in the drinking chocolate powder and liqueur. Finally, add the cream and whisk in lightly. Pour at once into 2 warmed mugs. The cream will rise and make a foamy head on the drinks. Top each with a tiny pinch of drinking chocolate powder and a few chocolate dots.

Mexican coffee

(Illustrated opposite)

300 ml/½ pint (U.S. 1¼ cups) freshly made strong black coffee
25 g 1 oz bitter or plain chocolate (U.S. 1 square unsweetened or semi-sweet chocolate), roughly chopped
2 tablespoons (U.S. 3 tablespoons) Kahlua or Tia Maria
2 pinches of ground nutmeg
sugar to sweeten (optional)
3–4 tablespoons (U.S. 4–6 tablespoons) whipped cream
little grated chocolate
little grated orange rind

Divide the coffee between 2 warmed glasses or cups and stir half the chocolate into each until it has melted. Stir in the liqueur, nutmeg and sugar to taste if desired. Top each drink with a cap of whipped cream sprinkled with chocolate and orange rind. Sip the coffee through the cream layer and serve with delicate biscuits such as 'langues de chat' (U.S. thin sweet cookies).

Bali-hi

1 fresh coconut, sawn in half, reserving the 'milk'
150 ml/¼ pint (U.S. ⅔ cup) milk
150 ml/¼ pint soda water (U.S. ⅔ cup club soda)
150 ml/¼ pint (U.S. ⅔ cup) pineapple juice
1 egg white
1 tablespoon icing sugar (U.S. confectioners' sugar)
2 tablespoons (U.S. 3 tablespoons) Crème de cacao
little grated chocolate

Stand each coconut 'cup' in a grapefruit dish. Strain the coconut 'milk' through a fine sieve into a bowl. Scrape the coconut flesh in each half shell with a tablespoon and add the pulp to the bowl. Put in the milk, soda water and pineapple juice and whisk vigorously or process in a food processor or blender. Divide between the coconut 'cups'.

Whisk the egg white in a clean bowl until stiff, add the sugar and whisk until firm and glossy. Whisk in the liqueur and float the mixture on the drinks. Sprinkle with chocolate and insert 2 long straws into each drink through the topping.

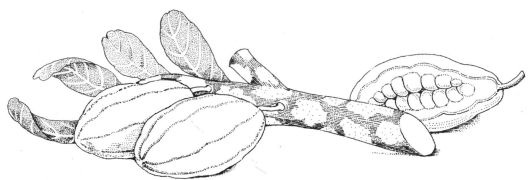

Mexican coffee

Rum warmer

SERVES 2

(Illustrated opposite)

300 ml/$\frac{1}{2}$ pint (U.S. 1$\frac{1}{4}$ cups) milk
2 teaspoons (U.S. 1 tablespoon) brown sugar, or to taste
1 egg yolk
2 teaspoons cocoa powder (U.S. 1 tablespoon unsweetened cocoa),
sifted
2 teaspoons (U.S. 1 tablespoon) freeze-dried instant coffee granules
1 tablespoon rum

Put the milk, sugar, egg yolk and cocoa in a pan and whisk over moderate heat until the mixture comes to boiling point. Remove from the heat and whisk in the coffee and rum. Pour immediately into 2 warmed glasses or cups.

Exotic cinnamon coffee

SERVES 2

(Illustrated opposite)

1 tablespoon (U.S. 4 teaspoons) freeze-dried instant coffee granules
300 ml/$\frac{1}{2}$ pint (U.S. 1$\frac{1}{4}$ cups) water
2 teaspoons (U.S. 1 tablespoon) brown sugar, or to taste
2 cinnamon sticks
2 teaspoons drinking chocolate powder (U.S. 1 tablespoon sweetened
cocoa)
2 tablespoons (U.S. 3 tablespoons) whipped cream

Put the coffee, water, sugar and cinnamon sticks in a pan and bring to the boil. Stir, draw off the heat and allow the bubbles to subside. Reboil the mixture again in the same way then remove from the heat and take out the cinnamon sticks. Whisk in the drinking chocolate powder and strain into 2 warmed glasses or cups. Serve at once topped with whipped cream. Serve with the cinnamon sticks as 'stirrers' if desired.

Iced chocolate egg nog

SERVES 2

2 eggs
50 ml/2 fl oz (U.S. $\frac{1}{4}$ cup) brandy
50 ml/2 fl oz (U.S. $\frac{1}{4}$ cup) chocolate syrup (see page 181)
350 ml/12 fl oz (U.S. 1$\frac{1}{2}$ cups) cold milk
6 ice cubes
little ground nutmeg

Put the eggs, brandy, chocolate syrup and milk in a blender and process until foamy. Place the ice cubes in 2 tall glasses and pour the egg nog over. Serve sprinkled lightly with nutmeg.

Left: Rum warmer. Right: Exotic cinnamon coffee

Bedtime spiced chocolate

SERVES 2

(Illustrated below)

450 ml/¾ pint (U.S. scant 2 cups) milk
50 g/2 oz plain chocolate (U.S. ⅓ cup semi-sweet chocolate pieces)
1 tablespoon soft brown sugar (U.S. light brown sugar)
2 pinches of ground cinnamon

Put the milk in a SilverStone pan and bring almost to boiling point. Remove from the heat, put in the chocolate and leave to stand until the chocolate has softened. Sprinkle in the sugar, replace the pan over the heat and whisk the mixture vigorously until it begins to rise in the pan. Pour into 2 warm mugs and sprinkle each drink with cinnamon before serving.

=== VARIATIONS ===

Fireside chilled chocolate Make the chocolate drink as before then leave to cool and chill in a covered container. Whisk again before pouring into mugs and add 2 ice cubes and a small chocolate flake to each before serving.
Night-time shake Chill the chocolate drink as above then whisk in 2 small scoops of vanilla ice cream, pour into long glasses and serve sprinkled with cinnamon.
Sundowners Make the chocolate mixture with 3 tablespoons (U.S. 4 tablespoons) malted chocolate drink powder instead of the chocolate. Serve in mugs and top each with a cap of whipped cream and cinnamon.

Banana ice cream floats

SERVES 2

350 ml/12 fl oz (U.S. 1½ cups) milk
75 g/3 oz plain chocolate (U.S. ½ cup semi-sweet chocolate pieces)
2 bananas, peeled and sliced
2 tablespoons (U.S. 3 tablespoons) advocaat (optional)
2 scoops vanilla or chocolate ice cream

Put half the milk in a pan, add the chocolate and heat gently, stirring, until the chocolate has melted. Stir until smooth then chill.
Drop 2 banana slices into each of 2 tall glasses. Put the rest in a blender with the remaining milk, the chocolate milk and advocaat. Process until frothy. Pour into the glasses and top with ice cream. Serve with long sundae spoon.

=== VARIATIONS ===

Strawberry ice cream floats Use 175 g/6 oz strawberries instead of the bananas, substitute Créme de cacao for the advocaat and use strawberry ice cream. Finish by sprinkling the top of each drink with ½ teaspoon drinking chocolate powder (U.S. sweetened cocoa).
Apricot ice cream floats Drain a 225-g/8-oz can of apricot halves and purée the fruit in a food processor or blender before adding the milk, chocolate mixture and advocaat. When frothy, pour into the glasses and top with chocolate ice cream and a little grated chocolate. You can use apricot syrup from the can instead of the liqueur if wished.

Hot mocha sundae sauce

SERVES 4

(Illustrated below)

4 tablespoons (U.S. 6 tablespoons) strong black coffee
4 tablespoons golden syrup (U.S. 6 tablespoons light corn syrup)
100 g/4 oz plain chocolate (U.S. ⅔ cup semi-sweet chocolate pieces)
TO SERVE
scoops of ice cream
chopped toasted hazelnuts (U.S. chopped toasted filberts) for
sprinkling

Put the coffee, syrup and chocolate in a SilverStone pan and heat
very gently, stirring frequently, until the chocolate has melted
and the mixture is smooth. Spoon immediately over dishes of ice
cream. This sauce is very thick even when hot and sets quickly to
a toffee-like consistency on contact with the ice cream. Serve
sprinkled with nuts.

VARIATION

Blackjack ice cream sauce Substitute 2 tablespoons black
treacle (U.S. 3 tablespoons molasses) for half the golden syrup
and add an extra 1 tablespoon of coffee. This sauce is best
served with a rich creamy vanilla or coffee ice cream. Sprinkle
with chopped walnuts or toasted flaked almonds (U.S. slivered
almonds).

Chocolate custard sauce

MAKES ABOUT 450 ML/¾ PINT (U.S. SCANT 2 CUPS SAUCE

2 tablespoons custard powder or cornflour (U.S. 3 tablespoons
Bird's English dessert mix or cornstarch)
3 tablespoons cocoa powder (U.S. 4 tablespoons unsweetened
cocoa), sifted
2–3 tablespoons (U.S. 3–4 tablespoons) sugar
350 ml/12 fl oz (U.S. 1½ cups) milk
1 egg yolk
15 g/½ oz (U.S. 1 tablespoon) butter or margarine
few drops vanilla essence (U.S. vanilla extract)

Put the custard powder, cocoa and sugar in a pan and gradually
blend in the milk. Bring slowly to the boil, whisking steadily,
until the sauce is smooth and thick. Simmer for 1 minute,
remove from the heat and whisk in the egg yolk, butter and
vanilla essence. Delicious with baked or steamed puddings.

Marshmallow chocolate sauce

SERVES 4–6

(Illustrated opposite)

25 g / 1 oz (U.S. 2 tablespoons) butter or margarine
100 ml / 4 fl oz golden syrup (U.S. ½ cup light corn syrup)
50 g / 2 oz cocoa powder (U.S. ½ cup unsweetened cocoa), sifted
2 tablespoons (U.S. 3 tablespoons) boiling water
1 teaspoon vanilla essence (U.S. vanilla extract)
25 g / 1 oz (U.S. ½ cup tightly packed) marshmallows, snipped into small pieces

Put the butter, syrup and cocoa in a pan and stir over gentle heat until smooth and hot. Do not allow the mixture to boil. Remove from the heat and stir in the water and vanilla. Fold the marshmallows into the sauce and transfer to a serving jug. Serve with ice cream or plain baked puddings.

Velvety hot fudge sauce

SERVES 4–6

(Illustrated opposite)

100 g / 4 oz plain chocolate (U.S. ⅔ cup semi-sweet chocolate pieces)
15 g / ½ oz (U.S. 1 tablespoon) butter or margarine
1 tablespoon golden syrup (U.S. light corn syrup)
75 ml / 3 fl oz double cream (U.S. ⅓ cup heavy cream)

Put the chocolate in a bowl with the butter, syrup and about a quarter of the cream. Stand the bowl over a pan of hot water until the chocolate has melted. Stir to blend. Remove from the heat and stir in the remaining cream. Leave to stand briefly until the sauce thickens slightly then transfer to a warm serving boat. Best spooned warm over ice cream and fresh fruit such as cherries or sliced bananas.

Choc and mallow crème

MAKES ABOUT 400 ML/14 FL OZ (U.S. 1¾ CUPS)

225 g / 8 oz plain chocolate (U.S. 1⅓ cups semi-sweet chocolate pieces)
225 g / 8 oz (U.S. ½ lb) marshmallows
150 ml / ¼ pint double cream (U.S. ⅔ cup heavy cream)

Melt the chocolate in a large bowl over a pan of hot water. Add the marshmallows and cream and fold the ingredients together gently until the marshmallows melt and the mixture is smooth. This will take several minutes. Remove from the heat and transfer to a container with an airtight seal. Allow to cool, cover and store in the refrigerator until required. Serve small scoops on warm milky drinks or ice cream.

Rich chocolate almond sauce

SERVES 4–6

300 ml / ½ pint (U.S. 1¼ cups) water
100 g / 4 oz plain chocolate, roughly chopped (U.S. ⅔ cup semi-sweet chocolate pieces)
1 tablespoon cornflour (U.S. cornstarch)
finely grated rind and juice of ½ orange
175 g / 6 oz caster sugar (U.S. ¾ cup granulated sugar)
pinch of salt
25 g / 1 oz (U.S. 2 tablespoons) butter or margarine
3 tablespoons (U.S. 4 tablespoons) Amaretto, Maraschino or sweet sherry
50 g / 2 oz flaked almonds (U.S. ½ cup slivered almonds), toasted

Put the water into a pan, add the chocolate and stir constantly over gentle heat until the chocolate has melted and the mixture is smooth. Blend the cornflour with the orange juice and add to the pan with the sugar and salt. Stir until the sauce boils and thickens. Simmer for 3 minutes. Remove from the heat, beat in the butter, liqueur, orange rind and almonds. Serve warm with ice cream or plain puddings.

Above: Marshmallow chocolate sauce. Below: Velvety hot fudge sauce

Index